The Poetics of Friendship in Early Modern Spain

The Poetics of Friendship in Early Modern Spain

A Study in Literary Form

Donald Gilbert-Santamaría

EDINBURGH
University Press

Edinburgh University Press is one of the leading university presses in the UK. We publish academic books and journals in our selected subject areas across the humanities and social sciences, combining cutting-edge scholarship with high editorial and production values to produce academic works of lasting importance. For more information visit our website: edinburghuniversitypress.com

© Donald Gilbert-Santamaría, 2020, 2022

First published in hardback by Edinburgh University Press 2020

Edinburgh University Press Ltd
The Tun – Holyrood Road, 12(2f) Jackson's Entry, Edinburgh EH8 8PJ

Typeset in 10.5/13 Adobe Sabon by
IDSUK (DataConnection) Ltd

A CIP record for this book is available from the British Library

ISBN 978 1 4744 5804 7 (hardback)
ISBN 978 1 4744 5805 4 (paperback)
ISBN 978 1 4744 5806 1 (webready PDF)
ISBN 978 1 4744 5807 8 (epub)

The right of Donald Gilbert-Santamaría to be identified as the author of this work has been asserted in accordance with the Copyright, Designs and Patents Act 1988, and the Copyright and Related Rights Regulations 2003 (SI No. 2498).

Contents

Acknowledgments	vi
Introduction: Toward a Poetics of Friendship	1
1. Boccaccio's Tale of Two Friends	27
2. Plotting Imperfections in *La Galatea*	52
3. The End of an Ideal: Cervantes's "El curioso impertinente"	77
4. Staging Intimacy in Guillén de Castro	109
5. María de Zayas's Good Friends	137
6. Guzmán de Alfarache's "Otro yo"	158
7. The Errantry of Friendship in *Don Quixote*	176
Works Cited	221
Index	229

Acknowledgments

When a project takes a decade to come to fruition, a full accounting of everyone who has contributed to the final outcome is difficult to achieve. A particular debt of gratitude is owed to the University of Washington for the institutional support that I have received over the years, especially from the University Libraries where all of the research for this project has taken place. I am also deeply appreciative of the encouragement and support of my colleagues in the Department of Spanish and Portuguese Studies. The University of Washington is home to an extraordinary community of scholars working across campus in various areas of early modern studies, many of whom have read draft chapters from this book. The final product owes much to the serious engagement with various aspects of this project received over the years from Louisa Mackenzie, Brigitte Prutti, Geoffrey Turnovsky, and especially Susan Gaylard. Many thanks are also due to Lorna Hutson, who read an earlier version of the chapter on *Guzmán de Alfarache* that I was kindly invited to write by Daniel Lochman and Maritere López for an edited volume on early modern friendship. Marshall Brown deserves special mention as the most attentive reader of an early draft of my Boccaccio chapter, as does Rebecca Wilkin, whose generous invitation to speak about *Don Quixote* provided me with a much-needed boost at a time when my efforts on this project were starting to flag. That the manuscript was ever finished is due in large part to the critical eye of Edward Baker, who patiently read every chapter in the lead-up to the submission of the revised manuscript. I also consider myself extraordinarily fortunate to have found a home for this book with Edinburgh University Press and an editor in Michelle Houston whose steadfast belief in this project has been indispensable to its successful completion. Finally, to my family, whose love *and* friendship make all things possible, my expression of gratitude here is but a feeble gesture toward that which words can never fully convey.

An earlier version of Chapter 6 appears in *Discourses and Representations of Friendship in Early Modern Europe, 1500–1700* and has been adapted for use here with permission from the publisher: Donald Gilbert-Santamaría, "Guzmán de Alfarache's 'Other Self': The Limits of Friendship in Spanish Picaresque Fiction," in Daniel T. Lochman, Maritere López, and Lorna Hutson, eds., *Discourses and Representations of Friendship in Early Modern Europe, 1500–1700* (Farnham, Surrey: Ashgate Publishing Limited, 2011), pp. 83–98.

For Nathalie

Introduction: Toward a Poetics of Friendship

Throughout the writing of this book, my interest in literary representations of friendship has been challenged by the immediacy of friendship in everyday life. Indeed, I find it impossible to conceive of a literature of friendship that does not, in some way, relate back to that real-world experience. At the same time, a full appreciation of the analysis that follows requires a suspension of habits of mind that would impose sociological or psychological criteria on what I propose to consider almost exclusively as a matter of literary form.[1] Thus, the notion of a poetics of friendship as I will develop it in the following pages is designed to capture a unique way of thinking about literary representations of friendship in the works of writers from the Spanish early modern period. While such representations are inextricably linked to the fact of friendship in the world, they are more significantly possessed of a critical autonomy that derives from their participation in a distinctive historical trajectory that can only be fully understood in literary terms.

To illuminate further this distinction between friendship in everyday life and its literary representation, I would point to the notion of exemplarity in its early modern usage. A key concept in early modern poetic theory more generally, exemplarity plays an especially important role in conceptualizing how the audience relates to literary representations of friendship in the period. There is, above all, the soft didacticism of literary representation as a model for human conduct in the world. With varying degrees of transparency, friendship narratives throughout the early modern period are driven by a kind of structural necessity to portray the ideal friend as the ultimate representation of what friendship *should* be. Conflicts between protagonists in these narratives frequently function as little more than a pretext for good friends to test their mettle, leading to the foregone conclusion of their moral superiority. While such an account of what Juan Bautista Avalle-Arce describes as the "tale of two friends" tradition is, as will become clear in the following chapters, somewhat reductive, the overall paradigm nevertheless persists in one form or another from the late Middle Ages through at least the early seventeenth century.

The longevity of the narrative tradition of writing perfect friendship may be attributed, at least in part, to its classical pedigree and, more specifically, to its close association with the taxonomy of friendship first formulated in Aristotle's *Nicomachean Ethics*. Aristotle's tripartite theory of friendship establishes perfect friendship—which is described as friendship among those "who wish goods to their friend for their friend's own sake"—as the most virtuous mode of voluntary communion between human beings.[2] This model carries an exemplary force that reaches a kind of moral apex, as we shall see, in the late medieval discourse of spiritual friendship in service to God. It is precisely this moral sensibility that persists most of all in the tales of perfect friendship that will be discussed in this study.

Yet even from the beginning there is a recognition of the practical limitations of this most exalted kind of friendship. Aristotle himself notes that perfect "friendships are ... rare" precisely because only a few are capable of the requisite "goodness" upon which such friendship is predicated.[3] This idea is taken up even more extensively in Cicero's more practically oriented *De amicitia*, in which Laelius, the wise elder who waxes nostalgic over his friendship with Scipio Africanus, dwells extensively on the difficulty of friendship in *practice*, noting at one point in an echo of Aristotle that "in the whole range of history only three or four pairs of friends are mentioned."[4] The problem, as becomes clear as one delves further into Cicero's treatise, is the fundamental inadequacy of most human beings to the demands of this highest, most celebrated form of friendship. Here, then, arises one of the central difficulties for the secular tradition of writing perfect friendship as it develops in the early modern period: How can a narrative based on the Aristotelian category of perfect friendship serve as an exemplum for a readership that is composed almost entirely of morally imperfect human beings?

As posited, however, this question carries a significant risk of presentist distortion. When applied to literary production in particular, the question implicitly privileges verisimilitude as the primary mode of reception along with a utilitarian understanding of exemplarity in which what is represented serves as a practical model for friendship in everyday life. Against this utilitarian vision, this study will propose a reading of exemplary friendship that takes into consideration other poetic principles at work in the literary culture of early modern Spain, especially as related to the central Renaissance preoccupation with *imitatio*. In the texts that I consider here, the soft didacticism that would hold up exemplary friendship as a model for human conduct is often complicated by a poetic practice that understands imitation as a mode of intertextuality and not as an imperative to represent life in the world beyond the text.[5] In these texts, what frequently matters most is affirming the Aristotelian model for perfect friendship even when doing so is at odds—often profoundly so—with the experience of friendship in everyday life.

From the perspective of a contemporary poetics that would privilege verisimilitude, this view of exemplarity admittedly makes little sense. Restored to the formal context of early modern literary practice more generally, however, the apparent contradictions in this view of exemplarity reflect a literary culture that derives much of its legitimacy from its relationship to earlier, classical forms. The significance of this point, however, is not limited to the early modern reverence for the classical *auctoritates*—although this is an important factor—but rather reflects complexities within the historical trajectory that leads from Aristotle and Cicero to the more properly literary texts that will be examined in this study. Thus, even in Cicero's Latin treatise, one already catches a glimpse of how exemplary friendship might operate within a poetics grounded in principles other than representational verisimilitude. Indeed, despite the practical cast of much of Laelius's comments on friendship, his reflection in one key passage on a theatrical representation of the mythical friendship of Orestes and Pylades exposes both a recognition of the practical limitations of exemplary perfect friendship as well as an implicit awareness of a very different understanding of how friendship operates in a literary context:

> Laelius: . . . Itaque, si quando aliquod officium exstitit amici in periculis aut adeundis aut communicandis, quis est qui id non maximis efferat laudibus? Qui clamores tota cavea nuper in hospitis et amici mei M. Pacuvi nova fabula, cum ignorante rege uter Orestes esset, Pylades Oresten se esse diceret, ut pro illo necaretur, Orestes autem, ita ut erat, Oresten se esse perseveraret! Stantes plaudebant in re ficta; quid arbitramur in vera facturos fuisse? Facile indicabat ipsa natura vim suam, cum homines, quod facere ispi non possent, id recte fieri in altero iudicarent.[6]

> [Laelius: . . . Whenever, therefore, there comes to light some signal service in undergoing or sharing the dangers of a friend, who does not proclaim it with the loudest praise? What shouts recently rang through the entire theatre during the performance of the new play, written by my guest and friend, Marcus Pacuvius, at the scene where, the king being ignorant which of the two was Orestes, Pylades, who wished to be put to death instead of his friend declared, "I am Orestes," while Orestes continued steadfastly to assert, as

was the fact, "I am Orestes!" The people in the audience rose to their feet and cheered this incident in fiction; what, think we, would they have done had it occurred in real life? In this case Nature easily asserted her own power, inasmuch as men approved in another as well done that which they could not do themselves.]

For Craig A. Williams, no other story "within the massive body of Greek mythological narrative adopted and adapted by Roman culture" more aptly represents "*the* mythic paradigm for friends in the Latin textual tradition" than the tale of Orestes and Pylades.[7] Cicero's brief recollection of Pacuvius's theatrical representation of that myth furnishes a concise summary of two of the principles of perfect friendship that will recur throughout later friendship narratives: The highest gesture of perfect friendship—the will to sacrifice one's own life for the sake of one's friend—is linked to a momentary confusion in the identity of the two men, that is, to the literal enactment of the defining metaphor of perfect friendship in both Cicero and Aristotle, the notion of the friend as a second self—an *alter ego*.[8]

At the same time, Laelius's description of the success of Pacuvius's theatrical staging may be said to confront a fundamental, philosophically significant doubt about the efficacy of the very model for perfect friendship celebrated by the audience in this anecdote from *De amicitia*. Even as he evokes the enthusiastic response of the audience to the theatrical representation of the two mythic friends' shared gesture of self-sacrifice, Laelius's commentary reminds the reader of the story's ultimate origin in fiction: "Stantes plaudebant in re ficta." The prepositional phrase that Laelius attaches to the audience's embrace of the spectacle of self-sacrifice—"in re ficta"—leads to what becomes one of the defining difficulties for the tale of two friends tradition as it will later emerge in the early modern period: "quid arbitramur in vera facturos fuisse?" In highlighting the distinction between everyday life and fiction, Laelius implicitly questions the limits of idealized exemplarity as a guide for practice in the real world. This audience, so enthusiastic in its reception of the idealized narrative of perfect friendship, is ultimately incapable of living up to the expectations of the model: "In this case Nature easily asserted her own power, inasmuch as men approved in another as well done that which they could not do themselves."

Despite the brevity of Cicero's reference to the myth of Orestes and Pylades, the full significance of Laelius's words here finally emerges as a critique of moral exemplarity applied to the theatrical representation of the Aristotelian ideal of perfect friendship. In the same way that the dialogue of *De amicitia* as a whole reveals the tension between idealized theory and the practical considerations of everyday life, this passage articulates the logical extension of this tension to the domain of fiction. The telling of made-up stories about perfect friendship—whether mythic or literary in origin—is here, more than a millennium before the full development of the early modern tradition, revealed as an exercise in exemplarity of dubious practical relevance. While the observation remains unstated in Cicero's text, it cannot be ignored as an implied query at the end of this passage: What does it finally matter that fictional characters are capable of extraordinary acts of self-sacrifice in the name of friendship if, in the end, those who witness these acts are constitutionally unable to emulate such moral perfection in their own lives?

As I will have occasion to explore in the following pages, this is a complicated question that involves the very essence of what I propose here as a poetics of friendship. For more than an exercise in superlative personal virtue, the narrativization of perfect friendship invariably depends on a host of structural elements that go well beyond the characterization of the perfect friend's absolute moral integrity; in addition to the idealized will to friendly self-sacrifice, such narratives also construct idealized opportunities for the successful acting out of that will. Hence, even in his abridged account of the myth of Orestes and Pylades, Cicero hints at the special circumstances that finally allow for an exalted moment of self-sacrifice in the service of friendship that also, as it turns out, gives symbolic expression to the fundamental ideal of the friend as a second self. In effect, the turn of events—even as briefly sketched in this passage—that facilitate Pylades's attempted sacrifice of his own life for that of his friend is highly scripted, that is, it is inherent to the formal structure of Pacuvius's representation of this mythic relationship.

From Boccaccio through Cervantes's early prose pastoral novel, *La Galatea*, and the theatrical works that will be considered in this study, this sense of scriptedness persists as a prominent feature in the poetic practice of writing perfect friendship. Yet the tenacity of the ideological claims of Aristotelian perfect friendship is hardly absolute and, in the Spanish context, those claims come under increasing pressure in the late sixteenth and early seventeenth centuries. Through an evolving process of contestation, the trajectory that I trace in this study reveals how new ways of thinking about literary imitation—and by extension exemplarity—undercut the representation of Aristotelian perfect friendship. The result is an erosion in the viability of the categorical ideal even in those works—like *La Galatea*—that remain, at least in principle, ideologically committed to the Aristotelian concept of the perfect friend. At the same time, however, the emergence of representational verisimilitude as an increasingly important aspect of the poetic practice in both prose narrative and the Spanish *comedia* is accompanied by a concurrent interest in depictions of friendship that draw inspiration from the far messier reality of friendship in everyday life. More than a mere epiphenomenon of representational verisimilitude, however, the reappraisal of friendship in much of the literature of early modern Spain emerges as a locus of poetic innovation in its own right. Indeed, what begins in Boccaccio and the early Cervantes of *La Galatea* as a mode of contestation to the scriptedness of the traditional paradigm leads in later texts to a radical transformation in the representation of friendship that ultimately comes to operate as an independent poetic force, a conclusion, as will become clear, that finds its most powerful instantiation in Cervantes's portrayal of the unlikely friendship between Don Quixote and Sancho Panza.

Much of the impetus for this study derives from Juan Bautista Avalle-Arce's groundbreaking 1957 article on "the tale of two friends." While the bulk of his account is taxonomic—including descriptions of an extended list of specific works—there are nevertheless glimpses of a deeper analysis that come out at key moments, no more so than in his description of a pivotal historically determined reorientation within the tradition of writing perfect friendship that he identifies, not coincidentally, with the Renaissance. Referring to the earliest, largely medieval stories from his own catalogue of tales of perfect friendship, he writes:

> Hasta aquí, las versiones del cuento sacrifican las posibilidades novelísticas a la moral. Esta escala de valores les impide diferenciarse, pues, para sus autores el verdadero interés no está en el contenido narrativo, sino en el contenido simbólico. Pero en el Renacimiento todo sufre un desplazamiento; lo que Lovejoy llama "the great chain of being" recibe un duro golpe y varios de sus eslabones saltan para no ser reemplazados más. Se deja de mirar al cielo; el mundo se vuelve inmanente y el hombre, libre de opresiones jerárquicas, se contempla a sí mismo, asombrado del hallazgo.[9]

> [Up to this point, versions of the story sacrifice novelistic possibilities to moral ones. This value system makes it difficult for them to differentiate themselves, since, for their authors the true interest is not in the narrative content, but in the symbolic content. But in the Renaissance everything suffers a displacement; what Lovejoy calls "the great chain of being" receives a harsh blow and several of its links fall out never to be replaced. One stops gazing at the heavens; the world becomes immanent, and man, free from hierarchical oppressions, contemplates himself, shaken by the discovery.]

The thumbnail sketch of the early modern worldview on offer here is at best limited in its rehearsal of an essentially Burckhardtian notion of the liberated Renaissance individual. Moreover, from the perspective of a poetics of friendship, the notion of a direct opposition between "moral" and "novelistic possibilities" can hardly ever be as complete as Avalle-Arce's statement here suggests. Nevertheless, the identification of a shift away from moral concerns toward "novelistic possibilities" in the Renaissance paradigm for the tale of two friends raises what will be one of the main concerns of my own study here, namely, the central role that poetics play in the evolution of early modern friendship narratives as an independent locus of critical interest. The shift that Avalle-Arce describes in the passage above, and that he significantly locates in the first text that I will consider in my own study—Boccaccio's tale of friendship from Day Ten of the *Decameron*—necessarily forces a reconsideration of moral didacticism not merely as a legitimate end of this kind of narrative, but more profoundly, in terms of its formal viability.[10] Moreover, whatever we finally decide the Renaissance to be, the mere invocation of such a term historicizes the experience of reading, underscoring in the process the audience's historically conditioned expectations that provide a source of tension with the text's formal attributes. In privileging the Renaissance reader as "free from hierarchical oppressions" in order to engage in self-contemplation, Avalle-Arce points to the sense of self-consciousness that so many scholars have associated with the early modern period and that, by extension, might explain why moral exemplarity would in this epoch of self-examination come under greater scrutiny.

From this more historically sensitive perspective, we can appreciate Cicero's precociousness in the passage cited earlier. Laelius seems to recognize, even if Pacuvius's audience may not, the limits of idealized moral exemplarity as a guide to human behavior. For writers in the early modern period, such a recognition is slow in coming, but it does finally arrive, and even reaches a kind of dialectical turning point in *Don Quixote*. Furthermore, as with all dialectical turns, the implicit contradictions that finally lead to this seemingly radical break are already evident well before the fated moment, if one just knows where to look. Boccaccio's tale of perfect friendship from the *Decameron*, which is often hailed as paradigmatic within the tale of two friends tradition, nevertheless displays many such contradictions. Existing as fault lines within the text, they are exposed to even greater stress in Cervantes's pastoral novel, *La Galatea*, only to explode in the violent denouement of the interpolated tale from *Don Quixote*, "El curioso impertinente."

Despite Cicero's prescient observations, a recognition of the ultimate impracticality of moral didacticism through idealized exemplarity represents a rather late development within the evolving discourse of early modern friendship. It depends, most of all, on the privileging of representational verisimilitude over other considerations, something that is, as I will argue here, not fully developed in Boccaccio or even in *La Galatea*. Where such a formal poetic shift has not yet occurred, one observes something quite distinct, and arguably more classical, namely texts that function in a rhetorical rather than what we might call, in a modern sense, a literary register. The very mythic nature of the friendship between Orestes and Pylades already guarantees an inevitable distancing between their idealized existence and the quotidian concerns of Pacuvius's audience. That distancing is not only expected, it is, I would argue, central to the success of the performance as an exercise in hyperbolic rhetoric in the service of an ideal. Such an interpretation helps to explain a subtle but crucial feature of Cicero's critique: While he notes the distinction between the audience's warm reception of the play and that same audience's implied inability to live up to the standards of the mythic protagonists, he never goes so far as to admit this distinction as explicitly contradictory. For Cicero, the inadequacy of idealized exemplarity to the practical demands of everyday life is not so much a problem as a peculiar characteristic of such theatrical representations. Indeed, in the Ciceronian context, the gap between the mythic friends and the audience is available for a rhetorical treatment that inspires respect, even awe for the ideal.

This rhetorical inflection within the representation of perfect friendship also helps to illuminate another feature of the tale of two friends tradition, namely, the problem of the friend's unknowability. In a literary context, the notion of knowability, even more so than the concept of moral exemplarity, is only intelligible under the auspices of a poetics that privileges verisimilitude. Only with an expectation of self-identification grounded in the audience or reader's robust sense of subjective autonomy does such an idea even make sense. In other words, the idea that the characters, in some profound epistemological sense, know each other, depends on our own sense as readers that they are knowable to *us*. In contrast, the rhetorical orientation, so aptly captured in Cicero's analysis of Pacuvius's theatrical representation of Orestes and Pylades, renders such preoccupations with knowability as fundamentally irrelevant to the exemplary function. Like the classical gods—or, as will become clear later, God himself—these perfect friends inhabit a mythic space that is unavailable for an analysis that would compare them directly to worldly standards of human understanding. Moreover, within this unassailable realm of perfect friendship, the core classical ideal of the friend as a second self emerges as perhaps the ultimate rhetorical flourish, a notion that remains beyond scrutiny in any empirical sense. It functions, as Avalle-Arce himself notes in relation to the earliest moralizing tales of perfect friendship, as "symbolic content" that is finally unintelligible to modern habits of reading with expectations of representational verisimilitude.

How this classical legacy is finally challenged and, in certain instances, overcome will be a major focus of the following chapters. Avalle-Arce, for his part, provides something of a preview of this process in his limited remarks comparing Cervantes's *La Galatea* with the interpolated story of "El curioso impertinente" from *Don Quixote* in which he argues that the literary idealism of the early work gives way in his later masterpiece to an almost cynical assertion of the final exhaustion of "el cuento de los dos amigos" as a relevant force within literary history. Where the tale of the two friends—Timbrio and Silerio—in Cervantes's pastoral novel bears witness to the traditional Aristotelian notion of idealized friendship—about which I will have more to say in a later chapter—the story of Anselmo and Lotario in "El curioso impertinente" ends with a flourish of violence that, as Avalle-Arce observes, mocks with "tremenda ironía" this promise of idealized friendship. In their mutual betrayal leading to death, these two friends embody nothing less than the demise of "el cuento de los dos amigos":

Así, *El curioso impertinente* es lógico desarrollo, y superación, del cuento de Timbrio y Silerio. Más aún: las acciones de Lotario, paralelas en sentido inverso a las de Silerio, se justifican con su triunfo, y esta victoria inmoral provoca el derrumbamiento del mito. Considerado en esa forma, *El curioso impertinente* es etapa última en el desenvolvimiento de la historia de los dos amigos, y al mismo tiempo su destrucción.[11]

[Thus, *El curioso impertinente* is the logical development and overcoming of the story of Timbrio and Silerio. Better: the actions of Lotario, parallel in an inverted sense to those of Silerio, find justification in his triumph, and this immoral victory provokes the destruction of the myth. Considered in this way, *El curioso impertinente* is the final step in the development of the tale of two friends and, at the same time, its destruction.]

Avalle-Arce's reference to the "myth" of perfect friendship recalls his reference later in the same essay to the "symbolic content" of these tales, that is, to their association with what is arguably the same mode of exemplarity that was observed earlier in Cicero's brief critique of Pacuvius's dramatic representation of the mythic friendship between Orestes and Pylades. Read against this background, the destruction of the "cuento de los dos amigos" signifies not just the end of a literary tradition, but more significantly, the final unravelling of the hermeneutics upon which that tradition depends. With Cervantes as the pivotal figure in his narrative, this passage stands out in Avalle-Arce's study as offering the most explicit example of a trajectory within the logic of the tale of two friends so that, paradoxically, in describing the effective exhaustion of the paradigm itself of the perfect friendship narrative, he reveals its status as a formal structuring force within a defined space of literary production. Whatever label one chooses to append to the tale of two friends as a literary category, its formal significance for Avalle-Arce's analysis rises to the surface at this point in his analysis with striking clarity.

Yet despite the insight of this passage, Avalle-Arce ultimately refrains from exploring the more radical implications of his reading of Cervantes's engagement with the tale of two friends tradition. After insisting that "El curioso impertinente" marks the "final step in the development of the tale of two friends," he nevertheless proceeds to describe several more post-Cervantine tales of friendship that embody a continuation of that same tradition, a move that he makes without explanation. More specifically, he fails to note that the interpolated tale that he will later call in a revised version of this article "the limit of absolute finality, after which it makes no sense to speak of the tale of two friends as a problem," occurs within the framework of a longer prose narrative that gives voice to arguably the most famous story of friendship in all of early modern European letters.[12] Having persuasively identified the end of one paradigm for literary friendship, he overlooks the emergence of an entirely different model for friendly communion in the main narrative of *Don Quixote*.

For my own purposes here, these oversights constitute something of a distraction that obscures the larger significance of Avalle-Arce's study. Critics interested in the formal attributes of *Don Quixote* have long debated Cervantes's inclusion of interpolated stories in his novel, with objections typically raised to the seeming incompatibility between these stories and the main narrative.[13] In the case of "El curioso impertinente," however, Avalle-Arce's analysis reveals such incompatibilities as symptomatic of the radical modernity of Cervantes's grand literary experiment. The betrayal and death of the two friends, Anselmo and Lotario, and the attendant destruction of the tale of two friends paradigm, may be read from this perspective as a symbolic act designed to clear the way for the new literary order of the novel's main narrative. Rather than a defect in Cervantes's literary vision, the apparent dissonance that accompanies the inclusion of "El curioso impertinente" within the larger narrative of *Don Quixote* thus becomes a new source of meaning in its own right, the symbolic embodiment of a literary-historical shift as expressed through a rupture within the poetics of friendship.

In the *Nicomachean Ethics*, Aristotle constructs a hierarchy of three levels of friendship. The lower levels include friendship based on pleasure and friendship based on utility, while the highest level—perfect friendship—may only exist between individuals who are defined as good. As Aristotle puts it, "But complete friendship is the friendship of good people similar in virtue; for they wish goods in the same way to each other in so far as they are good, and they are good in themselves."[14] Central to this Aristotelian notion of perfect friendship is the idea of the individual's selfless devotion to a friend for that friend's own sake: "Now those who wish goods to their friend for the friend's own sake are friends most of all; for they have this attitude because of the friend himself, not coincidentally."[15] While there is in this section of the *Ethics* a sense of friendship as mutually reinforcing the friends' shared virtuousness—an idea that will be replicated in the medieval tradition of spiritual friendship—the primary emphasis is on selflessness rooted in the desire for the good of one's friend as its own end, that is, on an unconditional love that prioritizes the interests and needs of the friend above one's own. This idea—and ideal—motivates much of what occurs in the traditional tale of two friends. As will become clear in my discussion below of both Boccaccio and *La Galatea*, the main characters are effectively defined in the tale of two friends tradition through hyperbolic displays of self-sacrifice in the interest of friendship. One might even say that such selflessness is the defining gesture of friendship throughout the entire tradition.

At the same time, however, the Aristotelian ideal is subject to alternative readings that, as the work of A. W. Price suggests, complicate our understanding of perfect friendship in ways that impact greatly the later evolution of the narrative tradition. Citing the ambiguity of Aristotle's definition of perfect friendship in the *Nicomachean Ethics*, Price argues for "a shift from the familiar 'loving someone for his sake' to a newly inflected 'loving someone for *his* sake,' that is for the sake of the person who he is . . . ; that is accompanied by an unargued assumption that *how* one is is part of *who* one is, that one's character is part of one's identity."[16] In Price's reading, the attributes that define a friend are seamlessly integrated into identity so that to know a friend's good qualities—goodness and virtue—is tantamount to knowing the friend. As the following discussion will demonstrate, the point is not a trivial one for subsequent developments in the discourse of early modern friendship.

As Ullrich Langer has explored at length, the fusion of identity—"*who* one is"—with attributes—"*how* one is"—later comes under significant pressure in the scholastic tradition, especially in relation to the question of humanity's relationship to God.[17] In the original Aristotelian context, the goodness of the two friends is a necessary prerequisite for perfect friendship. Virtue is, in this way, built into the Aristotelian schema, a fact that explains, at least in part, the conflation of identity and attribute in Price's reading of the key phrase "for *his* sake."

In contrast, drawing a line from Augustine (354–430) to Peter Lombard (1096–1160) and Thomas Aquinas (1225–1274), Langer demonstrates the sharp distinction within scholastic thinking between moral virtues, which "are always means to something else, never an end in themselves," and God, who is the "highest end" and "who cannot except metaphorically be said to perform moral acts."[18] As Langer puts it most succinctly, "God is not loved *because* of his goodness, but in himself."[19] God is thus divorced from any concrete association with specific moral virtues, that is, with attributes that might define him as a concrete individual—arguably an impossibility given his divine nature. Rather, he emerges in Langer's reading of the scholastic tradition as fundamentally unknowable in his radical uniqueness.

This sharp demarcation between moral virtue and identity in the figure of God plays a key role in Langer's account of the resurgence of an early modern discourse of perfect friendship. Initially within the scholastic tradition as Langer describes it, the paradigm of God as the "highest end" coincides with a parallel insistence on the instrumentality of all normal human friendship. In effect, Aristotelian perfect friendship between individuals, in its original sense, as an end in itself, is excluded from this tradition: Human beings, Langer summarizes, "are to be loved as a step toward God, not for themselves."[20] Thus, even as the scholastic tradition extols the exalted status of fellowship in the service of God, it marks that friendship as necessarily inferior to the love humanity owes to God which is finally revealed as the only truly selfless affection.

The subordinated status of this kind of spiritual friendship, however, is not absolute, and Langer notes as early as Lombard "a loosening of the categorical difference between instrumental human friendship and the non-instrumental love of God."[21] This is the pivotal moment in Langer's analysis, for rather than "a return to the conditional perfect friendship in goodness envisaged by Aristotle," this "loosening of the categorical difference" leads to "the possibility of conceiving of human relationships as ends in themselves *irrespective* of their motivation through virtue or goodness."[22] Having subjected the Aristotelian concept of perfect friendship to the requirements of scholastic theology, a newly forged understanding of loving another "for his own sake" as it relates to the deity is transferred back to the domain of purely human relationships. The implications of this move within the scholastic tradition for the original notion of Aristotelian perfect friendship, however, are deeply problematic, as the perfect friend—in direct contradiction to Price's analysis of the original Aristotelian formulation—is no longer definable through particular attributes.

Langer delves at some length into the ethical consequences of this turn within the scholastic tradition, noting in particular how the disassociation between attributes and identity in the case of human friendships leads to the unavoidable conclusion that "the individual human being does not have to be virtuous in order to be treated as an end, *propter seipsum*":[23]

> What this means is that ultimately the individual perfectly loved cannot be given any attributes by which he or she could be known to others as an individual. You cannot say, "I love the person who is good, generous, courageous," for the suggestion always is that those attributes constitute the person, who is, then, less of an individual and by the same token less perfectly loved. In other words, objects in their individuality can be pointed to, named (in the sense of a proper name), but not described . . . This brings us back to the problem of literary representation and motivation.
>
> If the perfect ethical relationship relies on the love of another for his own sake, as an end beyond which there can be no other end, then literary representation can only do justice to such a relationship if somehow it deprives itself of motivation. For the other to be invoked as a radically individual end in himself or herself, the recourses are few: incoherence, the prevalence of referring over signifying, silence. This is what some writers of the early modern period have resorted to, when attempting to represent what was felt to be the ideal ethical relationship, friendship.[24]

Langer's analysis illuminates the influence of the scholastics on Avalle-Arce's tale of two friends tradition. Not only is a lack of motivation one of the key features of this tradition, so is an erosion of the signifying function and, by extension, the paradox of the final unknowability of the friend as a radically unique individual. Among other things, this profoundly counter-intuitive finding serves as a reminder of the inadequacy of contemporary habits of reading in evaluating the early modern tradition of writing friendship. Driven by the lingering influence of the Aristotelian paradigm, the notion of the unknowable perfect friend is completely unintelligible to a methodology that would attempt to rationalize the narrative friendship tradition in terms of sociological or psychological accounts of how friendship operates in everyday life.

Furthermore, from the perspective of a poetics of friendship, this reconstituted Aristotelianism helps to explain many of the formal attributes typically found in the tale of two friends tradition. Above all, it lends insight into the peculiar altruism in the service of perfect friendship that is one of that tradition's most important features: In effect, acts of self-sacrifice and hyperbolic rhetoric in support of a static notion of perfect friendship come to operate as a palliative for a literary form in which the basic narrative function of character description and development has been seriously constrained. To the extent that these works lack motivation beyond the rarefied fact of perfect friendship itself, the friend is transformed into a kind of idealized cipher whose radical uniqueness serves to alienate rather than explain. At the same time, this breakdown in the signifying function finds an indirect compensation of sorts through the appeal to hyperbolic praise for extreme acts of self-sacrifice that—in an echo of Cicero's commentary on Pacuvius's theatrical representation of the mythic friendship between Orestes and Pylades—far exceed the readers' own capacity for virtuous action.

The line that Langer traces from Aristotle through the scholastics to the tale of two friends tradition is not, however, exhaustive of the ways in which the representation of early modern friendship may be understood historically, and the problem of the perfect friend's essential unknowability, while certainly a key element in traditional narratives of perfect friendship, nevertheless finds relief in alternative genealogies that are of particular interest to the arguably more modern representations of friendship that find their first most complete expression in *Don Quixote*. Of particular note in this regard is the trajectory leading from Cicero through Petrarch and Renaissance humanism. The discursive detour through scholasticism that culminates in the paradoxical result of the friend's unknowability runs counter to what Williams has described as "one of the most persistent and memorable of ideals about [classical] *amicitia*: One's friend is another self (*alter ego, alter idem*)." He continues, "The Latin adjective *alter* ('the other of two') points to a bond that joins precisely two individuals, and in perhaps the grandest of all idealizations, a pair of friends could be imagined as one soul divided between two bodies."[25] This reading of the friend as a second self could not be more distant from the kind of alienation that Langer associates with later scholasticism and the tale of two friends tradition.

In *De amicitia*, Cicero liberates this Aristotelian principle from its theoretical straitjacket, recasting the idea of the friend as an *alter idem* within the fluid reality of human experience. The result is a contextualized understanding of what it means to know one's friends that will indelibly mark the trajectory of this alternative humanist genealogy:

> Cumque plurimas et maximas commoditates amicitia contineat, tum illa nimirum praestat omnibus, quod bonam spem praelucet in posterum, nec debilitari animos aut cadere patitur. Verum etiam amicum qui intuetur, tamquam exemplar aliquod intuetur sui. Quocirca et absentes adsunt et

egentes abundant et imbecilli valent et, quod difficilius dictu est, mortui vivunt; tantus eos honos memoria desiderium prosequitur amicorum, ex quo illorum beata mors videtur, horum vita laudabilis.[26]

[Now friendship possesses many splendid advantages, but of course the finest thing of all about it is that it sends a ray of good hope into the future, and keeps our hearts from faltering or falling by the wayside. For the man who keeps his eye on a true friend, keeps it, so to speak, on a model of himself. For this reason, friends are together when they are separated, they are rich when they are poor, strong when they are weak, and—a thing even harder to explain—they live on after they have died, so great is the honor that follows them, so vivid the memory, so poignant the sorrow. That is why friends who have died are accounted happy, and those who survive them are deemed worthy of praise.]

Cicero's placement of the notion of the friend as a second self in a context that is sensitive to the temporal dimension of human relationships signals a significant movement beyond the stasis of the Aristotelian ideal. One here detects an awareness of change as an essential element in friendship, as new affective states like hope and regret emerge in a context where previously one had only discerned the perfection of shared virtue. Elsewhere, Cicero discusses the problem of finding friends, keeping them, and, when the necessity arises, breaking off from them, that is, he contemplates the practice of friendship in highly dynamic terms. Indeed, despite the didacticism that occasionally encumbers his dialogue, the overall effect is nonetheless to provide a glimpse into how friendship works in the world beyond the text both as practice and affective experience.

Above all, the efficacy of Cicero's alternative vision of friendship depends on a rejection of the idealistic claims of the Aristotelian model. While Laelius in his discourse on the topic cites the rarity of true friendship—as already indicated—he nevertheless embraces a highly practical understanding of how such relationships operate in the real world. Having echoed the Aristotelian premise "that friendship cannot exist except among good men," he proceeds to temper the idealistic baggage of Aristotle's model for perfect friendship: "I, however, am bound to look at things as they are in the experience of everyday life and not as they are in fancy or in hope."[27] With its emphasis on dynamic practice over idealized and inaccessible theoretical constructs, Cicero's dialogue on friendship may be said to define the notion of the friend as a second self in a way that avoids the problem of epistemological alienation that, in Langer's analysis, permeates the scholastic tradition. Where the radical uniqueness of Aristotle's perfect friend culminates under the pressure of scholastic thought in his theoretically determined, implacable unknowability, the emphasis on the temporal dimension of friendship that one discovers throughout Cicero's dialogue reveals perfect friendship in terms that are surprisingly sensitive to the vicissitudes of everyday life: "Now he, indeed, used to say that nothing was harder than for a friendship to continue to the very end of life; for it often happened either that the friendship ceased to be mutually advantageous, or the parties to it did not entertain the same political views; and that frequently, too, the dispositions of men were changed, sometimes by adversity and sometimes by the increasing burdens of age."[28] Here, the problem of the friend's unknowablity that Langer discovers at the heart of the tale of two friends tradition gives way to a narrative of evolution within friendship that is implicitly predicated on imperfect, but nevertheless, real knowledge of one's companion.

The practical emphasis within Cicero's account of friendship in *De amicitia* finds even fuller expression in his extensive correspondence, a body of writings that plays a central role in the transmission of this other classical paradigm for friendship into early modern literary consciousness. Williams attempts to characterize the importance of friendship to Cicero's epistolary writing in objective terms, noting the high frequency with which references to terms like *amici* and *amicitia* appear throughout his collected letters.[29] Yet as Amanda Wilcox's recent study of his correspondence suggests, Cicero's letters demonstrate little interest in the theoretical questions that preoccupy the interlocutors of *De amicitia*. Rather, these writings operate in a semi-public domain as part of a larger practice of exchange that mixes the rhetorical aspirations of the Ciceronian-Aristotelian ideal with the requirements of real-life social and political relationships. In fact, Wilcox's discussion of Cicero's correspondence engages in extensive close readings that show precisely how these letters work within the context of what she describes as a "gift exchange."[30] As such, the letters frequently display an instrumentalism of purpose despite repeated appeals to the idealized discourse of perfect friendship. Thus, in one notable example, Wilcox shows how the notion of the friend as second self—again, one of the abiding concepts of classical perfect friendship—operates in Cicero's letters as a rhetorical trope within a discourse that is highly self-serving.[31]

For Wilcox, the apparent tension between idealizing rhetoric and instrumentalism in Cicero's engagement with friendship in his letters reflects his preference for synthesis over Aristotle's tripartite hierarchical categories.[32] Where the Aristotelian categories isolate perfect friendship from other, less virtuous modes of human interaction, Wilcox suggests that Cicero's view of friendship, both in *De amicitia* and in his epistolary writings, imagines friendship as a single enterprise whose various facets do not necessarily demean the ideal. From this perspective, the rhetoric of perfect friendship is arguably not at odds with the more practical aims of his correspondence. Consistent with his view of friendship as an active, even political enterprise, Cicero integrates the rhetorically driven exaltation of perfect friendship with the demands of real life in the world beyond the text. Although contradictions remain in this Ciceronian synthesis, it nevertheless opens a space for a new appreciation of the literary dimension of his correspondence as rhetorical gestures in the service of perfect friendship necessarily aestheticize his letters without negating their more pragmatic function.

Of special interest for my study here, this Ciceronian synthesis is a key factor in the emergence of an alternative humanist understanding of early modern friendship more generally. Kathy Eden's recent work on Renaissance "intimacy" supplies a useful conceptual framework for describing the historical trajectory leading from Cicero into the early modern period, her analysis of Petrarch's discovery of Cicero's lost letters to Atticus in 1345 illuminating the historical dialectic that, even today, largely defines our understanding of the rise of Renaissance humanism. That "famous encounter between Petrarch and the epistolary Cicero," she argues, "sets the primal scene for the Renaissance rediscovery of intimacy" and helps define an alternative model of fictional friendship that, as will become clear later in this study, echoes in the later works of Cervantes and others.[33] Eden continues:

> For in response to his lucky find, Petrarch takes three decisive steps: first, he decides to write *like* the intimate Cicero; second, he decides to write directly *to* Cicero; and third, following Cicero, he decides to include this letter along with many others in a single letter collection, the *Familiares*. Taken together, as we will see, these steps thoroughly transform the cultural landscape of early modern Europe insofar as they reinvigorate a genre—the familiar letter—that will come to dominate the histories of education, literature, and printing, thereby changing the way the humanists and their successors read and write. As a consequence of his discovery in Verona, in other words, Petrarch bequeaths to future writers and readers not only an intimate Cicero but, as I will argue, rhetoric and hermeneutics of intimacy.[34]

In elucidating this account of the development of early modern intimacy, Eden points more specifically to Petrarch's stated interest in Cicero's letters as reflections on "personal matters of *familiaria*," and to his further assertion, following Cicero—and here she quotes Petrarch directly—that "'the true characteristic of an epistle is to make the recipient more informed about those things that he does not know'" including, most significantly for Eden's analysis, what Petrarch describes as the correspondent's "'state of mind' (*animi status*)."³⁵ Eden concludes: "So closely aligned is his letter writing with *familiaria* . . . that he eventually decides to call the collection *Familiarium rerum liber*."³⁶

At the same time, the three-step process that Eden outlines above also introduces a second essential element into her study of Petrarch's epistolary writing that is central to my own analysis of the representation of friendship in a more strictly literary context. As Eden's summarizing statement makes abundantly clear, the rise of early modern intimacy in Petrarch's letters is conceived as both "a rhetoric and hermeneutics," that is, in terms that privilege the mediated space of the text. The source for this conclusion, as Eden explains in her introduction, is Gadamer's *Truth and Method*: "Understanding any written text, Gadamer affirms . . . necessarily involves the reader as interpreter in the 'miracle' of understanding what the writer had in mind, and this understanding inevitably creates some kind of intimacy (*Vertrautsein*) between them."³⁷ Here, then, one begins to see the connection with Petrarch, as Gadamer's theoretical conception of familiarity resonates with Petrarch's own statements on the nature of epistolary discourse, more specifically with the idea of communicating, once again, the writer's "state of mind." In his study, Langer explicitly excludes consideration of the epistolary tradition, opposing such "humanist or other epistolary friendships" to the "imaginary worlds that literature represents."³⁸ From the perspective of Eden's analysis, however, the distinction seems somehow misplaced. Indeed, Eden identifies Gadamer's "special attention" to "*epistolary* reading and writing" with a recognition "that how we understand a letter serves as a paradigm for how we understand literature more broadly."³⁹

This idea discovers support in Nancy Struever, who argues that "the domain of intimate exchange" associated with Petrarch's epistles delimits "a space where conversation and letter are hegemonic practices."⁴⁰ While Struever's claims for Petrarch's letters are perhaps more expansive than Eden's—she sees his letters as providing a paradigm for all forms of philosophical inquiry, not just on literary matters—the primacy that she ascribes to epistolary writings for a particular strain of humanism supports the specific genealogy for early modern friendship that I would identify with Eden's analysis: "Petrarch not only announces the failure of the medieval university as context, but proceeds to replace the formal and dysfunctional academic constraints of the university with the informal and intimate relations of friendship, of a community conceived as a circle of friends devoted to *litterae*, literate wisdom . . ."⁴¹ Here, then, lies the fullest significance of Petrarch's letters to Cicero in which, as Struever asserts, "Cicero is called to account not simply as an *auctoritas*, an authoritative text, but as an interlocutory life."[42] Thus it is that Petrarch renders complete his resurrection of the great classical rhetorician.

The hegemonic status of epistolary writings in Petrarchan humanism is for Eden understood in terms of a stylistics of letter writing within which the question of subjective individuation plays a critical role. As Eden puts it, "style, and especially intimate style as an exclusive belonging, will emerge as both a source of individuation and a key marker for differentiating one writer from another."[43] Significantly for my purposes here, both the notion of belonging and individuation offer an alternative to the logical conundrum of Langer's radically unknowable friend. Eden's idea of intimacy, while no less a matter of rhetoric than Langer's reading of early modern friendship narratives, nevertheless creates the possibility of knowing the individuated subject and, by extension, opens a space for the modernized interpretation of friendship that one discovers most fully in *Don Quixote*. Indeed, the rhetorical emphasis of Eden's analysis highlights a feature of Cicero that is preserved, and arguably even expanded by Petrarch and the humanists: Appeals to the ideal of perfect friendship are maintained through discursive practices that are themselves a reflection of a more realistic appreciation of how friendship works in the world beyond the text. This is perhaps the most important implication of Eden's emphasis on a stylistics of intimacy, a concept that, in the end, may be easily extended to the literary depiction of friendship.

In fact, where difficulties of knowability and uniqueness are camouflaged by extravagant displays of selfless devotion in the traditional tale of two friends, the very real possibility of mutual recognition, however limited, becomes arguably the central trope in the emerging, more recognizably modern incarnation of the friendship story. In place of the almost ritualized enactment of self-sacrifice in the interest of perfect friendship that characterizes the traditional tale of two friends, one discovers increasingly in the texts of this period representations of friendship that are explicitly linked with the notion of the friend's unique identity as a source of narrative dynamism rather than an ossified relic of Aristotelian theoretical commitments. The rigid Aristotelian categories give way in these texts to an understanding of friendship as an ongoing process of getting to know the other that is necessarily open-ended, and therefore always incomplete. As Sancho puts it, "bien dicen que es menester mucho tiempo para venir a conocer las personas."[44] Perhaps more than any other, this statement defines the basis of friendship in *Don Quixote*, a novel that takes a thousand pages to recount the adventures of two characters whose relationship is defined by an ongoing struggle to know each other. In place of the static, idealized discourse of self-sacrifice—of a relationship that has existed, as Langer puts it, "*ab aeterno*"—the very long story of Don Quixote and Sancho Panza redefines friendship in terms of the practical day-to-day experience of coexistence that displaces the Aristotelian ideal onto an aspirational goal of knowing one's friend as well as possible.[45]

From the perspective of Langer's own analysis of perfect literary friendship, however, the shift to aspirational narratives that strive toward mutual knowing necessarily involves a retrenchment from the more austere demands of a theoretical posture that premises uniqueness on the subject's radical unknowability. The key here, however, is not a return to categorical thinking in terms of attributes, but rather a move toward action, and the consequences of action in self-definition. The Cervantine lemma that "cada uno es hijo de sus obras" here offers in the context of friendship a formula for Renaissance self-fashioning as a dynamic response to the more static Aristotelian search for definitions.[46] Set against the growing anonymity of social existence, this new model of friendship may be described using the language of Struever's assessment of Petrarch's epistolary discourse, about which she writes: "Authority, authenticity, and authentication are products of the activated relationship, rather than of the autonomous self."[47] In place of a paean to the abstraction of Aristotelian perfect friendship, the new poetics of friendship exemplified in *Don Quixote*—but also visible in a more attenuated form in other works from the period—responds to the subject's demand for recognition in a world in which imperfection underscores the inimitability of modern identity.

Furthermore, by replacing the ideal of perfect knowledge with an aspiration that is, in practice, never fully realized, this new model of friendship lends itself to a mode of literary representation that focuses almost exclusively on lived experience. I have discussed at length elsewhere how the poetics of Renaissance *imitatio*, with its emphasis on literary models drawn from the great works of classical antiquity, is displaced in Spain in this period by an emerging interest in representational verisimilitude as filtered through the writer's imagination.[48] The poetics of friendship, as I hope to show toward the end of this study, offers one of the most powerful measures of this foundational shift within the literary production of early modern Spain. Cervantes, once again, provides the strongest evidence for this assertion. It is, I would argue, no coincidence that the most robust assertion of a modern literary subjectivity drawn from the experience of life itself springs up in a novel that represents in unprecedented detail the course of a long and unlikely friendship between a mad would-be knight-errant and his earthy peasant squire. Here, then, arises the more radical claim that I would make for a poetics of friendship: The central place of modern friendship in *Don Quixote* creates formal demands within the narrative that help drive a reorientation of the Renaissance principle of *imitatio* away from the more traditional emphasis on literary intertextuality—especially as it relates to the prestigious tradition of classical antiquity—and toward an intense engagement with novel practices involving representational verisimilitude. Put simply, I will argue here for the primacy of the poetics of friendship as a central influence in the rise of the new poetics of representational verisimilitude.

This more radical claim recognizes friendship as an instrument for the literary representation of modern subjectivity. The legacy of early modern studies going back as far as Jacob Burckhardt's influential theory of the Renaissance individual depends upon an erosion of the traditional mechanisms through which identity is conferred and maintained. From this perspective, the obsessive concern with honor throughout the literature of early modern Spain—in both the theater and prose fiction—reflects the underlying anxiety that accompanies the slow degradation of increasingly obsolete notions of identity as fixed through birth and social position. Figures as disparate as Don Juan Tenorio, Guzmán de Alfarache, and Don Quixote reveal Renaissance self-fashioning in the Spanish context as exuding a neurosis extending at times to the edge of madness. The Spanish version of Renaissance self-fashioning never quite reaches the status of normalcy, but rather almost inevitably runs up against an entrenched social hierarchy that refuses to let the subject go its own way. In such a world, and in particular in the literary representations that emerge out of such a world, the subject frequently suffers a radical alienation whose most concrete manifestation is a kind of existential loneliness. Viewed in this light, the rise of a modern poetics of friendship may be said to offer a poetic compensation of sorts for the subject's seemingly inevitable alienation in the literature of the Spanish early modern period. As a voluntary association between unrelated individuals, friendship offers the possibility of overcoming, however imperfectly, the constraints of socially prescribed identities—of lineage, class, and rank. This is most noticeable in *Don Quixote*, where the hierarchical relationship between a master and his servant gives way to a sense of personal intimacy born of hundreds of pages of shared experiences and, perhaps more importantly, the dialogue through which those experiences come to shape the identity of both Don Quixote and Sancho Panza. But it is also evident, in at least a partial sense, in other works that will be examined in the following pages: in the sentimental attachment between Lotario and Camila in Guillén de Castro's theatrical rewriting of the interpolated tale "El curioso impertinente" from

Don Quixote; in the title character's yearning for a true friend in Mateo Alemán's picaresque narrative, *Guzmán de Alfarache*; and, finally, in María de Zayas's exploration of friendship between women in her unpublished play, *La traición en la amistad*. In all three of these works, one detects poetic innovations that mark a clear dialectical shift away from the rigid formulaic tendencies of Avalle-Arce's tale of two friends tradition and toward representations of friendship—grounded to varying degrees in verisimilitude—that are far more suggestive of the notion of interpersonal intimacy described by Eden and Struever in their analysis of Petrarch's letters.

Notes

1. The focus on a poetics of friendship distinguishes this study from other recent scholarship, much of which examines how larger historical forces influence literary representations of friendship. Thus, while I have been greatly influenced by the work of scholars like Hutson and Shannon, whose scholarship draws explicit connections between economic and political discourse and the literary representation of friendship in the English Renaissance, my study looks at the representation of friendship from within a more narrowly defined literary–historical perspective that grants poetic forces a greater degree of self-determination. See Hutson, *The Usurer's Daughter* and Shannon, *Sovereign Amity*. Hutson's work, in particular, will figure prominently in my chapter on Boccaccio's tale of friendship from the *Decameron*.
2. Aristotle, *Nicomachean Ethics*, 1156b10.
3. Ibid. 1156b25.
4. Cicero, *De amicitia*, iv.15. "...quod ex omnibus saeculis vix tria aut quattuor nominantur paria amicorum..."
5. Thomas Greene provides one of the most elegant accounts of humanist *imitatio* as it relates to the notion of intertextuality in the Renaissance. See especially, "Imitation and Anachronism," in *The Light in Troy: Imitation and Discovery in Renaissance Poetry*, pp. 28–53.
6. Cicero, *De amicitia*, vii.24.
7. Williams, *Reading Roman Friendship*, p. 148.
8. Ibid. pp. 6–7, provides a helpful explanation of the context for Cicero's reference to Pacuvius's staged representation of the mythic friendship of Orestes and Pylades: "The land of the Taurians was the setting of a stirring scene which thematizes precisely the difficulty of distinguishing between the two, a scene frequently and lovingly evoked in stories about the pair. When Thoas demands to know which one is Orestes so that he may kill him, each of the two identifies himself as Orestes in order to spare the other. The episode was dramatized by the second-century BC tragedian Pacuvius in a

scene which proved to be memorable. Pacuvius' play has not survived, but Cicero's Laelius evokes both the scene and its reception, pointedly describing Pacuvius as his own *hospes et amicus*, one with whom he shares the intertwined bond of hospitality and friendship."
9. Avalle-Arce, "Una tradición literaria: El cuento de los dos amigos," p. 34.
10. An awareness of the formal dimension of Boccaccio's turn toward storytelling is evident in much of the critical literature on the *Decameron*. Marcus, *An Allegory of Form*, p. 2, writing more than a generation ago, gives a sense of this critical interest: "Salvatore Battaglia's study of genre history gives a vivid idea of how Boccaccio transformed the medieval *exemplum*, which was relegated to the illustration of abstract truths, to the *novella*, a form capable of expressing the problematic of a changing world, free from subjugation to any external systems of interpretation. In his study of Boccaccio's prose style, Auerbach shows how the storyteller creates a vernacular worthy of this newly ennobled literary form. And in the architectonic design of the *Decameron* we have further proof that Boccaccio takes this erstwhile 'inferior' narrative art quite seriously." The idea also arguably underpins much of the more recent work of Robert Hollander, about which I will have more to say below.
11. Avalle-Arce, *Una tradición literaria: El cuento de los dos amigos*, p. 22.
12. Avalle-Arce, *Deslindes cervantinos*, p. 207. The original Spanish reads: "Es el tope de finalidad absoluta, después del cual no cabe plantearse el cuento de los dos amigos como problema."
13. This is a topic with a long and distinguished pedigree, especially as it relates to the most notorious of the interpolated stories, "El curioso impertinente." Beyond the metacriticism on this topic offered by Cervantes's novel itself, Américo Castro in *El pensamiento de Cervantes*, pp. 126–7, traces the roots of the debate over "El curioso impertinente" to such illustrious figures as Clemencín, Schevill, and Unamuno, among others. Within more contemporary Hispanism, the topic is revisited starting, perhaps most famously, with Bruce Wardropper in an article whose title captures by way of a pun the major point of debate in this tradition: "The Pertinence of *El curioso impertinente*." The topic is taken up by later Hispanists including Edwin Williamson, "Romance and Realism in the Interpolated Stories of the *Quixote*" and Diana de Armas Wilson, "'Passing the Love of Women': The Intertextuality of *El curioso impertinente*." I will have an opportunity to examine this critical history in greater detail in a later chapter.
14. Aristotle, *Nicomachean Ethics*, 1156b5–10. For a more extensive discussion of the three kinds of Aristotelian friendship, see Pangle, *Aristotle and the Philosophy of Friendship*, pp. 37–56.
15. Ibid. 1156b10–15.
16. A. W. Price, *Love and Friendship in Aristotle and Plato*, p. 104–5.
17. Langer, *Perfect Friendship*, pp. 51–64.
18. Ibid. p. 53.
19. Ibid. p. 61.

20. Ibid. p. 52. Reginald Hyatte's study of medieval spiritual friendship, *The Arts of Friendship*, p. 50, underscores Langer's point: "Proof of God's love on earth takes the forms of visions, spiritual messages, miracles, and special signs, all of which serve to make the mortal more fervent in her or his love, more eager to enjoy God's company in the afterlife. One gift which God may offer as encouragement to fervent love is a human friend. Spiritual friendship—that is, two or a few mortals' confident love of one another for the sake of God Who joined them in spirit—is represented and rationalized in some of the twelfth and thirteenth-century texts which we will examine as an earthly aid to the attainment of ever-greater benefits of divine love. In his dialogue on spiritual friendship, Aelred of Rievaulx claims that there are thousands of pairs of Christian martyrs who, through faith in Christ, were willing to sacrifice themselves for friendship. In comparison, the classical ideals, once prized because rare, are disappointing if one considers the quantity of those who can be called 'true' friends—few Romans, less Greeks, and no women. From this one might conclude that the multitude of flesh-and-blood Christian friends gives proof of the superabundance of God's love." Implicit here are both the instrumental nature of spiritual friendship and the sense in which God's implicit unknowability is assuaged by symptoms of his divine love.
21. Ibid. p. 53.
22. Ibid. pp. 53–4.
23. Ibid. p. 54.
24. Ibid. p. 62.
25. Williams, *Reading Roman Friendship*, p. 15.
26. Cicero, *De amicitia*, vii.23. Copley's translation, which I cite here, while less literal than Falconer's, does a better job of capturing the sense of Cicero's original.
27. Ibid. v.18. The original reads: "Nos autem ea quae sunt in usu vitaque communi, non ea quae finguntur aut optantur, spectare debemus."
28. Ibid. x.33. The original reads: "Quamquam ille quidem nihil difficilius esse dicebat quam amicitiam usque ad extremum vitae diem permanere: nam vel ut non idem expediret incidere saepe, vel ut de re publica non idem sentiretur; mutari etiam mores hominum saepe dicebat, alias adversis rebus, alias aetate ingravescente." By way of comparison, consider what Langer, *Perfect Friendship*, pp. 29–30, has to say about "friendship and time": "Friendship conveys a sense of completeness and completion that in linguistic terms is perhaps most characteristic of the perfect tense. It is present to us, but has always already actualized itself, 'perfected' itself. The development of friendship is the unfolding of what is already there, a sort of repeated showing of its completedness: just as the similarity of the friends ties them to each other, so does temporal development fail to introduce anything different, for each successive event is a confirmation, a demonstration of what has been perfected." The contrast here with Cicero could not be clearer.

29. Williams, *Reading Roman Friendship*, p. 219, where he notes on the matter of friendship in Cicero's *Epistulae ad familiares*, "The terms *amici* and *amicitia* are especially prominent on the landscape of Cicero's correspondence—a search of the PHI *Classical Latin Texts* database yields 409 occurences of the two nouns in the letters, along with 265 of *familiaris/familiaritas/familiariter*, and 196 of *necessarius/necessitudo*—and pervading them all is *amor*. It is only a slight oversimplification to say that in the speech genre of letters the verb *amare* signals the existence of *amicitia* just as the verb *odi* signals the existence of *inimicitiae* . . ."
30. Wilcox, *The Gift of Correspondence in Classical Rome*, pp. 9–10, notes that Cicero's more theoretical musings on "gift exchange" in friendship are found extensively in "Book I of the *De officiis*."
31. Ibid. p. 34.
32. Ibid. pp. 65–6.
33. Eden, *The Renaissance Rediscovery of Intimacy*, p. 50.
34. Ibid. p. 50. Eden's use of the term "rediscovery" in her title is noteworthy. Where Langer's analysis of the Aristotelian concept of friendship as processed through scholasticism stresses a long historical arc of continuity, Eden's study of early modern intimacy enacts an alternative model—so familiar throughout early modern studies—of a lost classical legacy that is, in this case, literally rediscovered, as Eden notes, p. 49, "in 1345 in the cathedral library of Verona."
35. Ibid. pp. 52–3.
36. Ibid. p. 53. Eden, p. 52, attributes the original critique of Cicero's "inclusion of personal matters or *familiaria* in his epistolary writing" to Seneca. According to Eden, this idea is then picked up in a more positive sense by Petrarch, whom Eden quotes directly.
37. Ibid. p. 6.
38. Langer, *Perfect Friendship*, p. 26.
39. Eden, *The Renaissance Rediscovery of Intimacy*, p. 5.
40. Struever, *Theory as Practice: Ethical Inquiry in the Renaissance*, p. 15.
41. Ibid. p. 6.
42. Ibid. p. 29.
43. Eden, *The Renaissance Rediscovery of Intimacy*, p. 9. Eden's analysis here resonates with Struever's understanding in *Theory as Practice*, p. 26, of the new mode of inquiry inaugurated by Petrarch's correspondence: "To address a friend as 'pars mei' (XXIII, 18, 42-3) and 'alter idem' (IX, 9, 31) defines the friend as inquirer in a very special manner; it imposes first-personal considerations. Intimacy is an investigative parameter, it enjoins a certain tone of voice in investigational exchange."
44. Cervantes, *Don Quixote*, I.15. All passages from *Don Quixote* are adapted from Rodríguez Marín's 1917 edition. Understood in context, Cervantes may be said to underplay the significance of the observation: it is made in reference to Don Quixote's horse, Rocinante. This ironizing gesture is consistent with the novel's reluctance to theorize in any serious way on matters

of friendship—with the one significant exception of the interpolated story of "El curioso impertinente."

45. Langer, *Perfect Friendship*, p. 46. Langer here is referring to the friendship between Tito and Gisippo, but the idea is a general feature of the tale of two friends tradition.
46. The expression from *Don Quixote* occurs twice in the novel, in chapters I.4 and I.47. The term "Renaissance Self-Fashioning," of course, is borrowed from Stephen Greenblatt's book of the same name. As Greenblatt, p. 1, puts it succinctly in the opening lines of that study, ". . . my starting point is quite simply that in sixteenth-century England there were both selves and a sense that they could be fashioned."
47. Struever, *Theory as Practice*, p. 11.
48. This is a major theme of *Writers on the Market*, my earlier study of Lope's *comedia*, Alemán's *Guzmán de Alfarache*, and *Don Quixote*.

Chapter 1

Boccaccio's Tale of Two Friends

Avalle-Arce traces the origin of the tale of two friends in Spain to the second story in Pedro Alfonso's popular twelfth-century *Disciplina clericalis*, the *Exemplum de integro amico*. Noting that "La *Disciplina clericalis* es, ante todo, un manual de ética," Avalle-Arce draws a compelling map of the relationship in Alfonso's text between exemplarity, entertainment, and the poetics of writing perfect friendship:

> Pero el moralista, en el caso de Pedro Alfonso, va de la mano con el hombre de letras consciente de su oficio, y los dos buscan, con propósito deliberado, cautivar al gran público. Ambas personalidades se complementan y contrarrestan, pero, como sucede en los demás ejemplarios medievales, no se integran en el cuerpo de la obra sino que proceden por separado: primero expone el moralista, después narra el literato. El principio jerarquizador, tan caro a la mentalidad medieval, supedita el relato a la exposición moral; la fábula queda relegada a segundo plano y su desarrollo artístico sufre en consecuencia.[1]

> [But the moralist in the case of Pedro Alfonso goes hand in hand with the man of letters, conscious of his role, and both seek, with deliberate intent, to captivate the larger public. Both personae complement and counter each other, but, as happens in other medieval exemplary narratives, they are not integrated within the body of the work, but rather arise separately: First, the moralist explains, then the writer narrates. The hierarchical priniciple, so dear to the medieval mindset, subordinates the story to moral exposition; the tale is thus relegated to the second order and its artistic development suffers as a consequence.]

The desire to "cautivar al gran público," which in this instance may be read as an appeal to entertainment as the means to moral instruction, underscores the exemplary function of the *Disciplina clericalis*. That exemplarity, in turn, imposes a hierarchy on Alfonso's dual role as "moralista" and "hombre de letras," in which the moralizing imperative dominates.[2] Finally, as Avalle-Arce suggests a bit later in the same paragraph, the privileged demands of moral exemplarity necessarily "se despoja el relato de toda superfluidad, y la narración, así aligerada, se nos ofrece descarnada, reducida a sus líneas esenciales. Los personajes tienen sólo valor simbólico, y en este plano actúan [strips the tale of all superfluity, and the narrative, thus lightened, is offered to us stark, reduced to its essential elements. The characters only have a symbolic meaning, and act accordingly]."[3] Moralism thus is finally revealed as a determinant factor in poetics, as the stories that comprise the *Disciplina clericalis*—and the *Exemplum de integro amico* in particular—are reduced to that which is essential to their exemplary function.

While it addresses the structural dynamic underlying the austere aesthetic of the *Exemplum de integro amico*, Avalle-Arce's analysis leaves open the question of precisely how Alfonso's tale of exemplary friendship relates to the practical reality of its intended audience. Here, as with my discussion in the last chapter of Pacuvius's dramatic staging of the story of Orestes and Pylades, one must resist the temptation to interpret exemplarity as simply providing practical knowledge applicable to the real circumstance of everyday life. In fact, from the very opening lines, Alfonso's *Exemplum de integro amico* exhibits a strangeness that compels a reassessment of the notions of both exemplarity and friendship:

> Relatum est michi de duobus negociatoribus, quorum unus erat in Egypto, alter Baldach, seque solo auditu cognoverant et per internuncios pro sibi necessariis mittebant.
>
> [I have been told of two merchants of whom one lived in Egypt, and the other in Baghdad. They knew each other solely by hearsay, and used messengers to inform each other of necessary business.][4]

Important aspects of this opening sentence stand out in contrast to the early modern tradition of writing perfect friendship that, according to Avalle-Arce, would grow up around this foundational tale. First, there is Langer's problem of the friend's unknowability, which is translated here into the practical fact of two men who literally have never met. There is the suggestion that they are, in some sense, medieval pen pals who correspond via intermediaries, but even that idea is undermined by Alfonso's insistence that their communication is limited to matters that are *necessarius*. This is not the selfless voluntary communion that marks Aristotle's highest mode of friendship but rather, as the use of the descriptive term *negotiator* confirms, a utilitarian relationship that is confined to commercial interests.

Taken as a whole, these indicators signal a curious rejection of friendship as a motivating force in the narrative. Nor does the subsequent story fill in that causal lacuna with additional details that might explain the extreme acts of selflessness that dominate later in the story. In the very next sentence, the merchant from Baghdad is described as taking a business trip to Egypt—"Contigit autem ut qui erat Baldach, in negociacionem iret in Egyptum"—at which point the merchant from Egypt "welcomed him joyfully into his house and served him in all things for eight days, as is the custom amongst friends [suscepit eum gaudens in domum suam et in omnibus ei servivit sicut mos est amicorum per VIII dies]."[5] Even here, as the narrative shifts from describing the two as business associates to an initial reference to friendship, a certain degree of ambiguity remains; the direct appeal to social customs—"mos amicorum"—necessarily embeds this new friendship within the fabric of established social rituals. In this sense, the two merchant-friends remain steeped in a kind of cultural formalism that arguably inhibits the kind of social transcendence normally reserved for Aristotelian perfect friendship.

Yet despite the almost deliberate resistance to a more robust rhetorical defense of these two characters as embodiments of perfect friendship, the approximately 600 words that make up the remainder of the *Exemplum de integro amico* stage a pair of reciprocating scenes of extreme self-sacrifice in the name of friendship that may be said to exemplify the pure selflessness of the Aristotelian model. First, the visiting merchant from Baghdad falls ill to the point of death, and when the merchant from Egypt discovers that this illness derives from an infatuation with a woman that he himself had planned to marry, he yields to his guest's passion, granting "him the noble maiden as wife, together with everything that was with her as dowry."[6] Then, in the second part of the story, the merchant from Egypt, having fallen into poverty, travels to Baghdad, but before he can locate his old friend, is falsely accused of murder, at which point, in an echo of Pacuvius's representation of Orestes and Pylades, the merchant from Baghdad offers to take his place on the cross, confessing to a crime that he did not commit. All is well in the end, however, thanks to a forgiving king, and the two men part as the embodiment of perfect friendship, while the narrator concludes, referring to the merchant from Baghdad, "It is scarcely likely that a man could find such a friend [Vix poterit talis reperiri amicus]."[7] With this final echo of both Aristotle and Laelius from Cicero's *De amicitia*, the *Exemplum de integro amico* finally assumes a rhetorical register that is recognizable within the Aristotelian-Ciceronian tradition.

Read against the backdrop of the tale's opening lines, the depiction of these two reciprocating acts of extreme self-sacrifice in the name of friendship lends the entire story a sense of profound unreality. Unlike the story of Orestes and Pylades, however, where the mythic status of the two friends tends to elevate their behavior beyond the realm of mundane human affairs, Alfonso's initial negation of any pre-existing friendship between his two merchants leads to a disarticulation with everyday life of a very different kind. The anonymous merchants from Egypt and Baldach are not mythic ideals, but rather oddly, empty ciphers whose acts of self-sacrifice in the name of friendship exist as symbols of an ideal that has no practical relation to human affairs in the world. If the spectacle of Pylades's grand gesture of selflessness in order to save his friend inspires admiration in the audience for, as Cicero notes, "that which they could not do themselves," the narrative account of two anonymous acquaintances with no personal history who engage in similar acts transforms the entire enterprise of perfect friendship into an abstract set of relational equations.[8]

While it operates according to a different logic than the mythic friendship of Orestes and Pylades, the representation of completely unmotivated acts of self-sacrifce in the name of friendship in the *Exemplum de integro amico* nevertheless raises familiar questions about the underlying function of exemplarity. Where Joseph Ramon Jones and John Esten Keller make a presentist retreat into a reading of the *Disciplina clericalis* as a collection of "pleasant fictions," an interpretation of the story that would take its exemplary pretensions seriously is confronted with an alien landscape in which the model for perfect friendship is reduced to a series of structural conceits that are completely disconnected from the experience of everyday life.[9] Purged of any discernible motivation, the friendship between these two medieval merchants is reduced to pure form, the manifestion not so much of an ideal as the enactment of an essentialized narrative paradigm. Read in this way, the exemplarity of the *Exemplum de integro amico* may be said to finally reside in the formal structure of this tale of reciprocating acts of self-sacrifice in the name of perfect friendship. Mythic friendship thus gives way to two-dimensional archetypes that are only intelligible as cogs within a narrative machine that resists more complex interpretative strategies that would locate deeper levels of meaning.

At the same time, the structural simplicity of the *Exemplum de integro amico* opens up the possibility for a very different kind of exemplarity that anticipates the later tradition of writing perfect friendship. In proposing the *Exemplum* as the originary tale of two friends, Avalle-Arce implicitly acknowledges its exemplary function as the model for a literary tradition. Here, the Renaissance discourse of *imitatio* as a species of intertextuality finds a limited reflection in what is arguably a new poetics of friendship. Yet, as the foregoing analysis suggests, it is not the concept of friendship itself or even affective states related to that concept that defines this new poetics, but rather a formal narrative paradigm within which friendship serves as an abstract driving force.

Understood in this way, this first iteration of the poetics of friendship may be said to possess a formal purity that underscores the thesis of my entire study. At the same time, this emphasis on structure—which, in the end, is nothing more than the rehearsal of certain fixed elements of plotting in the service of friendship as an unmotivated abstraction— comes under tremendous pressure in later renditions of Avalle-Arce's tale of two friends. Increasingly, the demands of writing longer and more complex narratives of friendship expose the limits of Alfonso's original paradigm, leading in the end to the symbolic implosion of the formal conceit of perfect friendship in Cervantes's "El curioso impertinente." Yet, as the remainder of this chapter will show, many of the internal tensions that will eventually lead to Cervantes's far more radical response to the difficulties of writing perfect friendship are already on display in one of the earliest Renaissance heirs to the *Exemplum de integro amico*, Boccaccio's fourteenth-century tale of Gisippo and Tito from Day Ten of the *Decameron*.[10]

A perspicacious reader of Boccaccio, Robert Hollander, offers a circumspect interpretation of friendship in the *Decameron*. Having noted the brief reference to friendship in the opening lines of the *Proemio*, he goes on to argue that, outside the tale of Gisippo and Tito, friendship is, in fact, not a topic of great interest to Boccacio: "Filomena's last *novella*, with its nostalgic championing of *amistà* (the word has ten of its twenty-eight occurrences in the *Decameron* in X.viii [one, retrospective in X.ix]), reminds us how little true friendship we have found in the cento *novelle*."[11] Instead, for Hollander, the importance of this tale derives from a more general reinterpretation of the *Decameron*'s tenth day of storytelling, which he describes in terms of "an interrogation of the myth of order."[12] Borrowing his terminology from the work of Frank Kermode, he elaborates what he means with this statement:[13]

> It is our view that too many of Boccaccio's readers tend to turn his fictions into "myths" and thus fail to take into full account precisely his ability, as fiction-maker, to irradiate the apparently contradictory yet utterly normal patterns in the behavior of humankind. It is the power of the satirist, prepared by instinct and experience to avenge himself upon mythmakers, that we find at the core of Boccaccio's magnificent achievement in the *Decameron*.[14]

Hollander's emphasis on fiction reminds us of Avalle-Arce's discovery of new "novelistic possibilities" in Boccaccio, that is, he constructs his reading of the *Decameron* in terms of the emergence of a new kind of storytelling.¹⁵ And while Hollander never makes the point explicitly, one recognizes in his belief in the capacity of Boccaccio's fiction to "irradiate the apparently contradictory yet utterly normal patterns in the behavior of humankind" an allusion to something akin to representational verisimilitude.

Yet for Hollander, it is not merely fiction that defines the formal space of the *Decameron*, but a subspecies of fiction that has been subjected to "the power of the satirist" acting against "the mythmakers." This is, according to Hollander, what "too many of Boccaccio's readers" fail to recognize, presumably because they are reading in the wrong way. Hollander's criticism here would seem to be localized to the critical tradition surrounding the *Decameron*. However, his observations arguably illuminate the broader historical narrative that I am attempting to construct in this study. Considered in that context, the failure to properly identify the turn to satirical fiction may be understood in historical terms as a symptom of Boccaccio's close proximity to the scholastic tradition of spiritual friendship. Unable to fully escape the shadow of that tradition, Boccaccio's fiction emerges, at least in part, as a reaction to its genealogy in myth and idealized exemplarity. Indeed—and here my reading departs from Hollander—it carries that genealogy along with it, the satirical elements of Boccaccio's tale co-existing with the Aristotelian ideal even as that ideal is subject to a kind of internal critique. Understood in this way, those readers who fail to see the satire in Boccaccio's tale of perfect friendship should be offered a partial redemption; for despite the critique of "mythmaking," the myth itself of perfect friendship subsists as an important foundation for Boccaccio's turn to fiction.

This historical reading of the internal dynamic of Boccaccio's tale of perfect friendship highlights, once again, the formal basis of literary innovations relating to the representation of friendship. Hollander's identification of Boccaccio's fiction with satire, in this respect, is crucial. However, as Hollander's own analysis implies, that satire must finally be understood not in its more customary usage as a mode of social criticism—although there may well be elements of this—but more fundamentally as a critique of form. In the end, it is not the hypocrisy of real friends that comes under scrutiny in the tale of Tito and Gisippo, but rather the exhaustion of the Aristotelian model for perfect friendship in a narrative landscape that privileges storytelling over idealized moral exemplarity. There are historical motivations for this that go beyond the text itself, to be sure, but the underlying critique of representation is self-directed. What is at stake, then, is not the functioning of friendship as myth—obviously it does function for some readers, as Hollander himself acknowledges—but rather an evolutionary process within the formal possibilities for a poetics of friendship.

The story of Tito and Gisippo occurs rather late in the *Decameron*, as the eighth tale from the tenth and final day of storytelling, and revolves around a friendship between two men that is tested through rivalry in love. Set in classical antiquity, the tale describes how the Roman Titus Quintus Fulvius, having been sent to study in Greece under the tutelage of Gisippo's father, befriends his master's son based on common interests.[16] In a manner consistent with the Aristotelian highest ideal of friendship, the two young men are described as inseparable—"nor knew either rest or solace save when he was with the other [niun di loro aveva né ben né riposo, se non tanto quanto erano insieme]"—and united in their devotion to the highest aims of education: ". . . and with even pace and prodigious applause [they] scaled together the glorious heights of philosophy [. . . e parimente ciascuno d'altissimo ingegno dotato saliva alla gloriosa altezza della filosofia con pari passo e con maravigliosa laude]."[17]

From a structural point of view, this commitment to Aristotelian orthodoxy constitutes one of the unifying formal attributes of the story as a whole, not only informing the shape of the narrative, but also punctuating it at key moments with passages that provide strong philological evidence of the story's genealogical nexus to the Aristotelian-scholastic tradition of perfect friendship. Consider, for example, this passage in which Gisippo asserts his desire to cede his betrothed, Sofronia, to his friend as a token of their abiding friendship:

«Sarà adunque Sofronia tua, ché di leggiere altra che così ti piacesse non troverresti; e io, il mio amore leggiermente ad un'altra volgendo, avrò te e me contentato. Alla qual cosa forse così liberal non sarei, se così rade o con quella difficoltà le mogli si trovasser che si truovan gli amici; e per ciò, potend'io leggerissimamente altra moglie trovare ma non altro amico, io voglio innanzi (non vo' dir perder lei, ché non la perderò dandola a te, ma ad un altro me la trasmuterò di bene in meglio) trasmutarla, che perder te.»[18]

["Sophronia, then, shall be yours; for you would not lightly find another so much to your mind, and I shall readily find another to love, and so shall content both you and me. In which matter, peradventure, I might not be so liberal, were wives so scarce or hard to find as are friends; wherefore, as 'tis easy a matter for me to find another wife, I had rather—I say not lose her, for in giving her to you lose her I shall not, but only transfer her to one that is my *alter ego*, and that to her advantage—I had rather, I say, transfer her to you than lose you."]

This passage asserts the primacy of friendship over love—a recurring feature, as will become evident, in many early modern friendship narratives—while simultaneously transforming Sofronia into an object of exchange through which Gisippo realizes his act of friendly self-sacrifice.[19] However, from the perspective of a poetics of friendship the exchange of Sofronia is assimilated into a much more orthodox Aristotelian formula, namely, that of the friend as "un altro me"—a second self. As Langer puts it in his remarks on this same passage: "One is tempted to say that, if indeed the friend is another self, it is immensely easier to find a different spouse than another I."[20] Read in this way, the narrative's internal structure displays a remarkably close adherence to the expectations of the Aristotelian ideal.

Not only does the narrative's engagement with the notion of the friend as a second self constitute a kind of genetic trace of Boccaccio's debt to the long tradition of Aristotelian perfect friendship, the complexities of its deployment mirror in important ways Langer's analysis of the Aristotelian-scholastic tradition, discussed in the previous chapter. On the one hand, the narrative's explicit invocation of this theme consistently serves to distinguish the two perfect friends from everyone else around them, an idea that provides a deeper explanation for Sofronia's abject objectification, as perhaps best exemplified in the passage describing the moment of her deception on her wedding night:

> Il quale, come nel letto giunse, presa la giovane, quasi come sollazzando, chetamente la domandò se sua moglie esser voleva. Ella, credendo lui esser Gisippo, rispose di sì; ond'egli un bello e ricco anello le mise in dito dicendo: «E io voglio esser tuo marito». E quinci consumato il matrimonio, lungo e amoroso piacer prese di lei, senza che ella o altri mai s'accorgesse che altri che Gisippo giacesse con lei.[21]

> [Now no sooner was Titus abed with the lady, then, taking her in his arms, he, as if jestingly, asked in a low tone whether she were minded to be his wife. She, taking him to be Gisippus, answered, yes; whereupon he set a fair and costly ring on her finger, saying:—"And I am minded to be your husband." And having presently consummated the marriage, he long and amorously disported with her, neither she, nor any other, being ever aware that another than Gisippus lay with her.]

Throughout this passage, the narrator places special emphasis on Sofronia's utter lack of conscious participation in this marriage arrangement, effectively undermining her agency and affirming her role as passive object of exchange. Indeed, the narrative's rehearsal of an idealized moral exemplarity demands no less, as any intervention by Sofronia as an independent voice within the narrative would necessarily introduce complications into the perfect fulfillment of Gisippo's act of self-sacrifice in the name of friendship.[22]

Equally significant, however, Sofronia's lack of agency in this scene bolsters the defining Aristotelian notion of the friend as a second self. What ultimately deprives her of agency is not a lack of will, but rather a self-conscious act of deception by her would-be lover. Tito deliberately misrepresents himself to Sofronia, and Sofronia—somewhat incredibly— misrecognizes the man whom she finds in her bed. Sofronia's inability to distinguish between her betrothed and his friend works to confirm their symbolic self-identity. Once he enters the marriage bed Tito becomes, in a manner that underscores the Aristotelian logic of the tale's plotting, Gisippo's second self. Sofronia's silence at this point only serves to confirm this Aristotelian symbolism, especially as this fundamental confusion of identities persists for a time after the the consummation of her marriage.

Moreover, the symbolic logic that would affirm Tito as Gisippo's *alter ego* gives rise to a necessary corollary in Sofronia's absolute alientation from her husband, creating in the process a structural counterpoint to the Aristotelian ideal of self-identification between friends. Indeed, by the end of the passage, the problem of misrecognition takes on universal proportions as neither Sofronia "nor any other" is ever made "aware that another than Gisippus lay with her." In this way, the internal dynamic of the friend as a second self finds a complement in the radical segregation of the perfect friends from all other social relations, even marriage.

The full significance of this radical differentiation between Gisippo and Tito's perfect friendship and all other social relations comes into fuller view in the next section of the narrative in which Tito, sensing his new in-laws' dissatisfaction after they discover the truth of Sofronia's fate, confronts his wife's family with a very long speech—so long, in fact, that it comprises almost a third of the text for the entire story. The speech is rhetorically quite complex, no more so than in Tito's careful parsing of distinctions between divine providence, free will, and fortune. On the one hand, Tito suggests that his marriage to Sofronia was "ordained from all eternity [che *ab etterno* disposto fosse]," the product, as the context for these words makes clear, of the will of "the Gods, by whom . . . we and our affairs are swayed and governed with uniform and unerring wisdom [gl'Iddii, il quali . . . con ragion perpetua e senza alcuno errore dispongono e governan noi e le nostre cose]."[23]

This notion of divine providence, however, gives way to a somewhat different formulation when Tito turns his attention to the topic of friendship, the ties of which, he argues, "should be more more binding than that of blood or kinship" because "our friends are of our own choosing, whereas our kinsfolk are appointed to us by Fortune."[24] Here, talk of divine providence is replaced by an almost Machiavellian notion of fortune as chance, or the random forces of the universe, against which the free will to choose one's friends emerges as a locus of exalted resistance.

Taken independently, Tito's statements on the topic of marriage and friendship would seem to lean on two distinct philosophical schemes: friendship is portrayed in Tito's speech as both an instrument of divine providence as embodied in his marriage to Sofronia and as an expression of individual will—the choice to be a friend—in defiance of the chaotic forces of fortune that rule the rest of the world. Divine providence and fortune here operate in somewhat contradictory ways—exposing a more general philosophical tension within the Renaissance that would later lead Machiavelli to explicitly disregard the former in his political theory. Boccaccio, however, finds a way to fuse these two schemes, as Gisippo's freely willed act of self-sacrifice in the name of friendship becomes the key gesture in the fulfillment of the divine plan for Tito's marriage to Sofronia. In this way, perfect friendship itself is imbued with a divine element that further alienates the two friends from everyone else whose lives and relationships are necessarily subject to the vicissitudes of capricious fortune. Indeed, so far are the two friends, Tito and Gisippo, removed from the world of normal human interactions that the logic informing their exalted status is unintelligible to mere mortals. Tito captures something of this idea when he complains of his in-laws' inability to discern "the secret providence and purposes of the Gods [della segreta provvedenza e intenzion degl'Iddii]" and in his disparaging refusal to explain to his unenlightened intelocutors "after what sort the sacred laws of friendship prescribe that friend shall entreat friend [Quello che le sante leggi della amicizia vogliono che l'uno amico per l'altro faccia . . .]."[25]

With the successful resolution of Tito's claim to Sofronia—about which I will have more to say shortly—the narrative accelerates towards a second, and arguably more dramatic, scene of friendly self-sacrifice. From the perspective of the narrative's commitment to the Aristotelian model of perfect friendship, the scene is something of a structural necessity, providing Tito with an opportunity to reciprocate Gisippo's early "transfer" of Sofronia. Indeed, there is much evidence that this structural demand is the driving force in the final pages of the story, as narrative details and dialogue are scaled back in the interest of pushing the plot along its necessary course: Gisippo, having fallen into poverty and now banished from Athens, travels to Rome, where through no fault of his own he is accused of and confesses to a murder that he did not commit. At this key moment, Tito shows up, recognizes his friend and—in an echo of the story of Pylades and Orestes—publicly declares that he, not Gisippo, is responsible for the crime. Only a few lines later, however, this scene of self-sacrifice in the name of friendship is conveniently resolved when the true culprit—"so sore at heart was he by reason of their innocence [tanta fu la tenerezza che nel cuor gli venne per la innocenzia di questi due"]—steps forward to acknowledge his guilt, in response to which Octavianus decides to set all three men free, "the two by reason of their innocence, and the third for love of them [li due, per ciò che erano innocenti, e il terzo per amor di loro]."[26] In a final flourish of friendly communion, Tito grants Gisippo his younger sister in marriage and makes him a citizen of Rome, where "long and happily they lived together . . . growing, if possible, greater friends day by day [. . . sempre in una casa gran tempo e lietamente vissero, più ciascun giorno, se più potevano essere, divenendo amici]."[27]

As if to underscore the story's singularity of purpose, nearly every aspect of the narrative described above contributes to the enactment of perfect Aristotelian friendship. In fact, there is a structural economy in these last pages that approaches the terseness of the *Disciplina clericalis*, while the shift in focus from matters of the heart to questions of life and death raises the stakes in this final section of the narrative. The result is precisely the kind of rarefication that I associated in the last chapter with Cicero's account of the dramatic representation of the mythic friendship of Orestes and Pylades. Even the demands of moral exemplarity are fulfilled in the narrative's denouement as Tito's willingness to make the ultimate sacrifice leads not to his death, but to a final reunion between friends, symbolically sealed by Gisippo's marriage and formal acceptance into Roman society as a citizen, thereby confirming the abiding equality between the two men, that is, their status as one another's *alter ego*. Such symbolic marks of friendship may be said to signal the final reaffirmation of the bond between Tito and Gisippo in quintessentially Aristotelian terms, as a paucity of narrative detail combined with heavy symbolic content gives rise to a representation of two friends who inhabit an idealized state of perfect communion.

My analysis so far has attempted to demonstrate the extent to which the tale of Tito and Gisippo fulfills the expectations of the Aristotelian paradigm of perfect friendship. This is a reading endorsed not only by many established critics but also, I would note, by Boccaccio's narrator, Filomena, whose concluding remarks insist on the tale's exemplarity:

> Santissima cosa adunque è l'amistà, e non solamente di singular reverenzia degna, ma d'essere con perpetua laude commendata, sì come discretissima madre di magnificenzia e d'onestà, sorella di gratitudine e di carità, e d'odio e d'avarizia nimica, sempre, senza priego aspettar, pronta a quello in altrui virtuosamente operare che in sé vorrebbe che fosse operato.[28]

> [Exceeding sacred then, is friendship, and worthy not only to be had in veneration, but to be extolled with never-ending praise, as the most dutiful mother of magnificence and seemliness, sister of gratitude and charity, and foe to enmity and avarice; ever, without waiting to be asked, ready to do as generously by another as she would have done by herself.]

The assimilation of ideal friendship in this passage into a discourse rife with religious references underscores Boccaccio's alignment with the Aristotelian-scholastic tradition of perfect friendship. The mythic register described above in the context of Pylades and Orestes is here Christianized through appeals to the sacred and, curiously enough, an association between friendship and the "golden rule." Viewed from this perspective, the dubious practical applicability of the tale of Tito and Gisippo arguably gives way to an exaltation of the mytho-religious quality of friendship: Filomena's praise effectively elevates the notion of friendship to a semi-divine status that resembles more the medieval notion of spiritual friendship than any practical understanding of its functioning in the real world.[29] Like the two mythic friends in Cicero's anecdote, Tito and Gisippo come to embody an idealized virtue whose value lies precisely in its inimitable transcendent perfection.

As I have already indicated, this reading of the tale of Tito and Gisippo, while clearly attractive to many readers of the *Decameron*, nevertheless displays an acute critical myopia that fails to account for Boccaccio's skeptical engagement with the idealizing premise of his own narrative. While the tale never abandons its overall commitment to the claims of the Aristotelian ideal, especially as realized in structural terms, the execution of that commitment is nevertheless disrupted at key moments in the story. As discussed above, these disruptions share a common origin in what Avalle-Arce describes as the literary mode of fiction, especially as directed toward an internal narrative self-critique. In this sense, these disruptions provide more than just a critical assessment of the ostensible claims of Aristotelian perfect friendship; more fundamentally, they constitute a formal response to the inadequacies, to borrow once again from Hollander, of the tale's mythmaking.

Perhaps the earliest sign of this countervailing tendency surfaces with Tito's internal deliberations over his feelings for his friend's betrothed. After a long internal monologue in which he struggles with the competing demands of love and friendship, Tito finally gives in to his amorous feelings:

> E poi, di Sofronia ricordandosi, in contrario volgendo, ogni cosa detta dannava, dicendo: «Le leggi d'amore sono di maggior potenzia che alcune altre: elle rompono, non che quelle della amistà, ma le divine . . . La bellezza di costei merita d'essere amata da ciascheduno; e se io l'amo, che giovane sono, chi me ne potrà meritamente riprendere? Io non l'amo perché ella sia di Gisippo, anzi l'amo ché l'amerei di chunque ella stata fosse.»[30]

> [But then, as he remembered Sophronia, his thoughts took the contrary direction, and he recanted all he had said, musing on this wise: "The laws of Love are of force above all others; they abrogate not only the law of human friendship, but the law Divine itself . . . So beauteous is this damsel that there is none but should love her; and if I love her, who am young, who can justly censure me? I love her not because she is the affianced of Gisippus; no matter whose she was, I should love her all the same."]

Two things stand out in the passage. First, as both Giuseppe Mazzotta and Hollander have observed, there is a fundamental contradiction between Tito's estimation of the claims of love in this passage and his assertations elsewhere that he privileges his friendship with Gisippo above all else.[31] Confronted with the first real test of his friendship with Gisippo, Tito seems already poised to fail in his loyalty to his perfect friend. Second, beyond Tito's self-serving arguments to justify his betrayal, the passage ends with a statement that illuminates the complexity of Boccaccio's engagement with the topic of Aristotelian perfect friendship. In his long speech to his in-laws, already mentioned above, Tito argues for his marriage as the fulfillment of divine will through the instrument of perfect friendship. Here, however, he ends with a declaration that effectively cleaves his love for Sofronia from any such higher purpose—". . . l'amerei di chunque ella stata fosse." With these words, Tito insists that his love for Sofronia exists independent of his friendship with Gisippo. Given that he finally yields to his amorous desires at the expense of his duty to friendship, the end result is not only a subordination of that friendship to his love for Sofronia, but more significantly, an effective denial of the special place of this one friendship in his life.[32]

Tito's revelation of his internal deliberations displays a psychological richness that carries over into his relationship with his friend Gisippo. The problem of the perfect friend's unknowabilty that Langer identifies with the late medieval tradition, if not completely relieved, is at least assuaged somewhat at those moments in Boccaccio's text where his protagonists are depicted as sharing a kind of nascent intimacy—in Eden's sense of the word. The result is a paradox of sorts in which a breakdown in the structural purity of Tito's claim to embody Aristotelian perfect friendship opens up a space for new ways of knowing one's friend. Nowhere is this more evident than in Gisippo's response to his friend's admission of his amorous disposition toward Sofronia in the course of their one and only extended dialogue:

> «Tito, se tu non fossi di conforto bisognoso come tu se', io di te a te medesimo mi dorrei, sì come d'uomo il quale hai la nostra amicizia violata, tenendomi sì lungamente la tua gravissima passione nascosa. E come che onesto non ti paresse, non son per ciò le disoneste cose, se non come l'oneste, da celare all'amico, per ciò che chi amico è, come delle oneste con l'amico prende piacere, così le non oneste s'ingegna di torre dello animo dello amico; . . .»[33]

> ["Titus . . . but that you are in need of comfort, I should reproach you, that you have offended against our friendship in that you have so long kept close from me this most distressful passion; and albeit you did deem it unseemly, yet unseemly things should no more than things seemly be withheld from a friend, for that, as a friend rejoices with his friend in things seemly, so he does endeavor to wean his friend from things unseemly . . ."]

This confessional moment is certainly pivotal to the narrative's overall plotting: Tito's confession of his love for Sofronia facilitates Gisippo's grand act of self-sacrifice for the sake of his friend which, in turn, fulfills the structural requirements for Aristotelian perfect friendship as an expression of ideal moral exemplarity. At the same time, however, the confession of "unseemly things" in order that they may be corrected implies a departure from the Aristotelian ideal of the perfectly virtuous friend toward a more practical conception of friendly communion.[34] One hears in this passage echoes of Cicero and the alternative humanist genealogy for early modern friendship as the rigid structural requirements of the Aristotelian paradigm give way to a notion of friendship that is decidedly aspirational in nature. Above all, this passage demonstrates the extent to which Boccaccio has moved beyond the abstract epistemological problem of Langer's radically unknowable perfect friend toward a mode of storytelling that would represent the practical difficulties of mutual comprehension within friendship.

To understand this last point, a comparison with Boccaccio's probable source material in the *Disciplina clericalis* is instructive. While rivalry in love in this medieval story also provides the pretext for an expansive gesture of self-sacrifice in the name of friendship, the psychological dimension of the characters' predicament is completely ignored. Arguably a characteristic of medieval narrative in general, this complete disregard for the psychological dynamic between these two friends nevertheless guarantees the Aristotelian purity of their relationship, but only at the cost of any serious interest in a more textured representation of the two main characters. In contrast, by confronting Tito's moral failings as an independent source of narrative interest, Gisippo's remarks in the passage above necessarily diminish the tale's effectiveness as a morally pure example of Aristotelian perfect friendship. Comparing the two tales, one even detects in Boccaccio an interest in exploring—if not exploding—the discourse of ideal friendship through its exposure to the practical idiosyncrasies of human desire. Instead of burying the difficulty of Tito's morally defective desires, Boccaccio seems intent on exposing them as a kind of counterpoint within what is otherwise an orthodox rehearsal of the Aristotelian-scholastic tradition.

A similar tendency toward undermining the force of Aristotelian perfect friendship is equally on display in Tito's long speech to his in-laws.[35] Immediately following his arguments in support of friendship as a manifestation of divine providence—as discussed above—Tito rather abruptly alters the rhetorical emphasis of his speech, offering a far more pragmatic defense of his union with Sofronia. Asserting that his in-laws know nothing "of the providence of the Gods [della providenzia degli Iddii]," Tito goes on to recount the aspects of his personal history that render him a superior candidate for marriage to Sofronia. He cites his wealth, social rank, and even the status of Rome—"I am of a city that is mistress of all the world, and he of one that is subject to mine [io dirò che io sia di città donna di tutto 'l mondo, ed egli di città obbediente alla mia]"—as factors that should lead his in-laws to favor him over his friend Gisippo.[36] As he puts it in his concluding remarks, "but not a whit less should you prize an alliance with me at Rome, considering that there you will have in me an excellent host, and a patron apt, zealous and potent to serve you as well in matters of public interest as in your private concerns [ma io non vi debbo per alcuna cagione meno essere a Roma caro, considerando che di me là avrete ottimo oste, e utile e sollicito e possente padrone, così nelle pubbliche opportunità come ne' bisogni privati]."[37]

The import of this second set of arguments within Tito's speech is somewhat ambiguous. They are framed rhetorically, as already indicated, as a response to his in-laws' inability to conceive of the higher logic of love and friendship, and in this sense may be taken as a further sign of the exalted status of both. Yet the arguments themselves are distinctly pragmatic, appealing to a more historically grounded understanding of marriage as a social institution and, by extension, to a mode of storytelling based, at least in part, in the principles of representational verisimilitude. In particular, Tito's invocation of his status as a Roman citizen carries an implicit reference to the asymmetric power relations at work in this scene, an observation, as Hollander notes, that is borne out in his final words to his in-laws:[38]

> «... o piacciavi o non piacciavi quel che è fatto, se altramenti operare intendeste, io vi torrò Gisippo, e senza fallo, se a Roma pervengo, io riavrò colei che è meritamente mia, mal grado che voi n'abbiate; e quanto lo sdegno de' romani animi possa, sempre nimicandovi, vi farò per esperienza conoscere.»[39]

> [" ... whether this, which is done, like you or not, if you are minded to contravene it, I shall take Gisippus hence with me, and once arrived in Rome, shall in your despite find means to recover her who is lawfully mine, and pursuing you with unremitting enmity, will apprise you by experience of the full measure and effect of a Roman's wrath."]

Faced with this implicit threat of violence, Sofronia's family understandably accedes to her marriage to Tito.

Despite Tito's framing of this second part of his discourse as a response to his audience's constitutional inability to comprehend the force of his first set of arguments, his words nevertheless have a corrosive effect on his claim to Aristotelian perfect friendship.[40] In extolling his superior qualities as a match for Sofronia, Tito self-consciously introduces a stark note of difference into his relationship with Gisippo that contradicts the fundamental Aristotelian notion of the friend as a second self. Moreover, by characterizing that note of difference through an appeal to concrete social circumstances, Tito undermines the mythic foundations that supported his earlier assertation of his friendship as a manifestation of divine providence. In effect, he makes it very difficult for the reader to accept the mystification of his perfect friendship with Gisippo in the manner of the audience for Pacuvius's theatrical depiction of the mythic Orestes and Pylades, a fact that is only underscored by the final warning to his in-laws with which he ends his long harangue.[41]

So far everything that I have written about Boccaccio's internal critique of the Aristotelian ideal of perfect friendship has circulated around narrative details—principally in the form of what characters say to themselves and each other. These details, I have suggested, are grounded in a nascent interest in a more textured mode of storytelling that is also more attentive to the experience of everyday life. Perfect friendship is, in this way, subject to the limitations of human existence as both a social and psychological phenomenon. Tito, who, not coincidentally, does most of the speaking, is no perfect model of virtue, a fact that enriches the reader's experience of him as a character while it also necessarily impedes his ability to embody the highest ideals of Aristotelian friendship.

Understood from the perspective of Hollander's formal distinction between "mythmaking" and "fiction," my analysis so far shows how narrative details grounded in more complex character development may be said to undermine the mythic drive that organizes the narrative at a macro level. This is true, at least, for the first, and longest, section of the narrative in which Tito's love for Sofronia and Gisippo's sacrifice on behalf of his friend are described in significant detail. It is not true, however, of the story's ending.

I have already commented on the accelerated pacing of the final pages that lead from Gisippo's arrival at Rome and Tito's gesture of self-sacrifice at Gisippo's murder trial to the final rehabilitation of the two friends as equals. In contrast to the rest of the story, this final section has been purged of the kind of narrative detail that is so fundamental to the narrative's internal critique up to this point. What remains is a far more schematic narrative that evokes the structural simplicity of the *Exemplum de integro amico*. Coming in at just over 1,100 words, the second half of the tale of Tito and Gisippo is constrained almost entirely to a recitation of the plotting that leads to Tito's extreme act of self-sacrifice in the name of friendship. Of particular note in these final pages is the almost complete lack of reflection by the characters themselves. The internal monologues and extensive dialogues that saturate the first part of the story are almost completely absent in the second. While there are a couple of brief exchanges between the praetor, Marcus Varro, and the two friends as well as a single intervention by Tito in which he offers Gisippo the option of staying with him in Rome, there is almost nothing in these final pages that would provide a deeper understanding of the relationship between Boccaccio's protagonists.

What one discovers instead in these final pages are hints that the narrative has somehow moved beyond its previous interest in exploring the underlying motivations driving the story's plot. Nowhere is this more evident than in the scene at court when Tito recognizes his friend for the first time since their previous parting in Athens:

> Era Tito per ventura in quella ora venuto al pretorio; il quale, guardando nel viso il misero condennato e avendo udito il perché, subitamente il riconobbe esser Gisippo, e maravigliossi della sua misera fortuna e come quivi arrivato

fosse; e ardentissimamente disiderando d'aiutarlo, né veggendo alcuna altra via alla sua salute se non d'accusar sé e di scusar lui, prestamente si fece avanti...[42]

[But Titus, who happened at that moment to come into the praetorium, being told the crime for which he was condemned, and scanning the poor wretch's face, presently recognized him for Gisippus, and marvelled how he should come to be there, and in such a woeful plight. And most ardently desiring to succour him, nor seeing other way to save his life except to exonerate him by accusing himself, he straightway stepped forward...]

This passage describes the critical development that will provide Tito with the required opportunity to reciprocate Gisippo's earlier act of self-sacrifice. Yet the circumstances for this development are contrived to a degree that exceeds almost anything experienced in the narrative so far. The exaggerated sense of coincidence here tends to undermine the believability of the entire scene and, in this way, implies a sharp deviation from more subtle movements in the narrative witnessed earlier in the story. The narrator, Filomena, betrays this sense of farfetched coincidence in a passing reference of ambiguous significance—"Era Tito *per ventura* in quella ora venuto al pretorio ...." Here, earlier appeals to providence as an affirmation of the divine nature of the friendship between Tito and Gisippo are reduced in a brief instant of narrative self-consciousness to a matter of pure chance. Beneath Tito's act of self-sacrifice in the name of friendship lurks an awareness of the structural imperative that necessarily conjures up the opportunity for such grand gestures out of thin air.

A similar analysis may be applied to the cursory allusion to Tito's puzzlement over his friend's destiny—"e maravigliossi della sua misera fortuna e come quivi arrivato fosse"—and its immediate dismissal in an assertation of what finally matters most in this scene: "e ardentissimamente disiderando d'aiutarlo...." Taken together, these musings imply a definitive negation of the narrative's motivational fabric beyond the structural requirements of its underlying commitment to Aristotelian perfect friendship. How Gisippo ends up in his current straits is of no significance to the story's ultimate aim while, from the perspective of the Aristotelian ideal, Tito's "most ardent" desire to help his friend is sufficient to explain what happens next. Indeed, it is not so much that Gisippo's circumstances are unmotivated—a superficial motivation is offered, after all—but that the revelation of motivations is self-consciously discarded as a point of narrative interest.

Hollander's analysis of Boccaccio circulates primarily around the tension between "mythmaking" and "parody." The lack of motivation that accompanies the end of this tale of perfect friendship, however, arguably marks a move beyond either of these two alternatives, recalling instead the emphasis on narrative structure that was observed in the *Exemplum de integro amico*. It is certainly true that Filomena's concluding words exalting friendship as "a most sacred thing, not only worthy of singular reverence" signal an explicit return to the mythic discourse that would, on first glance, justify Victoria Kirkham's conclusion that "Tito and Gisippo shoud be read . . . as exemplars of the most noble classical virtue, friendship."[43] By this point in my analysis, however, such appeals to the narrative's exemplary function seem inadequate to the larger circumstances of Boccaccio's tale. Not only does Filomena's assessment of the story she has just told fail to account for the irony that pervades the first part, it also seems somewhat incongruent with Boccaccio's withdrawal into a kind of structural formalism in the novella's final pages. In effect, Filomena's rhetoric floats so far above the substance of Boccaccio's narrative that its claims on behalf of exemplarity are rendered essentially meaningless.

It is here, perhaps, that a return to the sense of a poetics of friendship as it first emerges in the *Disciplina clericalis* is in order. Beyond more superficial discussions of the story's message—to the extent that one may be identified—what stands out in the second part of Boccaccio's tale of perfect friendship is its close adherence to the structural paradigm of the *Exemplum de integro amico*. In the absence of the narrative complexity that marks the first part, Boccaccio's representation of Tito's offer to die in his friend's place stands out primarily as the fulfillment of the pre-existing expectations of Alfonso's originary narrative. The result is not so much a disavowal of a more didactic exemplarity as an implicit rehearsal of the structural paradigm for writing perfect friendship.

Such an interpretation of the story's ending, however, does not negate the parodic elements that contest a more mythic reading of friendship throughout the narrative's first part. Rather, these final pages serve more as a reminder of the extent to which Alfonso's paradigm constitutes the conditions of possibility for everything else that happens in the story. While the question of what it means to be a friend is at issue in this tale in a way that it was not in the *Exemplum de integro amico*, the practical import of that question remains in the end unresolved not because of a lack of will on the part of the narrator—who does after all offer a rhetorical assessment of this central problem—but because the structural paradigm on which the story is built is itself incapable of making sense of that question in terms that a modern reader might recognize.

The importance of this recognition of Boccaccio's structural debt to Alfonso's *Exemplum*, however, is not limited to such practical matters.

Equally if not more significant is the impact that this recognition has on the Aristotelian model for perfect friendship. While Filomena's reading of the friendship between Tito and Gisippo certainly supports contemporary critical interpretations that emphasize the mythic quality of their relationship, the repeated reminders of the structural imperative that drives the story's second half tend to undercut the very premise of a mode of storytelling that might provide anything other than rhetorical support for the Aristotelian ideal. In this sense, the ending to the tale of Tito and Gisippo largely confirms the primacy of structure first evident in the *Exemplum* as formal considerations ultimately overpower both the mythic and parodic aspects of Boccaccio's storytelling. Despite Boccaccio's more textured narrative, the ultimate fate of his two friends resembles greatly that of the merchants from Egypt and Baghdad.

The primacy of structural forces is arguably the most formidable obstacle to rendering friendship in terms that would evoke Eden's discourse of intimacy. Even as later narratives aspire toward representations that might somehow evoke the conditions of friendship in everyday life, the structural demands of writing perfect friendship, now emptied of any remaining mythic potential, continue to anchor these texts to a formalism that is alien to modern sensibilities. At the same time, however, it is important to recognize the underlying congruence between this formalism and the idealized model of Aristotelian perfect friendship that it supports. Both Langer and Boccaccio describe the Aristotelian ideal as having existed "ab aeterno," a formulation, I would submit, that is functionally equivalent to declaring that such friendships are, in their essence, unmotivated. It is thus not an accident that the fullest expression of Tito and Gisippo's friendship as an ideal only occurs through and within the formalism of the story's ending. Only when allowed to flourish uninterrogated by questions over motivations and causality can they finally realize their fullest symbolic potential as representatives of an unachievable ideal.

Notes

1. Avalle-Arce, "Una tradición literaria: El cuento de los dos amigos," p. 3.
2. Irrespective of Avalle-Arce's analysis, there is in fact considerable debate over Alfonso's underlying purpose in writing the *Disciplina clericalis*. Extrapolating from the enormous popularity of Alfonso's text, many critics have speculated on the relative weight of entertainment versus didacticism as motivating factors in its production. Jones and Keller, *The Scholar's Guide*, p. 18, for example, have argued that the *Disciplina clericalis* "was meant

to be what it appears to be today, that is, a group of pleasant fictions and philosophical ideas cleverly wrapped in a mock-serious didacticism." They conclude, p. 19: "The lessons in the stories are there for those who wish to find them, but the stories themselves are obviously what really count in the mind of the teller." Alternatively, Tolan, *Petrus Alfonsi and His Medieval Readers*, p. 82, has taken a somewhat more nuanced view; arguing that "the term 'exemplum' is loaded with the meaning later given to it by thirteenth-century preachers" who "saw the *Disciplina* primarily as a mine for *exempla* to be used in their sermons," Tolan emphasizes the storytelling element in these tales which, he asserts, served "to inspire the student to wisdom and decorum," suggesting in this way a somewhat different understanding of the stories' didactic potential.

3. Avalle-Arce, "Una tradición literaria: El cuento de los dos amigos," p. 3.
4. Alfonso, *Disciplina clericalis*, p. 4, trans. p. 107. All English quotes for the *Disciplina clericalis* are taken from P. R. Quarrie's translation in *The* Disciplina Clericalis *of Petrus Alfonsi*.
5. Ibid. p. 4, trans. p. 107.
6. Ibid. trans. p. 107. The original medieval Latin, p. 5, reads: "Quo audito dedit ei puellam nobilem in uxorem cum omnibus que erat cum ea accepturus."
7. Ibid. p. 6, trans. p. 109.
8. See Introduction.
9. Jones and Keller, *The Scholar's Guide*, p. 18.
10. Writing about the tale of Tito and Gisippo, Lee, *The Decameron: Its Sources and Analogues*, p. 330, notes, "The original of this tale is to be found in the second tale of the 'Disciplina clericalis' of Alphonsus . . ." Citing some early twentieth-century sources, Sorieri, *Boccaccio's Story of Tito e Gisippo*, p. 12, draws a direct link between the *Exemplum de integro amico* and the tale of Tito and Gisippo from the *Decameron:* "The second story of the *Disciplina*, which could be entitled 'Of True Friendship,' has been considered the probable model which Boccaccio had before him, or in mind, when writing his novella of *Tito e Gisippo*." In a more recent study, Brown, *Boccaccio's Fabliaux*, p. 87, asserts that "whether or not Boccaccio was directly familiar with this Latin composition would be difficult to prove because the *Disciplina Clericalis* inspired vernacular translations and adaptations in the second half of the twelfth century that were as popular and accessible to Boccaccio as the Latin text." Neverthless, she goes on to cite the authority of Marcus Landau's nineteenth-century study as maintaining that "Boccaccio derived four *novelle* from the *Disciplina Clericalis*, or rather a French translation of it," p. 88. She concludes, pp. 88–9: "In spite of the isolated retelling and recopying of certain parts of the *Disciplina Clericalis* by Boccaccio and others, it is still possible for Boccaccio to have known the work as a compilation."
11. Hollander, *Boccaccio's Dante and the Shaping Force of Satire*, pp.79–80. The problem of friendship is by no means a settled matter among Boccaccio

scholars. Hollander's interpretation of the story of Tito and Gisippo, from which I will be drawing extensively in the following pages, may be read as a reaction to contemporaries, like Kirkham, for whom the exemplary status of Aristotelian friendship is seen to flourish in this tale from late in the *Decameron*. Kirkham, *The Sign of Reason*, pp. 239–40, writes: "For him [Boccaccio], Tito and Gisippo are models of magnanimity and generosity, motif of the *Decameron*'s final day. Their well-planned response to an unlucky circumstance resolves a life-threatening conflict, reconfirming what Cicero had called the 'natural fraternity' where men are united by reason and speech. Tito and Gisippo should be read, not as miscreants in a morally repugnant situation, but as exemplars of the most noble classical virtue, friendship." Nor does Hollander provide the last word on the subject; Sherberg, *The Governance of Friendship*, p. 1, has recently published an entire book devoted to the topic: "This study takes its title from two observations about the *Decameron*: first, that it traces its origins to a gesture of friendship, and second, that its initial focus on friendship opens onto a wide-ranging exploration of the relationship between friendship and governance, both in the household and the state."

12. Ibid. p. 113.
13. As cited by Hollander, p. 113, Kermode describes the distinction between myth and fiction in the following terms: "We have to distinguish between myths and fictions. Fictions can degenerate into myths whenever they are not consciously held to be fictive. . . . Myth operates within the diagrams of ritual, which presupposes total and adequate explanations of things as they are and were; it is a sequence of radically unchangeable gestures. Fictions are for finding things out, and they change as the needs of sense-making change. Myths are the agents of stability, fictions the agents of change. Myths call for absolute, fictions for conditional assent. (39)" The original passage is from Kermode, *The Sense of an Ending* (as per Hollander).
14. Ibid. p. 114.
15. See Avalle-Arce, "Una tradición literaria," p. 34. Critics of the literature of early modern friendship frequently cite the tale of Tito and Gisippo as occupying a special place within the history of the tradition as a kind of originary text. See, for example, Hutson, *The Usurer's Daughter*, Langer, *Perfect Friendship*, and Avalle-Arce, "Una tradición literaria." My own analysis here argues for the formal basis for such an assessment of Boccaccio's story, underscoring the intricate relationship between the thematics of perfect friendship and its articulation as a poetics.
16. Blackbourn, "The Eighth Story of the Tenth Day of Boccaccio's *Decameron*," pp. 5–13, argues at some length about the importance of the tale's classical setting. In particular, she emphasizes how that classical context requires that one be especially attentive to the use of rhetorical strategies in this story.
17. Boccaccio, *Decameron*, vol. 2, p. 592; trans. vol. 2, p. 354. All citations in English have been adapted from the translation by Rigg with modernized pronouns.

18. Boccaccio, *Decameron*, vol. 2, p. 599; vol. 2, trans. pp. 358.
19. Hutson, *The Usurer's Daughter*, p. 77 argues for the exchange element in Tito's marriage as the starting point for Boccaccio's engagement with the question of friendship: "Boccaccio's original was a traditional test-of-friendship story; it was he who transformed the tale of eventual compensation for extreme self-sacrifice into a celebration of the potential power of friendship conceived as humanistic *amicitia*—dialectical counsel and persuasive communication in emergency."
20. Langer, *Perfect Friendship*, p. 46.
21. Boccaccio, *Decameron*, vol. 2, p. 601; trans. vol. 2, pp. 359–60.
22. Hutson, *The Usurer's Daughter*, p. 61, highlights the importance of Sofronia's lack of agency as a more general feature of the novella, noting how it persists even after she discovers the true identity of her husband: "the subjectivity of Sophronia in Boccaccio is so limited by her function in the narrative, that her ability to make a virtue of necessity and switch her affection from Gisippus to Titus is commended as being *savia*, wise."
23. Boccaccio, *Decameron*, vol. 2, pp. 602–3; trans. vol. 2, p. 361.
24. Boccaccio, *Decameron*, trans. vol. 2, pp. 361–2. The passage from the original Italian, vol. 2, p. 604, reads: ". . . essendo contento d'avervi tanto solamente ricordato di quelle, che il legame della amistà troppo più stringa che quel del sangue o del parentado, con ciò sia cosa che gli amici noi abbiamo quali ce li eleggiamo, e i parenti quali gli ci dà la fortuna."
25. Ibid. vol. 2, pp. 603, 604; trans. vol. 2, p. 361.
26. Ibid. vol. 2, pp. 612, 613; trans. vol. 2, pp. 367, 368. As Filomena relates in her opening remarks, *Decameron*, trans. vol. 2, p. 354, the story is set in the period when "Octavianus Caesar, not as yet named Augustus," was "in the office called Triumvirate."
27. Ibid. vol. 2, p. 613; trans. vol. 2, p. 368.
28. Ibid. vol. 2, pp. 613–14; trans. vol. 2, p. 368.
29. Hyatte, *The Arts of Friendship*, p. 159, offers a nuanced reading of Filomena's speech that recognizes both its religious overtones and secular function: "There is a strong hint of Christian moralizing in the first part's praise of charity as well as in the last words, where the Golden Rule and the first law of *amicitia* in *Laelius* 13,44 are combined. Nevertheless, the virtues of *amistà* which she describes are strictly secular, in no way spiritual, since there is no suggestion that they derive from God or love of God . . ."
30. Boccaccio, *Decameron*, vol. 2, p. 594; trans. vol. 2, p. 355.
31. Mazzotta, *The World at Play*, p. 258, writes: ". . . Tito's mind is a theater on the stage of which a genuine moral debate is played out. The terms of the *psychomachia* (the text explicitly refers to Tito's thoughts and '. . . la battaglia di quegli . . .' p. 904) are the age-old contrast between *amor* and *amicitia*, passion and reason, pleasure and duty. Love's hegemony is undisputed and its anarchic power is said to shatter all restraints and order, incite incestuous passions and, a fortiori, violate the bonds of friendship (p. 903)." Hollander, *Boccaccio's Dante*, p. 132, extends this reading

through an analysis of Tito's rhetoric: "What is more important to keep in mind, however, is that what matters is not only the argument itself—that is, the argument for love over friendship or the one for friendship over love—but also Tito's presentation of it. Having been schooled in the arts of rhetoric and ratiocination, Tito can exploit his craft by devising cogent arguments that will allow him to satisfy his personal desires. Boccaccio thus reveals not only an ironic view of this version of the myth of friendship but also an ironic sense of rhetorical persuasion."

32. The full implications of this final declaration are perhaps somewhat more complex than my comments above imply. Mazzotta, *The World at Play*, p. 258, recognizing the Girardian potential of this scene, offers a more nuanced reading of Tito's concluding statement: "Tito's disclaimer in his soliloquy ... betrays the suspicion, above and beyond Tito's denial, that theirs is a love triangle, wherein the woman is the passive focus of displacement of the two friends' rivalries: for Tito, this is a way of owning what Gisippo owns and, at the same time, of establishing the difference between themselves, but in his terms."

33. Boccaccio, *Decameron*, vol. 2, p. 596; trans. vol. 2, pp. 356–7.

34. While there is at least one moment in the *Nicomachean Ethics* where Aristotle contemplates the possibility of correcting the errors of one's friends (1165b15–20), the overall thrust of his arguments mitigates against such a possibility. The coincidence between attribute and identity—see my discussion of Price in the previous chapter—implies that such errors are fundamentally errors of character. When a perfect friend acts in a less than virtuous manner, the more typical Aristotelian response would invoke the language of misrecognition and conclude that the friend is not the person whom we thought them to be. Thus, 1165b20–5, "the friend who dissolves the friendship seems to be doing nothing absurd. For he was not the friend of a person of this sort ..."

35. Hollander, p. 132, n. 42, following Kirkham, indicates that this is, in fact, "the longest speech in the *Decameron*." See Kirkham, *The Sign of Reason*, p. 238.

36. Boccaccio, *Decameron*, vol. 2, pp. 604, 605; trans. vol. 2, p. 362.

37. Ibid. vol. 2, pp. 605–6; trans. vol. 2, p. 363. On Tito's appeal to his superiority over Gisippo, Hollander, p. 133, offers the following critique of earlier scholarship: "... even though Tito himself admits that he will violate the rules of epideictic rhetoric in praising himself (X.viii.60), the fact that he does so in such flagrantly jingoistic and crass terms ... should surely have caused more uncomfortable notice than it has."

38. For Hollander's interpretation of Tito's speech, especially as it relates to the power relations between Tito and his interlocutors, see *Boccaccio's Dante and the Shaping Force of Satire*, pp. 133–4.

39. Boccaccio, *Decameron*, vol. 2, pp. 608–9; trans. vol. 2, p. 365.

40. In his detailed analysis of Tito's speech, Hyatte, *The Arts of Friendship*, p. 155, argues that "Titus' apparent immodesty in talking about his own nobility,

wealth, and influence illustrates in an exaggerated manner an important feature of Cicero's oratory, that of the speaker's ethos or moral character as a persuasive force." This assessment fits with his overall appraisal of the story, pp. 147–8: "In other words, a good part of the originality of Boccaccio's representation of perfect friends in the antique mold is his revision of classical *amicitia vera* according to the standards of the orator's virtue and his identification of ethically superior friendship with the ideal orator's ethos, or character." In contrast, my analysis here focuses on Tito's rhetorical deviations from the principles of perfect Aristotelian friendship as a function of Boccaccio's interest in storytelling. Read in this way, no amount of Ciceronian oratory can compensate for the morally corrosive effect of Tito's implied threats.

41. In his final assessment of Tito's speech to his Greek in-laws, Hollander, *Boccaccio's Dante*, p. 134, argues that Boccaccio's intent was "to portray something other than munificence, something that masqurades as munificence but is better understood as self-love."
42. Boccaccio, *Decameron*, vol. 2, p. 611; vol. 2, trans. p. 366.
43. Kirkham, *The Sign of Reason*, pp. 239–40.

Chapter 2

Plotting Imperfections in *La Galatea*

Spanish pastoral lovers are never free. They inhabit a world that is defined by their subjugation to frustrated passions, unrequited love, and irremediable loss. The "dulce lamentar" of Garcilaso's shepherds in *Égloga I*—perhaps the purest expression of the Spanish pastoral—is a song of suffering with no end, a *canto* that echoes in a closed and timeless place whose idyllic beauty cannot conceal the lover's profound isolation.[1] Nor is that isolation merely physical; it is built into the formal conventions of a genre that requires that the lover's suffering persist for all eternity. As Garcilaso's pastoral lovers suspend their "triste lloro" at day's end and gather up their flock, the eclogue's closing lines anticipate the perpetual recurrence of a timeless diurnal cycle that is also built into the structure of the poem: It may be read over and over again, with each new reading serving to confirm the shepherds' confinement within an emotional prison from which there is no escape.

This fundamental notion of the shepherd lover's lack of freedom persists in what is arguably the sixteenth century's most important contribution to the form, the hybridized pastoral novel.[2] Tracing its origins to the Italian Jacopo Sannazaro's *Arcadia* (1502–4), Jorge de Montemayor's *Los siete libros de la Diana* (1559) embeds the pure lyricism of the eclogue form within the prose frame of a longer novelistic narrative.[3] With the pastoral novel's liberal use of prose, the theme of the shepherd lover's essentially unfree nature is made available for new kinds of representational analysis, as Montemayor demonstrates near the very beginning of *La Diana*:

> Pues llegando el pastor a los verdes y deleitosos prados, que el caudaloso río Ezla con sus aguas va regando, le vino a la memoria el gran contentamiento de que en algún tiempo allí gozado había, siendo tan señor de su libertad, como entonces subjeto a quien sin causa lo tenía sepultado en las tinieblas de

su olvido. Consideraba aquel dichoso tiempo que por aquellos prados y hermosa ribera apacentaba su ganado, poniendo los ojos en sólo el interese que de traelle bien apacentado se le seguía; y las horas que le sobraban gastaba el pastor en sólo gozar el suave olor de las doradas flores, al tiempo que la primavera, con las alegres nuevas del verano, se esparce por el universo, tomando a veces su rabel, que muy pulido en un zurrón siempre traía; otras veces una zampoña, al son de la cual componía los dulces versos con que de las pastoras de toda aquella comarca era loado.[4]

[And arriving at the delightful green meadows that the abundant river Esla irrigates with her waters, he recalled the great happiness that in a previous time he had enjoyed there, being lord of his freedom, as his was now subject to her who without cause had entombed him in the darkness of her forgetting. He considered those happy times when he had grazed his sheep on those meadows and the beautiful banks, placing his eyes solely on his interest in keeping them well-fed, and the hours that were left to him, he spent exclusively in enjoying the soft fragrance of the golden flowers, that, anticipating the happy news of summer, spring scatters throughout the world; sometimes taking his rebec in hand, that he kept highly polished in his bag, and at other times his rustic flute, to the sound of which he composed sweet verses for which he was praised by the shepherdesses of that entire region.]

In a departure from the Garcilasan tradition, the shepherd Sireno here imagines the time before he loved as a kind of prelapsarian paradise.[5] Drawing a clear contrast between Sireno's past freedom—"siendo tan señor de su libertad"—and his current thralldom to the object of his desire, Montemayor cracks open the structural unity of Garcilaso's pastoral world, replacing the ontological isolation of the lovers from *Égloga I* with a direct reference to the problem of the shepherd's agency. Sireno is unfree not as a function of the timeless idyllic world he inhabits, but because of the weight of his emotional enslavement to his beloved.[6] In this sense, he is more recognizable as a modern protagonist, a character with whom a reader might identify, or at the very least, understand in terms of real human motivations; for while Montemayor's pastoral lover may be no less able to escape the bonds of his love than his Garcilasan predecessors, the reasons for that failure are presented in terms that preserve a much greater sense of his individual subjectivity.

In reframing the pastoral lover's lack of freedom as a problem of individual agency, Montemayor opens a space for Cervantes's arguably more radical reassessment of the genre in *La Galatea* (1585).[7] Despite the hyperbole that is a defining attribute of the pastoral lover's complaint, the passivity of his state is generally rendered in terms that are, comparatively speaking, quite benign, an artifact of the intense formalism of the genre's more purely poetic origins in the shepherd's "dulce lamentar."[8] For Cervantes, the shift to a hybrid form that privileges narrative prose over pure poetry provides an opportunity for innovations that call into question this essential feature of so much of earlier pastoral literature. With a new focus on the pastoral lover's lost freedom in terms of personal agency, Cervantes makes clear from early on in *La Galatea* that he will not be content to merely rehearse the conventions of the past:

> Ya se aparejava Erastro para seguir adelante en su canto, quando sintieron, por un espesso montezillo que a sus espaldas estava, un no pequeño estruendo y ruido; y, levantándose los dos en pie por ver lo que era, vieron que del monte salía un pastor corriendo a la mayor priessa del mundo, con un cuchillo desnudo en la mano y la color del rostro mudada; y que tras él venía otro ligero pastor, que a pocos passos alcançó al primero, y asiéndole por el cabeçón del pellico, levantó el braço en el aire quanto pudo, y un agudo puñal que sin vaina traía se le escondió dos vezes en el cuerpo . . .[9]

> [Erastro was preparing to continue with his song when they heard, from a dense wooded hill that was at their backs, a not insignificant uproar and commotion; and getting to their feet to see what was happening, they saw coming from the hill a shepherd running in great haste with a naked blade in his hand and his coloring altered; and behind him came another fleet shepherd, who quickly overcame the first; and seizing him by the collar of his sheepskin coat, the second shepherd lifted his arm as high as he could and stabbed the first twice with a sharp dagger . . .]

Here, the lyric "dulce lamentar" of one pastoral lover, Erastro, is cut short by the arrival of a second pastoral lover, Lisandro, whose drive for vengeance leads him to commit murder. The final scene of brutality in what is later revealed as a sordid tale of jealousy and treachery, the stark representation of Carino's murder upends the traditional pastoral conventions at work in Erastro and Elicio's placid rivalry in love for Galatea. As Elizabeth Rhodes remarks, "by knifing Carino to death in the present tense of the narration, Lisandro . . . bursts the idyllic bubble around Arcadia in two ways: by acting rather than contemplating and talking about his past, and by forcing a non-allegorical, extremely violent act directly on to the idyllic scene of Elicio and Erastro's amoeban song."[10] Indeed, where pastoral lovers—in Montemayor and elsewhere in *La Galatea*—typically show impressive restraint in their interactions and frequently even describe each other as friends, the characters that populate Lisandro's story exhibit a depravity that challenges even the most cynical readings of human nature; as we soon learn, Carino's death is just one of four acts of premeditated murder that characterize this unprecedented tale of pastoral love gone bad.[11]

At the very least, Cervantes's almost gleeful destruction of the idyllic world of Neoplatonic lovemaking in this scene suggests an underlying distaste for literary convention.[12] As a response to the intertextuality that defines so much of Renaissance *imitatio*, Cervantes's rewriting of the pastoral in this murderous scene exposes the fragility of pastoral love when subjected to the pressure of humanity's baser instincts. Indeed, in giving voice to those baser instincts, Cervantes not only exposes the darker side of love understood as a psychological state, he also offers a response, based in an implicit appeal to the principles of representational verisimilitude, to the more expansive pastoral vision of Neoplatonism as an ideology that would somehow bind the world in harmony under the auspices of love.[13]

Read from Lisandro's perspective, Cervantes's dark parody may be said to reveal what happens when lovers are truly out of control, that is, when the formalized constraints on their subjective autonomy as determined by literary form are converted into pathologies of "real" passionate rage whose outward manifestation upends the niceties of generic conventions.[14] Indeed, not only are imperfect pastoral lovers—their pathologies redefine them as such—exposed as unfree, their lack of freedom itself may be said to rend the generic fabric of the pastoral form. And while repairs are made in the end, the psychological trauma of this early violence can never be fully healed. The memory of that violence remains to haunt the text as an unspoken threat to the novel's formal integrity.

It is against this backdrop that I would begin to assess Cervantes's rewriting of the tale of two friends tradition from within the pastoral landscape of *La Galatea*. Like the pastoral itself, the paradigmatic tale of two friends, as explored in the previous chapter, is bound by formal conventions that impose rigid constraints on both plotting and character development. In both the pastoral and the tale of two friends tradition, the protagonist functions as an exemplary case whose comportment, at least in the paradigmatic instance, is finally judged by its enactment of the ideal.

In his implicit critique of the pastoral, Cervantes leverages the symbolic potential of the pastoral lover whose subjugation to the power of love leads to an essential loss of freedom. Thralldom to love becomes, in this reading, a metaphor for the constraints that pastoral form necessarily imposes on subjective autonomy. In the case of the tale of two friends tradition, however, the situation is necessarily different. Perfect friendship, unlike love, is defined through an act of free will; as Aristotle, Cicero, and Boccaccio—through the voice of Tito—make clear, we choose our friends as an expression of our good will. Yet, as my analysis of Boccaccio in the previous chapter reveals, that essential and necessary claim to freedom is, in practice, undermined by formal requirements that script the narrative of perfect friendship in ways that call that claim into question. For this reason, perfect Aristotelian friendship, in contrast to love, cannot give symbolic representation to the genre's formal limitations. Rather, in the novelistic rendering of the tale of two friends tradition, the idea of the perfect friend strains under the weight of the inherent contradiction between lofty assertions to free will and the genre's origin in a categorical definition of ideal friendship that, when given narrative expression, admits little room for the protagonists' subjective expression. It is this contradiction, more than anything else, that informs Cervantes's rewriting of the tale of two friends from within the pastoral landscape of La Galatea.

In the last chapter, I proposed, following Hollander, that Boccaccio's response to the tale of two friends paradigm may be productively understood under the auspices of parody. The same may be said for Cervantes. However, where Boccaccio takes aim at the mythmaking inherent in the categorical ideal of perfect friendship, Cervantes's energies are directed primarily toward exposing the fundamental incompatibility between the orthodox tale of two friends and emerging narrative practices founded, to varying degrees, on the principles of representational verisimilitude. Like the irruption of violence within the scene of Erastro's pastoral lament, representations of the chaos, unpredictability, and complexity of everyday life repeatedly disrupt the fulfillment of the orthodoxy of perfect friendship. These repeated disruptions undermine the very ontological basis of the Aristotelian ideal, which is finally revealed under the pressures of Cervantes's narrative practice to be little more than rhetorical posturing.

Understood in this way, the prestigious Aristotelian ideal of perfect friendship may be said to function as a foil for a meditation on the poetics of narrative fiction more generally. Arguably the purest expression of a transcendent vision of subjective autonomy—the choice of friends as a manifestation of the will unfettered by worldly preoccupations— Aristotelian perfect friendship embodies a conception of the individual that is fundamentally at odds with the human condition and, for this reason, constitutionally incompatible with representational verisimilitude. In a later chapter, I will demonstrate precisely how this realization leads Cervantes to embrace an entirely new narrative poetics of friendship. For the moment, however, I will focus on how the representation of perfect friendship in La Galatea exposes the ultimate insufficiency of perfect friendship to the demands of modern narrative, revealing in the process the inherent contradiction that resides at the very heart of the implied exemplarity that is a constitutive element of the tale of two friends tradition.

Cervantes's tale of the two friends Silerio and Timbrio in *La Galatea* operates as a running subplot in the novel that is recounted in two distinct parts, functioning in this way as an interpolated story within the larger pastoral narrative.[15] First, Silerio recites a long narrative that provides the backstory for his relationship with Timbrio. Set largely outside the novel's pastoral frame, that story includes many key elements of the friendship narrative tradition, but ends inconclusively with the two friends' separation and no clear resolution in their relationship.[16] Then, after a significant delay, the main narrative takes up the story of these two lost friends anew through the direct narration of their seemingly happy reunion much later in the novel. The story thus culminates in an explicit reaffirmation of the bonds of perfect friendship.[17] At the same time, however, there are irregularities, especially in Silerio's initial narrative, that call into question the efficacy of the tale's happy ending, a result, as will become clear through the following analysis, of Cervantes's interest in disrupting the generic conventions of both the pastoral form and the tale of two friends tradition, especially through the application of poetic principles based in an interest in representational verisimilitude.

As in the earlier tale from Boccaccio, the friendship between these two characters is summarized in cursory fashion at the very beginning of Silerio's long, and frequently interrupted, first narrative:

—En la antigua y famosa ciudad de Xerez, cuyos moradores de Minerva y Marte son favorescidos, nasció Timbrio, un valeroso cavallero, del qual, si sus virtudes y generosidad de ánimo huviesse de contar, a difícil empresa me pondría. Basta saber que, no sé si por la mucha bondad suya, o por la fuerça de las estrellas, que a ello me inclinavan, yo procuré, por todas las vías que pude, serle particular amigo, y fueme el cielo en esto tan favorable que, casi olvidándose a los que nos conoscían el nombre de Timbrio y el de Silerio—que es el mío—, solamente *los dos amigos* nos llamavan, haziendo nosotros, con nuestra continua conversación amigables obras, que tal opinión no fuesse vana. Desta suerte los dos, con increíble gusto y contento, los moços años passávamos, ora en el campo en el exercicio de la caça, ora en la ciudad en el del honroso Marte entreteniéndose . . .[18]

["In the ancient and famous city of Jerez, whose inhabitants are favored by Minerva and Mars, Timbrio was born, a valiant *caballero*, of whom, if one had to enumerate his virtues and generosity of spirit, it would entail a very difficult undertaking. Suffice it to say that, whether because of his goodness or the force of the stars, which is what I suspect, I attempted, by all means at my disposal, to be his special friend, and the heavens were so favorable to my cause that almost forgetting that they knew us by the names of Timbrio and Silerio—which is mine—they called us simply "the two friends," and we, with our continuous conversation and friendly deeds worked so that this opinion would not be in vain. In this way, the two of us, with incredible pleasure and contentment, passed our youthful years, either in the country in the exercise of the hunt, or in the city practicing the honorable arts of Mars . . ."]

Here, in the opening description, the origin of the friendship between the two young men is motivated rather weakly in the familiar terms of divine providence—what Silerio describes as "la fuerça de las estrellas"—and an appeal to their shared interest in the most conventional of youthful activities: hunting and the practice of arms. What is new, however, is the explicit link that Silerio draws between ideal friendship and the two friends' public reputation: "casi olvidándose a los que nos conoscían el nombre de Timbrio y el de Silerio—que es el mío—, solamente *los dos amigos* nos llamavan." Guaranteed by popular acclaim according to a formula that, as Avalle-Arce notes, will be repeated in "El curioso impertinente," ideal friendship is not merely a matter of personal virtue alone, but rather is defined through the judgment of public opinion.[19]

The link that Cervantes establishes between perfect friendship and public opinion marks a critical return to the discourse of exemplarity. In this instance, however, the exemplary function is for the first time clearly articulated within the specific circumstances of the friends' existence within the larger social fabric of the novel. The consequence of this latest move, however, is somewhat ambiguous. On the one hand, the act of naming by which they become "los dos amigos" leads, at least in part, to an erasure of their individual identities, which, as the passage just cited above indicates, have been essentially forgotten. One detects in this passage a hint of that mythologizing discourse that would, in the terms of Langer's analysis, render the perfect friend unknowable except as the embodiment of the transcendent Aristotelian ideal. And yet Cervantes's insistence that their status as "the two friends" is ultimately a function of some version of public opinion tends to ironize any such mythologizing claims. The obscuring of Timbrio and Silerio's individual identities in their collective image as "los dos amigos" is, in this case, hardly a function of their transcendence. Rather, it is suggestive of an entirely different mechanism for ascribing meaning, one in which the community's collective perception, however defined, is given far more influence over the assignation of value.

Above all, the invocation of public opinion—even if the public in this instance is comprised of a group of pastoral shepherds—necessarily sets Cervantes's text at variance with Aristotle, for whom perfect friendship is defined exclusively in terms of the two friends' inherent virtue and good will. Where perfect Aristotelian friendship—even to a large extent in Boccaccio—depends on the radical segregation of the perfect friend from the quotidian world of other, necessarily corrupted, human relations, Cervantes insists from the very beginning of his tale of friendship that such idealized notions only have meaning to the extent that they are defined as such through the power of their reception by a wider audience.[20] The idea of perfect friendship is, in this way, already degraded, its claims reduced to a matter of representation and rhetorical affect.

This revelation of Aristotelian good will as a rhetorical flourish that camouflages the functional link between exemplary perfect friendship and its public consumption may be understood as one possible manifestation of a more general interrogation of the limits of subjective autonomy that recurs with striking regularity throughout Cervantes's rewriting of the tale of two friends tradition in *La Galatea*. What makes Cervantes's innovation in this regard significant, however, is not just the fact that perfect friendship is revealed to depend on the external conditions of its reception, but more fundamentally, the way in which this move reflects a more general recognition—driven in large part by Cervantes's interest in verisimilitude—of friendship as inextricably bound up with the social experience of everyday life. The purity of intent that is central to the Aristotelian model is subject to the pressures of an approach to narrative that acknowledges the complex interactions between individual will and the practical realities of life in a social context that is unpredictable and replete with moral and epistemological ambiguity.

Perhaps the most palpable sign of this ambiguity may be discovered in the novel's plotting. Where the storyline in Boccaccio and Pedro Alfonso can seem sclerotic, a direct consequence of the subordination of events to the drive to confirm the requirements of perfect friendship, Cervantes's tale of two friends in *La Galatea* delights in submitting its protagonists to all manner of external shocks that disrupt the easy fulfillment of their professed claims to embody the Aristotelian ideal. Thus, early on in his long monologue, Silerio describes his arrival near Barcelona, where he discovers Timbrio bound as a prisoner and sentenced to death. In keeping with the idealized characterization of their friendship, Silerio boldly intervenes to help Timbrio escape his imprisonment, only to end up detained himself and subject to the same punishment that had been previously assigned to his friend:

> El atrevamiento mío, y el haverse escapado Timbrio, augmentó mi culpa y el enojo en los juezes, los quales, condenado bien el excesso por mí cometido, pareciéndoles ser justo que yo muriesse, y luego, luego, la cruel sentencia pronunciaron, y para otro día guardavan la execución. Llegó a Timbrio esta triste nueva allá en la iglesia donde estava, y, según yo después supe,

más alteración le dio mi sentencia que le havía dado la de su muerte, y, por librarme della, de nuevo se offrecía a entregarse otra vez en poder de la justicia; pero los sacerdotes le aconsejaron que servía de poco aquello: antes era añadir mal a mal y desgracia a desgracia, pues no sería parte el entregarse él para que yo fuesse suelto, pues no lo podía ser sin ser castigado de la culpa cometida.[21]

["My daring and the fact that Timbrio had escaped, increased my guilt and the judges' anger, who, condemning the excesses committed by me and thinking it just that I die, then passed down the cruel sentence and awaited another day for the execution. This sad news reached Timbrio there in the church where he had taken refuge and, according to what I later found out, my sentence affected him more than had his own sentence of death; and in order to free me he again offered to turn himself in to the authorities; but the priests advised him that this would serve little purpose, but rather add evil to evil and misfortune on top of misfortune, since turning himself in would not lead to my being freed, since I could not but be punished for my crime."]

At first glance, this passage preserves all the expected features of the test of ideal friendship. Silerio literally replaces his friend in prison and by facing the exact same punishment that had been reserved for Timbrio, demonstrates his commitment to the notion of the friend as an *alter ego*. Not to be outdone in displays of selflessness, Timbrio, in turn, "se offecía a entregarse otra vez en poder de la justicia," a sign here of the perfect correspondence between these two companions and of a mutual will to self-sacrifice in the name of friendship.

Having rehearsed the well-worn conventions of earlier friendship narratives, however, the passage ends on a much more ambiguous note: The *sacerdotes* at the church where Timbrio has taken refuge convince him that his proposed dramatic gesture of self-sacrifice to liberate Silerio will not save his friend and will, in fact, only make things worse. In effect, the priests convince him to postpone his valiant impulse to self-sacrifice on purely practical grounds. As Silerio puts it, "No fueron menester pocas razones para persuader a Timbrio no se diesse a la justicia; pero sossegóse con proponer en su ánimo de hazer otro día por mí lo que yo por él avía hecho, por pagarme en la mesma moneda, o morir en la demanda [It took some convincing to persuade Timbrio not to turn himself in; but, he consoled himself with proposing in his soul to do for me another day that which I had done for him, in order to pay me back in the same way, or die in the attempt]."[22] Both the material world and the practical advice of these other characters effectively disarm Timbrio's lofty intentions in the name of perfect friendship. And while Timbrio claims that he is only putting off for a more apt occasion the fulfillment of his duty to friendship, the ease with which he is convinced to abandon such a reckless act of self-sacrifice already suggests the inherent conflict between the transcendent Aristotelian ideal and the messy reality of the practical predicament in which this ostensibly perfect friend finds himself.

As if to emphasize this last point, the narrative, in true Cervantine fashion, quickly spins off in a new direction. In the middle of the night, with both Timbrio and Silerio awaiting their fate, the story takes an unexpected turn that calls into question the agency of both characters and, by extension, their inherent capacity to act the part of the ideal friend. In the middle of the night—which Cervantes describes as "the perfect time for wicked insults"—the village comes under attack by Turkish invaders.[23] A kind of *deus ex machina*, the arrival of "la turca gente" accomplishes that which Silerio's faithful friend Timbrio cannot:

> Mas, ¡ay!, que está tan llena de miserias nuestra vida, que en tan doloroso successo como el que os he contado, huvo christianos coraçones que se alegraron, y éstos fueron los de aquellos que en la cárcel estavan, que con la desdicha general cobraron la dicha propria, porque, en son de ir a defender el pueblo, rompieron las puertas de la prisión y en libertad se pusieron, procurando cada uno, no de offender a los contrarios, sino de salvar a sí mesmos, entre los quales yo gozé de la libertad tan caramente adquirida.[24]

> ["But, alas, how full of misery is our life, so that in a misfortune as painful as that which I have just described, there were Christian hearts that were pleased; and these were the hearts of those who were imprisoned, who with the general unhappiness achieved their own happiness because, under the guise of defending the village, they broke down the doors of the prison and conveyed themselves to freedom, each aiming not to offend the enemy, but rather to save himself, and among whom I finally enjoyed my freedom, attained so dearly."]

There is a delicious irony in Silerio's escape in the wake of this attack on the city, the result of a profound moral confusion that essentially mocks the inadequacy of Aristotelian good will to the requirements of his practical predicament as a prisoner of the state. *Fortuna*, as Cervantes reminds us throughout *La Galatea*, is the nominal culprit, suggesting the revival of a distinctly medieval suspicion of the humanist belief in the individual's capacity for action.[25] And unlike Boccaccio's earlier tale, where divine will and personal volition finally harmonize as a sign of the higher nature of ideal friendship, here a foreign enemy undermines the moral order: Innocent women and children are carried off by the invaders while criminals find their freedom in the ensuing tumult. What should have been accomplished by the perfect friend as an expression of his inherent goodness—at least according to the dictates of the formal requirements of the tale of two friends tradition—is thus finally achieved by violent chaos with absolutely no regard for the moral imperatives of the traditional exemplary friendship narrative.

From the reader's perspective, the impact of this scene is accentuated by its staging in a contemporary setting that, if not strictly speaking historical, has the ring of historical truth about it. Unlike Boccaccio's mythologizing narrative, in which the tale of two friends is cast in a remote, idealized classical past, as Francisco López Estrada puts it, "propia de un renacentista ingenuo," here we encounter the representation of a world that is much closer to the contemporary experience of Cervantes's audience—an observation that extends even to the two friends themselves, whose "vida de acción," as Aurora Egido notes, could hardly be more alien to the rarefied literary universe of pure pastoral.[26] A symptom of Cervantes's commitment to representational verisimilitude, this fact has the added effect of heightening the emotional impact of the events depicted. The moral chaos generated by the arrival of the "turca gente" is thus arguably felt with an immediacy by Cervantes's reader that has no analogue in Boccaccio's classical rendering of the tale of two friends tradition.

The arrival of the Turkish invaders marks a sharp contrast to the contrived plotting of earlier narratives written in service of a transcendent vision of Aristotelian perfect friendship. In place of a carefully scripted storyline that might provide an opportunity for exalted acts of self-sacrifice, Cervantes emphasizes the role of uncontrolled external forces in human affairs, an idea that—as already suggested—might be historicized under notions of *fortuna* or *los hados*, but which from the perspective of verisimilitude may also be understood as a kind of indifference. This disruptive impulse in Cervantes's storytelling, however, is not limited to his manipulation of the narrative's plotting, but also shapes his depiction of the protagonists' inner lives, which through a nascent appeal to verisimilitude are infused with an unprecedented level of emotional complexity.

This new aspect of Cervantes's revision of the tale of two friends tradition comes into view when the two friends are later reunited in Naples. Cured of the wounds he received in his precarious escape, Silerio discovers his friend literally sick with love for the beautiful Nísida—he is, as Silerio describes it, suffering "de una enfermedad tan estraña, que si yo a aquella sazón no llegara, pudiera llegar a tiempo de hazerle las obsequias de su muerte [from a disease so strange, that if I had not arrived at that moment, I could have arrived in time to perform his funeral rites]."²⁷ After some prodding, Silerio agrees to help Timbrio in his amorous pursuit of Nísida and with this determination the story lays the groundwork for a love triangle that will provide the major interest for what remains of the narrative.

The parallels with Boccaccio at this point become obvious, but with an important, albeit subtle, difference. Unlike the earlier Italian narrative, which emphasizes the divine origin of Tito's love for Sofronia, Cervantes's story begins with an invocation of the long tradition of love as a kind of mental illness, even madness, an association that, in the larger context of *La Galatea*, calls to mind the more specifically pastoral convention of the lover who is held in thrall to his beloved.²⁸ As I noted in the last chapter, the association of Tito's love with divine providence in Boccaccio reinforces, however imperfectly, the Aristotelian ideal of perfect friendship as it highlights Sofronia's special merits in an exchange between two perfect friends. In contrast, Cervantes's appeal here to the notion of love as an illness that deprives the lover of agency has a very different and far more disruptive effect: It undermines the foundation of Timbrio's claim to good will from within the psychic space of subjectivity itself. As becomes quickly apparent in what remains of Cervantes's story, this disabling of the perfect friend's agency—which will eventually affect both Timbrio and Silerio—corrodes the purity of their ideological claims, as it were, from the inside out.

In order to help his friend in the pursuit of his new love interest, Silerio offers to dress as a *truhán*, here understood as a kind of itinerant poet and musician, and by this means gains access to Nísida in order to advance Timbrio's suit. The narrator provides no explanation for this overly complicated scheme, but rather shifts quickly to the moment when Silerio, now dressed in his disguise, first sees Nísida:²⁹

> ... vi más cerca la justa causa que Timbrio tenía de padecer, y la que el cielo me dio para quitarme el contento todos los días que en esta vida durare. Vi a Nísida, a Nísida vi, para no ver más, ni ay más que ver después de averla visto. ¡O fuerça poderosa de amor, contra quien valen poco las poderosas nuestras!³⁰

> ["... I saw close up the just cause why Timbrio was suffering, and that which heaven gave to me in order to deprive me of happiness the rest of the days of my life. I saw Nísida, I saw Nísida, so that I might never see again, nor have anything more to see after having seen her. Oh, powerful force of love, against whom our powers are of so little use."]

Like Tito in the story from the *Decameron*, Silerio immediately falls madly in love with his friend's lover. And also like Tito, Silerio is racked by the conflicting claims of love and friendship: "A vuestra consideración discreta dexo el imaginar lo que podía sentir un coraçón a quien de una parte combatían las leyes de la amistad, y de otra las inviolables de Cupido . . . [For your discreet consideration, I leave it to imagine what a heart might feel in which on one side fight the laws of friendship, and on the other the inviolable laws of Cupid . . .]"[31] In contrast to the earlier tale, however, in which this conflict is resolved quickly through Tito's confession of his love and Gisippo's accession to his friend's presumably more fervent passion in the name of perfect friendship, Silerio keeps his feelings to himself. In effect, while he ostensibly fulfills his stated promise to serve as Timbrio's intermediary, Silerio, in fact, undertakes what is essentially an act of subterfuge. Refusing to disclose his true feelings to his *alter ego*, Silerio accepts a moral compromise that cannot help but corrode the purity of his commitment to the Aristotelian ideal.

At this point, Silerio's failure to overcome fully his feelings for Nísida in favor of his commitment to friendship may be interpreted to reflect the pastoral as a contaminating influence within Cervantes's rewriting of the tale of two friends tradition as the lover's essentially unfree nature comes into conflict with the Aristotelian orthodoxy of the friend's unencumbered good will. Formal distinctions thus set the stage for a deeper ontological crisis as Silerio's identity is overdetermined by his association with two distinct and, as it turns out, fundamentally incompatible literary traditions. Read in this way, the conflict between love and friendship arguably exposes Silerio as a scripted puppet whose apparent internal struggles are nothing more than an epiphenomenon of the competing formal claims of pastoral love and Aristotelian friendship. In effect, by highlighting Silerio's internal conflict, Cervantes forces the issue of literary determinism, revealing the vacuity of any claim Silerio might make to subjective autonomy.

While compelling, this interpretation is incomplete. As I have already indicated, the problem of subjective autonomy in Cervantes is almost invariably related to his overarching interest in representational verisimilitude, especially in later writings like the *Novelas ejemplares* and *Don Quixote*. In this instance, the irreconcilable claims of pastoral love and Aristotelian perfect friendship may also be read through the filter of verisimilitude in terms of an internal emotional struggle that reflects a level of complexity in the depiction of Silerio's inner life that is unprecedented in earlier narratives from the tale of two friends tradition.[32] Unable to extinguish his feelings for Nísida, Silerio's free will is necessarily divided, so that he is incapable of fulfilling his assigned role of exemplary perfect friend.

The import of this final observation quickly becomes apparent when one night, by accident, Timbrio chances to hear Silerio singing a lover's lament. Interpreting Silerio's verses—correctly—as a sign of his friend's secret love for Nísida, Timbrio resolves to absent himself that very night "e irse adonde de niguno fuesse hallado [and go where no one might find him]" in order to allow Silerio "comodidad de que solo a Nísida sirviesse [the convenience of serving Nísida alone]."[33] Timbrio's will to give up Nísida for the sake of his friend here recalls Gisippo's earlier sacrifice in favor of Tito in Boccaccio but with one important distinction: Unlike his Italian predecessor, Timbrio is uable to overcome the emotional trauma of this ultimate act of selflessness, so that in the end, his only remedy is to flee, abandoning both his lover and his friend.

This lack of a resolution in the conflict between love and friendship only deepens later when Silerio, now informed of Timbrio's decision to flee, discovers his disconsolate friend lying face down on his bed shedding "infinite tears" over his decision to give up Nísida as a sacrifice to his friendship with Silerio. Further undermining the resolution of the story's primary conflict, Silerio engages in another act of calculated deception: In order to allay his friend's suffering, Silerio lies about his feelings for Nísida, claiming that the true object of his verses was, in fact, Nísida's sister, Blanca. While this lie achieves its desired goal—"y súpelo dezir esto de manera que él lo tuvo por verdadero [and I knew how to say it in such a way that he took it for the truth]"—convincing Timbrio that Silerio is, in fact, not in love with Nísida, it does so in a way that leaves the underlying conflict between the two friends unresolved while also further complicating any claim that Silerio might make to exemplify the Aristotelian ideal of the perfect friend.[34] That ideal is now displaced by something far more ambiguous, and far more in keeping with the tenets of representational verisimilitude, a calculated decision to deceive as the lesser evil that reads very much like an exaggerated case study in situational ethics and that, in the end, does nothing to resolve Silerio's emotional struggle.

Having successfully deceived his friend into thinking that his amorous inclinations tend toward Nísida's sister Blanca, Silerio is soon back pressing Timbrio's case with Nísida. In keeping with the larger framework of the pastoral mode, the narrative trends back at this point to its arguably inevitable outcome as Nísida finally admits that she has fallen for her suitor, that is, Timbrio (and not Silerio): ". . . '¡Ah, Silerio, Silerio, y cómo creo que a costa de la salud mía has querido granjear la de tu amigo!' [Ah, Silerio, Silerio, how I believe that at the price of my health you have gained that of your friend!]"[35] The deliberately convoluted plotting of this tale comes to the fore at this moment in Nísida's confession here of her love for Timbrio as the awkward interjection of "Ah, Silerio, Silerio," underscores the intermediary Silerio's ambiguous role as Nísida's unacknowledged *de facto* suitor—something which, in the end, he both is and is not. Overwrought with possible interpretations, the notion of the friend as an *alter ego* is transformed at this moment from the defining characteristic of ideal friendship into a confused and contradictory signifier whose ultimate meaning is destabilized by new complications in the story's plot.

At the same time, Silerio's response to the news that he has finally succeeded in his attempt to seduce Nísida on Timbrio's behalf underscores, once again, the internal subjective dimension of the formal conflict between love and friendship:

> Quál yo quedé, pastores, oyendo lo que Nísida dezía y la voluntad amorosa que tener a Timbrio mostrava, no es posible encarecerlo, y aun es bien que carezca de encarecimiento dolor que a tanto se estiende, no porque me pesasse de ver a Timbrio querido, sino de verme a mí impossibilitado de tener jamás contento, pues estava y está claro que ni podía, ni puedo vivir sin Nísida . . .[36]

> ["How this affected me, shepherds, hearing what Nísida was saying, and the love that she showed for Timbrio, it is not possible to overstate; and it is well that a pain that reaches such depths cannot be overstated; not because it aggrieved me to see Timbrio loved, but rather to see myself precluded from ever being happy, as it was and is clear that I could not, nor can I live without Nísida . . ."]

The symbolic force of the scene, as Silerio literally comes to embody Timbrio's *alter ego* in his seduction of Nísida, is finally distilled here into an expression of internal emotional turmoil. In the end, the formal substitution of one friend for another in the service of the Aristotelian ideal of perfect—one might even say abject—selflessness, does little to assuage the suffering of the lovesick Silerio, for whom the thought of his friend's happiness provides small consolation, just enough to keep him from utter despair and death.[37]

Where in the earlier scene with the "turca gente," external events conspire to undermine the perfect friend's capacity to act in accord with the demands of perfect friendship, here Silerio's internal emotional tumult serves to disrupt that good will on behalf of one's friend that is arguably the single most important feature of the Aristotelian ideal. In both instances, however, the disruption of the conventions of perfect friendship may be traced back to Cervantes's growing interest in the principles of verisimilitude. The indifference of the external world to the moral demands of writing perfect friendship finds a complement in the complexity of Silerio's emotional state in the passage above as the mythologized moral clarity of the Aristotelian friend yields to a clear-eyed reckoning with the fundamental weakness of the human will. Compelled to pursue Nísida on his friend's behalf, Silerio ultimately gets swept up by his own amorous rhetoric. Read in this way, the notion of Silerio as Timbrio's *alter ego* is finally revealed not as a sign of an exalted transcendence of everyday human experience, but rather as a powerful confirmation of their shared human debility in the face of the illness that is love.

After describing a few more details of his relationship with Timbrio, Silerio's monologue concludes with an account of how they were finally separated. From this point on, the two friends remain apart until much later in the novel when they finally reunite in a scene that is narrated directly within the novel's present. In stark contrast to Silerio's long narrative, which repeatedly contests the Aristotelian ideal, the scene of Silerio and Timbrio's reunion demonstrates a significant and self-conscious interest in reanimating the conventional paradigm for writing perfect friendship. Thus, Timbrio, who is the first to learn of his friend's potential return, voices his excitement in language that explicitly evokes key tropes from the Aristotelian tradition:

> —¡Sanctos cielos! ¿Y qué es lo que oigo—dixo Timbrio—, y qué es lo que dizes, pastor? ¿Es por ventura esse Silerio que has nombrado el que es mi verdadero amigo, el que es la mitad de mi alma, el que yo desseo ver más que otra cosa que me pueda pedir el desseo? ¡Sácame desta duda luego, así crezcan y multipliquen tus rebaños de manera que te tengan envidia todos los vecinos ganaderos![38]

> ["My heavens! And what is this that I hear," said Timbrio, "and what is this that you are saying, shepherd? Is it possible that this Silerio that you have named is my true friend, he who is the other half of my soul, he who I desire to see more than anything that my desire could ask for? Relieve me of this doubt, and let your flocks grow and multiply so that all your neighbors envy you!"]

Timbrio's exaltation of his feelings for Silerio here prepares the way for a happy ending so that his hyperbolic—and highly conventionalized—language may be understood as serving a technical purpose within the narrative, signaling a return to the principles of ideal friendship. Moreover, the seemingly gratuitous reference in this passage to pastoral pursuits—"que crezcan y multipliquen tus rebaños"—reminds the reader of the formal framework for this return. Throughout much of Silerio's monologue, the struggle between love and friendship reflected a deeper formal conflict between the pastoral and the tale of two friends. Here, however, Cervantes reverses course: As a literary genre that largely eschews interest in representational verisimilitude in favor of idealized poetic formulae, the idyllic world of the pastoral lovers suddenly emerges as an especially suitable locus for the renewal of the equally idealized Aristotelian notion of perfect friendship.

In fact, the importance of the pastoral setting in restoring Timbrio and Silerio's ideal friendship is underscored throughout this last episode. Informed of Silerio's abode at a nearby hermitage, Timbrio, Nísida, and Blanca—Nísida's sister—rush to see him, at which point the narrative once again asserts the story's explicit pastoral context as the reunion between these two long-lost friends is staged as an exchange in verse reminiscent of the eclogue tradition. After overhearing Silerio recite in verse the story of his misfortunes in both love and friendship, Timbrio, whose identity remains hidden from his friend, arranges for Nísida to sing a lyrical response that gives poetic form to Timbrio's own sense of lost friendship:

> ... Aquel que, por buena suerte, / tú mesmo quisiste darme, / no ganó tanto en ganarme / quanto ha perdido en perderte. / Mitad de su alma fuiste, / y medio por quien la mía / pudo alcançar la alegría / que tu ausencia tiene triste.[39]

> [He whom, with great fortune, you yourself wanted to give me did not win as much in winning me as he has lost in losing you. You were half of his soul and the means by which mine, sad in your absence, could achieve happiness.]

Nísida, who throughout Silerio's own story has served as the source of conflict between two friends, now takes on an explicitly mediatory role in their final reunion, pressing the case for Timbrio's commitment to their friendship and infusing this final encounter with an unprecedented sense of optimism.

The final meeting between the two friends occurs a few pages later and, once again, lyric poetry provides the catalyst for the renewal of Aristotelian perfect friendship: Timbrio, who still has not revealed himself to his friend, begins to recite a sonnet, but only gets through the first stanza before Silerio recognizes his friend's voice. As the narrator makes clear, the ensuing scene of Timbrio and Silerio's emotional reunion completely dissipates the previous tension in their relationship: "Largo sería de contar las palabras de amor y contento que entre Silerio, Timbrio, Nísida y Blanca passaron, que fueron tan tiernas y tales, que todos los pastores que las escuchavan tenían los ojos bañados en lágrimas de alegría [It would take much time to relay all the words of love and happiness that passed between Silerio, Timbrio, Nísida, and Blanca, words that were so tender that all the shepherds who heard them bathed their eyes in tears of happiness]."[40] Evoking once again the public dimension of their friendship, their meeting is witnessed by teary-eyed shepherds who seem unable to resist the scene's melodramatic appeal. Yet the fact that the witnesses in this case are themselves idealized figures whose own relationship to the world of everyday life is tenuous at best only heightens the sense that we have now finally returned to a kind of pastoral literary self-sufficiency.

The end of the story is predictable in its respect for the categorical requirements of ideal friendship. After recounting at length his own experiences since their parting, Timbrio ties up the one remaining loose end in this tale of two friends by offering Blanca as wife to Silerio:

> ... aconsejó Timbrio a su amigo fuesse contento de que Blanca le tuviesse, escogiéndola y aceptándola por esposa, pues ya la conocía, y no ignorava su valor y honestidad, encareciéndole el gusto y plazer que los dos tendrían viéndose con tales dos hermanas casados. Silerio le respondió que le diesse espacio para pensar en aquel hecho, aunque él sabía que al cabo era impossible dexar de hazer lo que él le mandasse.[41]
>
> [... Timbrio advised his friend to be happy with Blanca, choosing her and accepting her as wife, since he already knew her and was not unaware of her value, honesty, praising her and the pleasure he and Silerio would have seeing themselves married to the two sisters. Silerio asked for space to think about this plan, even though he knew that in the end it was impossible not to do what Timbrio had ordered.]

The paradigm of ideal friendship here reasserts its primacy. No mention is made of Silerio's earlier feelings for Nísida, nor does the text reference the madness that these feelings provoked. Instead, the good friend accedes to a substitution that effectively salvages the requirements of such a friendship: The entrance of the stunningly beautiful Blanca resolves the story's problematic love triangle, her identity as Nísida's sister restoring—if somewhat imperfectly—the notion of the friend as a second self. Blanca becomes the consolation prize that allows for Timbrio and Silerio to share, at some level, in the same love.

The ending of the tale of Timbrio and Silerio's friendship, however, cannot completely undo the narrative experience of everything that has come before, a fact that is shrewdly acknowledged in the final sentence of the passage above. Silerio hesitates before accepting Blanca, and in the description of his assent to the marriage, one detects a note of resignation: "aunque él sabía que al cabo era impossible dexar de hacer lo que él le mandasse." Self-sacrifice at the altar of friendship is replaced at this moment by acquiescence to what looks suspiciously like a form of necessity. In conspicuously avoiding any mention of Silerio's feelings for Blanca—in stark contrast to his earlier expressions of irrepressible passion for Nísida—this passage underscores the purely formal nature of the story's denouement. Silerio's recognition that he must finally marry Blanca thus reflects a shift from the narrative's earlier experimentation with representational verisimilitude to an almost mechanistic deployment of the conventional plotting of the tale of two friends tradition. In the end, the very moment in the narrative that confirms the traditional paradigm of ideal friendship also serves to drain that moment of any claim to emotional authenticity.

Even more significant, however, this final scene brings us back to the central Cervantine focus on subjective autonomy. Beyond the question of emotional authenticity and representational verisimilitude, Silerio's hesitancy before the prospect of marriage with Blanca injects a paradoxical hint of coercion into an event that should mark the symbolic triumph of perfect friendship. Unlike the conflict over love that constitutes the narrative's main test of friendship, Silerio's equivocation here defies the logic of perfect friendship. He is not driven by some all-consuming mad passion that incapacitates his free will. Rather, his irresolution gives voice to a self-conscious meditation, however brief, on how friendship itself constrains his free will. In the end, Silerio will marry Blanca, but that marriage can never be understood as the manifestation of a pure and seamless expression of his freedom within friendship.[42]

For a writer who will later create one of the most robust expressions of early modern subjective autonomy in the figure of Don Quixote, the foregoing analysis is suggestive of the role the tale of two friends plays in the development of Cervantes's poetics. While the story of Silerio and Timbrio maintains the formal expectations of the narrative friendship tradition, it also finally calls into question one of the defining attributes of perfect friendship, namely, its basis in an absolutely unencumbered will. And while, in the end, Silerio does his duty as a friend and marries his good friend's wife's sister, the ambiguities of this final gesture open a space for even more radical questioning of the paradigm of perfect friendship in the story from *Don Quixote* that will form the basis of my next chapter, "El curioso impertinente."

Notes

1. It is worth noting that the source of pastoral suffering in *Égloga I* is not limited to the more traditional trope of unrequited love, but also, in the case of Nemoroso, includes the emotionally powerful image of his beloved Elisa's untimely death in childbirth. Indeed, Nemoroso's description of Elisa's final moments constitutes one of the most heart-wrenching passages in all of Spanish early modern letters. On the poetic perfection of Garcilaso's *Égloga I*, A. A. Parker, "Tema e imagen de la Égloga I de Garcilaso," p. 199, writes, "La Égloga I suele ser considerada como el más cumplido ejemplo de la conversión por Garcilaso del artificio bucólico en una armoniosa unidad de contenido y forma: no necesita insistirse en que el poema es de un arte exquisito." This sentiment is echoed by Rafael Lapesa, *La trayectoria poética de Garcilaso*, p. 140, who highlights the significance of *Eclogue I* to Garcilaso's overall poetic production: "La égloga I marca la más alta cima de la poesía garcilasiana. Otras creaciones posteriores la aventajarán acaso en perfección técnica y en riqueza sensorial; pero ninguna ha llegado a tan estrecha unión del sentimiento y la forma."
2. I employ the label "pastoral novel" with some trepidation. While I use the term throughout this chapter, I do so with an awareness that questions of nomenclature for texts likes Montemayor's *Los siete libros de la Diana* and Cervantes's *La Galatea* are far more complex than my usage here suggests. Writing of *La Galatea*, Rhodes, "Sixteenth-century Pastoral Books, Narrative Structure, and *La Galatea* of Cervantes," p. 352, provides a good summary of the problem: "To hesitate between 'romance' and 'novel' in reference to *La Galatea* and the books that inspired it is unnecessary because, as Wardropper has pointed out, in Cervantes' day, the word 'novela' was used to refer to short stories, not what we call 'novels,' and the Spanish word *romance* had been pre-empted to refer to something quite different from what we call 'romance.' 'Libros de pastores,' in English 'pastoral books,' seems to be the most acceptable solution. Use of that term makes it easier to identify the elements that distinguish these 'libros de pastores' from other types of sixteenth-century fiction; unhindered by the obligation to interpret them as novels or romances, realistic or idealistic, the critic can focus attention on what pastoral books consist of in themselves, with the understanding that the resulting list of characteristics will not correspond to any categories we have since imposed on literature." While I have chosen not to follow Rhodes's lead on the use of the expression "libros de pastores," her analysis is amenable to my approach here as it opens up the possibility for discussions of narrative structure that are not driven by conventional measures of genre. For another perspective on this question, see also Johnson, "Montemayor's *Diana*: A Novel Pastoral," p. 20: "Jorge de Montemayor never called his *Siete Libros de la Diana* a 'novela pastoril' nor indeed was the word *novela* applied by anyone in the sixteenth century to any works other than Italianate short stories. Nevertheless it seems clear that Montemayor was conscious of producing a new and even daring version of pastoral, by combining it with narrative in the tradition of the Italian *novella*."

3. The extent of Sannazaro's influence on Montemayor is a subject of some debate. As Avalle-Arce, *La novela pastoril española*, p. 73, notes in his classic study from the late twentieth century: "Ante el sentido y la forma de la *Diana*, la crítica, en general, ha presentado dos actitudes opuestas ... El positivismo, dadas sus preferencias metodológicas, acentuó, en forma desmedida, por lo general, los parecidos con sus antecedentes, dedicando especial atención a trazar paralelos con la *Arcadia* de Sannazaro. Por su parte, el revisionismo ambiental en que vivimos, producto de diversas corrientes que han ido ahondando su influencia en lo que va de siglo, ha preferido subrayar las divergencias con los modelos, en forma concordante con las nuevas tendencias críticas a buscar la partciularidad efectiva y no lo genérico inoperante."
4. Montemayor, *Los siete libros de la Diana*, pp. 109–10. Translation is my own.
5. See my previous analysis in "Love and Friendship in Montemayor's *La Diana*," especially the following remarks on the passage reproduced here: "At the same time, however, the Neoplatonic undercurrent of this passage is complicated by the narrator's reference to Sireno's former freedom compared with his present subjugation to his love for Diana. The prelapsarian vision that we are offered in this early scene associates the idyllic harmony of nature with Sireno's now lost *libertad*. In effect, the passage suggests an easy correlation between freedom and the harmonious integration of the individual within the universe while love is revealed as nothing less than a kind of enslavement," p. 749.
6. Mujica, "Antiutopian Elements in the Spanish Pastoral Novel," p. 266, captures something on this sense of emotional enslavement as a more general phenomenon in *La Diana*: "Montemayor's characters share a uniform view of life and love. Without exception, they see themselves as victims of irrational forces that are not subject to the human will and cannot be deciphered by human reason: 'Pues ¿quién es este Amor? Es una sciencia / que no la alcança estudio ni esperiencia' (p. 17). All Montemayor's characters believe themselves to be pawns of their own emotions, of destiny, and of fortune. The circle of which each shepherd forms a link (Ysmenia loves Montano; Montano loves Selvagia; Selvagia loves Alanio; and Alanio loves Ysmenia) is symbolic of the view of love as a trap that ensnares the individual."
7. As Avalle-Arce, *La novela pastoril*, p. 230, observes, Montemayor is not the only significant Spanish precursor to *La Galatea*: "Cuando Cervantes se inicia formalmente en el mundo de las letras, no le faltaban modelos en que inspirarse para escribir una novela pastoril. Entre varios otros de menor nombradía, ya lo habían precedido Montemayor, Alsonso Pérez, Gil Polo y Gálvez de Montalvo. Las características externas de su novela se modelan sobre aspectos de la técnica narrativa que hemos encontrado en todos estos escritores." For a more extensive discussion of *La Galatea* and the Spanish pastoral novel, see also López Estrada, *La "Galatea" de Cervantes: Estudio crítico*, pp. 64–81.
8. Rhodes, "Sixteenth-century Pastoral Books," p. 353, alludes to this quality of much of early modern pastoral and notes the distinction with

Cervantes: "The impulse behind the escape to Arcadia is a desire for sentiment, not activity. Since pastoral books are longer than verse eclogues, that impulse toward pure emotion through recollection was necessarily expanded in them ... As the eclogue in Spain passed from Garcilaso through Montemayor to Cervantes, the pastoral impulse was channelled through prose as well as poetry and through related events as well as feelings. History violated poetic Arcadia with the advent of the pastoral books, and each author of this type of fiction distributed the amount of action and contemplation in different percentages. In *La Diana*, for example, a decidedly lyric tone and passivity predominates. This is not the case in Cervantes's book."

9. Cervantes, *La Galatea*, vol. 1, pp. 12–13. The text of *La Galatea* has been adapted from the Schevill and Bonilla 1914 edition. All translations from *La Galatea* are my own.
10. Rhodes, "Sixteenth-century Pastoral Books," p. 355. Bruno Damiani, "The Rhetoric of Death in *La Galatea*," p. 53, reminds us of the ubiquity of "violence and death" in *La Galatea*, which he asserts are "dominant themes" that "are revealed through a highly developed rhetorical apparatus." In the case of Lisandro's tale, however, the rhetoric of death that attends so much of the love poetry from the period is displaced by a scene of real murderous violence, that is, by the literalization of that which in the Renaissance tradition of Spanish poetry had always functioned as either hyperbole or metaphor.
11. The complicated plotting of this episode is recounted by Lisandro in the aftermath of Carino's murder in *La Galatea*, vol. 1, pp. 22–39.
12. As Avalle-Arce, "La Galatea: La Novelistic Crucible," p. 14, puts it, "here in the *Galatea* we are confronted with an extraordinary, initial and inexplicable murder, which decidedly, forcefully and overtly breaks all literary canons." It is worth noting that Avalle-Arce, p. 15, sees the violent death on display in this early scene from the novel as a harbinger of Cervantes's interest in transcending the static idealism of earlier pastoral in a movement toward what I describe throughout this study as representational verisimilitude: "Death has entered Arcadia, led by the hand of Cervantes, and this more than fifty years before Nicolas Poussin saw her, hallucinated, murmuring to the shepherds, *Et in Arcadia ego*. But Death's hegemony is exercised only where there is Life, and its presence in the Cervantine Arcadia should make very clear the fact that Cervantes wanted to create live shepherds, flesh and blood beings, not the idealities that the *Diana* of Montemayor had brought into Spanish soil ... The shepherds of Cervantes live in the shadow of death precisely because they are alive (or such is the artist's intention), because they want to assert the fact that they are not theoretical creatures valid only as abstractions."
13. Significantly, Aurora Egido, *Cervantes y las puertas del sueño*, p. 81, detects this pastoral Neoplatonism in the opening scene between Elicio and Erastro in Book I: "Resulta asombrosa la ceguera de los detractores de *La Galatea* que han podido olividar el nexo neoplatónico que engarza los poemas con

la prosa en lazo indisoluble. La zampoña y el rabel de Elicio y Erastro acompañan sus voces poéticas, armónicamente concertadas con el atardecer. La microcosmía establece las analogías entre el hombre y el universo." I would stress once again, however, that it is precisely this idyllic Neoplatonism that is undone by the scene of Carino's murder.

14. Avalle-Arce, p. 34, captures something of this idea in the introduction to his edition of *La Galatea:* "Pero ni *La Galatea* ni el pensamiento de su autor se dejan encerrar en un rígido esquema platónico. El concepto del amor puede corresponder a veces a tales principios, pero en las otras ocasiones está tan hondamente enclavado en lo íntimo de la personalidad del pastor, que no se puede hablar más de teorías, sino de sufriente e ilógica humanidad. Basta repasar algunos de los «casos de amor» para ver cómo el concepto del amor empapa en vida concreta y se aparta de la teorización abstracta."

15. Avalle-Arce, *La novela pastoril española*, p. 234, includes the interpolated story of Timbrio and Silerio in the tale of two friends tradition: "Comencemos por las de Timbrio y Silerio, que relatan la misma anécdota y que son, en conjunto, una versión del cuento de los dos amigos, reelaborado ya con distinta intención y manera por Alonso Pérez (v. *supra*, págs. 112–14). La historia que comparten Timbrio y Silerio se identifica con el cuento tradicional por dos rasgos esenciales: un amigo se sacrifica para liberar a otro de una muerte segura, y los dos amigos se enamoran de la misma mujer, con las consiguientes preubas de amistad."

16. Muñoz Sánchez, "Un ejemplo de interpolación cervantina," p. 282, notes how the use of interpolated tales in *La Galatea* serves to extend the novel's reach beyond its formal pastoral setting: "Los episodios intercalados son los hechos sucedidos en el pasado y que se actualizan en el presente pastoril mediante la narración, más o menos extensa y en primera persona, de un personaje, que no es un pastor, aunque pueda ir disfrazado como tal, y que desempeña, entonces, las funciones de un narrador intradiegético o paranarrador . . . Al contar su biografía o su prehistoria amplían el tiempo, hacia el pretérito, y el espacio del reducido marco pastoril, ya que esos personajes-narradores no pertenecen a la bucólica, sino que van a para allí, como hemos dicho, por motivos de distinta índole, por lo que el relato de su historia se hace posible al ser encontrados por los pastores, habitualmente, encuentros motivados por el azar narrativo."

17. The connection between Boccaccio's story of Tito and Gisippo and Cervantes's rewriting of the tale of two friends tradition through the figures of Timbrio and Silerio is well documented. López Estrada mentions it in his extensive study of La Galatea, *La "Galatea" de Cervantes*, pp. 101–5.

18. Cervantes, *La Galatea*, vol. 1, pp. 118–19.

19. Avalle-Arce, *La novela pastoril española*, pp. 235–6. I will have more to say about this topic in the next chapter.

20. While it is true that Boccaccio's parody undermines Tito's claims to a pure Aristotelianism in his friendship with Gisippo, that parody never addresses the concept of perfect friendship itself. Rather the focus is consistently on

the ways in which both Tito and Gisippo fail to live up to that mythologized ideal. One might reasonably argue that there is an implicit critique of Aristotelian perfect friendship in Boccaccio, but certainly nothing like the kind of direct unraveling of the concept with which Cervantes confronts his readers in the story of Timbrio and Silerio.

21. Cervantes, *La Galatea*, vol. 1, pp. 123–4.
22. Ibid. vol. 1, p. 124.
23. Ibid. vol. 1, p. 126. The original reads: "Poco más de media noche sería, hora acomodada a facinorosos insultos . . ."
24. Ibid. vol. 1, p. 128.
25. For a more general discussion of *fortuna* in *La Galatea*, see López Estrada, *Estudio crítico de "La Galatea,"* pp. 39–44.
26. López Estrada, *La "Galatea" de Cervantes*, pp. 104–5, writes, "Por otra parte, el carácter clásico del escenario y de los personajes en la versión de Boccaccio, propia de un renacentista ingenuo, queda sustituido por la realidad geográfica de la Europa del siglo XVI: Jerez y Nápoles son las ciudades en que comienza y se desarrolla la acción de la novela. Y, enlazadas con ellas, las escenas de bandidos catalanes (que han de reaparecer en el *Quijote*) y las del asalto turco a una aldea catalana, suceso que se ha querido documentar en la realidad histórica." The expression, "que se ha querido documentar en la realidad histórica," captures the sense of historical truthfulness as that which really matters in this scene, the sense that these events are, in Aristotle's sense, probable, even if not literally true. Egido, *Cervantes y las puertas del sueño*, p. 335, for her part, describes Silerio alternatively as both an "ermitaño" and an "hombre de acción" who is "confundido a ratos con los pastores," a remark that captures his hybrid existence in the text.
27. Cervantes, *La Galatea*, vol. 1, p. 129.
28. Egido, *Cervantes y las puertas del sueño*, p. 25, asserts that the trope of "la enfermedad de amor tiñe de punta a cabo el curso y el discurso de *La Galatea*." This analysis echoes López Estrada, *La "Galatea" de Cervantes*, p. 28, from fifty years earlier: "Por los ojos queda el alma herida; y el cuerpo da los primeros indicios de la llaga de amor: se embebe y transporta en los propios pensamientos, viene obligado a suspirar y llorar. De ahí que se hable de *enfermedad* de amor, *mal* de amor, y *éticos* de amor. Los testimonios físicos del mal son: la amarillez del rostro, la flacidez del cuerpo; puede llegar al paroxismo declarado en el alma o manifestado en el cuerpo por desmayo; y da lugar también a extraños accidentes." López Estrada links all of these characterizations with specific sections of the text in his footnotes.
29. One detects a note of irony in Cervantes's description of this peculiar plot device: "Pero después que tuve bien conocida su enfermedad, y huve visto a Nísida y considerando la calidad y nobleza de sus padres, determiné de posponer por él la hazienda, la vida y la honra, y más si más tuviera y pudiera, y assí usé de un artificio el más estraño que hasta oy se avrá oído ni leído, y fue que acordé de vestirme como truhán, y con una guitarra entrarme en

casa de Nísida, que por ser, como ya he dicho, sus padres de los principales de la ciudad, de otros muchos truhanes era continuada," vol. 1, pp. 130–1. Muñoz Sánchez, "Un ejemplo de interpolación cervantina," p. 289, observes that Cervantes uses this same plot device in *El celoso extremeño*.
30. Cervantes, *La Galatea*, vol. 1, p. 133.
31. Ibid. vol. 1, p. 136.
32. López Estrada, *La "Galatea" de Cervantes*, p. 105, captures something of this emphasis on verisimilitude which he attributes, at least in part, to a difference in narrative structure in Cervantes's text as compared to Boccaccio: "Puede decirse, como resumen, que al relato *directo* de Boccaccio, Cervantes prefiere la narración *personal*, partida en varios parlamentos parciales que se complentan entre sí, cada uno de los cuales es la experiencia de un personaje distinto."
33. Cervantes, *La Galatea*, vol. 1, p. 148. Schevill and Bonilla render the adjective "solo" as the adverb "sólo." I follow the guidance of some modernized editions in using "solo" which I preserve in the translation. The distinction is important to the extent that it emphasizes the fact that Timbrio wishes to allow Silerio to pursue Nísida unencumbered by his earlier pledge to act as Timbrio's agent. See, for example, the edition of Juan Montero, p. 135.
34. Ibid. vol. 1, pp. 149–50.
35. Ibid. vol. 1, p. 168.
36. Ibid. vol. 1, p. 169.
37. Silerio states in this regard, ". . . y si alguno [gusto] la suerte en este trance me concedía, era considerar el bien de mi amigo Timbrio, y este fue parte para que no llegasse a un mesmo punto mi muerte," vol. 1, p. 169.
38. Cervantes, *La Galatea*, vol. 2, p. 78.
39. Ibid. vol. 2, p. 108.
40. Ibid. vol. 2, p. 113.
41. Ibid. vol. 2, p. 133.
42. Mujica, "Antiutopian Elements in the Spanish Pastoral Novel," p. 278, is even more dismissive in her interpretation of the story's ostensibly happy ending: "When at last they are reunited by a new trick of fortune, Timbrio courts Nísida and Silerio settles for Blanca, Nísida's younger sister. This is one of the few episodes that seems to end well. Yet the problem is not really solved. One friend wins the prize; the other loses it. Friendship has required sacrifice and one of the two friends has had to settle for second best. Perfection remains an unattainable ideal."

Chapter 3

The End of an Ideal: Cervantes's "El curioso impertinente"

Scholarly articles on "El curioso impertinente," Cervantes's interpolated story of friendship from the first part of *Don Quixote*, number in the hundreds.[1] Much of this critical interest circulates around what Wardropper describes in his groundbreaking 1957 article as "The Pertinence of *El curioso impertinente*." Pointing out the ambiguity in the story's title, Wardropper observes: "While it is logically the inquisitive man who is described as 'impertinent,' a secondary meaning—that the tale of this *Curioso* is 'irrelevant'—echoes from the words."[2] The origin of this alternative reading of the story's title may be traced back to Cervantes himself, who, in an early chapter from the second part of *Don Quixote*, explicitly raises the question of the relevance of "El curioso impertinente" to the main narrative of the knight-errant's adventures. Describing the public reception of the first part of *Don Quixote*, the *bachiller* Sansón Carrasco remarks, "Una de las tachas que ponen a la tal historia ... es que su autor puso en ella una novela intitulada *El curioso impertinente*; no por mala ni por mal razonada, sino por no ser de aquel lugar, ni tiene que ver con la historia de su merced del señor don Quijote [One of the faults they find with this history ... is that its author inserted in it a novel called 'The Ill-advised Curiosity'; not that it is bad or ill-told, but that it is out of place and has nothing to do with the history of his worship Señor Don Quixote]."[3]

From the perspective of my analysis here, the terms of this critical debate are perhaps less significant than the fact itself of the novella's possible impertinence. Wardropper voices the aesthete's mid-twentieth-century concern over the integrity of Cervantes's novel in a memorable passage: "... it is scarcely flattering to the world's idea of a masterpiece or of the genius who wrote it to suppose that he threw it together like a bad cook making a cake."[4] In the light of the post-structuralist wave in literary criticism, Wardropper's concerns may sound quaint. Nevertheless, the continued struggle of even the most theoretically sophisticated critics with the problem of how to understand the relationship between "El curioso impertinente" and the novel's main narrative reveals the extent to which the underlying formal question first posited by Sansón Carrasco remains unresolved.[5]

As I will show both here and in a later chapter, the formal incongruity between "El curioso impertinente" and the framing narrative of *Don Quixote* may be productively understood in terms of an evolution within the poetics of friendship. My analysis will expand upon Avalle-Arce's original assertion regarding the unique place of Cervantes's interpolated story within the history of the tale of two friends tradition. Starting with his suggestion that "El curioso impertinente" marks the "etapa última en el desenvolvimiento de la historia de los dos amigos, y al mismo tiempo su destrucción," I will explore how the representation of friendship in the main narrative constitutes a dialectical overcoming of the inherited conventions of the tale of two friends tradition.[6]

An important clue to Cervantes's rewriting of the tale of two friends tradition is already available in Sansón Carrasco's reference to the criticism that "El curioso impertinente" no "tiene que ver con la historia de su merced del señor don Quijote."[7] The *bachiller* never identifies the specific source of this criticism of Cervantes's narrative. Rather, his use of the third-person plural—"una de las tachas que ponen a la tal historia . . ."—refers in the most general terms to an anonymous reading public whom Sansón implicitly endows with the authority to critique Cervantes's work. This is not the first time that this idea finds expression in *Don Quixote* as the emphasis on the public reaction in this passage recalls the narrator's exhortation in the Prologue to the first part, in which Cervantes makes clear the reader's freedom to say "de la historia todo aquello que te pareciere, sin temor que te calunien por el mal ni te premien por el bien que dijeres della [what you will of the story without fear of being abused for any ill or rewarded for any good you may say of it.]"[8]

The importance of Cervantes's insistence on the reader's right to pass judgment on his work derives in large measure from how that new aesthetic authority relates to the representation of the characters that populate the narrative's fictional universe. In the case of Sansón Carrasco's critique of "El curioso impertinente," the reaction of the two central characters from the novel's main narrative is instructive. Sancho echoes the *bachiller*'s earlier criticism of the irrelevance of "El curioso impertinente" to the main narrative, calling the author a "son of a dog [hideperro]" and accusing him of having mixed "cabbages with baskets [berzas con capachos]."[9] Don Quixote, for his part, adds an insult of his own, describing the novel's author as "algún ignorante hablador [some ignorant chatterer]," whom he criticizes for writing "a tiento y sin algún discurso ... salga de lo que saliere, como hacía Orbaneja, el pintor de Úbeda, al cual preguntándole qué pintaba respondió: 'Lo que saliere' [in a haphazard and heedless way ... let it turn out as it might, just as Orbaneja, the painter of Úbeda, used to do, who, when they asked him what he was painting, answered 'What it may turn out.']"[10]

The invective that both characters launch at the author of their life stories signals a quick readiness to embrace the public's negative opinion of the decision to include the interpolated story within the main narrative. That willingness to pile on suggests a certain anxiety about the readership's claim to a right to pass judgment on the lives of the characters that populate the novel. Don Quixote's remarks on the "pintor de Úbeda" are especially enlightening in this respect. The painter's work, as he goes on to explain, is plagued by the problem of misrepresentation: "Tal vez pintaba un gallo, de tal suerte y tan mal parecido, que era menester que con letras góticas escribiese junto a él: 'Éste es un gallo.' Y así debe de ser de mi historia, que tendrá necesidad de comento para entenderla [Sometimes he would paint a rooster in such a fashion, and so unlike, that he had to write alongside of it in Gothic letters, 'This is a rooster'; and so it will be with my history, which will require a commentary to make it intelligible]."[11] In the wake of the author's loss of control over the reception of his work, Don Quixote posits the need for a commentary in an attempt to restore order. The implications for Don Quixote himself in this passage are clear enough: If the book's author is, indeed, like the "pintor de Úbeda," then Don Quixote also runs the risk of being misrepresented beyond recognition.[12]

Above all, the problem of misrepresentation pierces the heart of Don Quixote's project to achieve fame through the practice of the noble profession of knight-errantry, underscoring the extent to which his success or failure ultimately rests not just on the competence of his author, but also on the whims of the public's reception of the author's work. As he notes a bit earlier in his conversation with the *bachiller:*

—Una de las cosas—dijo a esta sazón don Quijote—que más debe de dar contento a un hombre virtuoso y eminente es verse, viviendo, andar con buen nombre por las lenguas de las gentes, impreso y en estampa. Dije con buen nombre, porque siendo al contrario, ninguna muerte se le igualará.[13]

["One of the things," here observed Don Quixote, "that ought to give most pleasure to a virtuous and eminent man is to find himself in his lifetime in print and in type, familiar in people's mouths with a good name; I say a good name, for if it be the opposite, then there is no death to be compared to it."]

At various points in the first part of Cervantes's novel, Don Quixote insists that his great deeds will define him as a knight-errant. Here, however, that notion is self-consciously reorganized in terms of Don Quixote's public reputation. No longer is it sufficient to undertake great feats of valor, nor is it even enough that those deeds be recorded for posterity. What is finally required in Don Quixote's quest for glory is the approbation of the public so that the knight-errant's good name might be carried along "por las lenguas de las gentes."

At the end of the passage above, Don Quixote hints at the broader implications of his meditation on his reputation when he declares that the consequences of losing one's good name are such that "ninguna muerte se le igualará." The choice of words here reflects the deeper significance of public opinion within his project to resurrect the values of knight-errantry; as the ultimate arbiter of meaning, the reading public is empowered to determine whether Don Quixote's knightly aspirations live or die. This idea, however, is not restricted to the public's power over Don Quixote's aspirations for literary fame. Understood in a more expansive sense, Don Quixote's declaration translates into a commentary on the power of public opinion to legislate matters of identity more generally. As a review of Cervantes's novel as a whole reveals, identity in *Don Quixote* invariably depends upon the speculations of external observers, a finding that, as will become clear later in this discussion, applies equally to the interpolated story of "El curioso impertinente." Don Quixote, as Cervantes's lemma has it, may claim to be "el hijo de sus obras," but the ultimate interpretation of that claim is transferred to the external authority of those who witness his strange antics.

The ensuing erosion of individual autonomy in *Don Quixote* may be productively understood from the wider historical perspective of what José Antonio Maravall describes as "una cosmovisión barroca."[14] In promoting the role of public opinion in the construction of identity, Cervantes appeals to a vision of identity that is purely discursive in nature, echoing in this way the cultural attitudes of the Spanish baroque, which, Maravall argues, are founded upon a profound epistemological uncertainty about the nature of the universe that is captured in the quintessentially baroque emphasis on appearances.[15] Under the auspices of this degradation of a more optimistic Renaissance concept of individual autonomy, the anxiety that Don Quixote expresses throughout his conversation with the *bachiller* Sansón Carrasco is justified by the very distinct possibility that his "good name" is, in a very real sense, all that he possesses.

More to the point of my study here, however, the revelation of the discursive foundation of Don Quixote's claim to embody the values of knight-errantry has profound implications for the tradition of perfect friendship. I have already referenced on several occasions the problem of the perfect friend's unknowability. In its highest Aristotelian formulation—as exemplified in the mythic friendship between Orestes and Pylades—that sense of unknowability recognizes the final inaccessibility of the perfect friend's claim to embody Aristotelian virtue. Like God himself, the perfect friend escapes mere human understanding. Read in the context of *Don Quixote*, however, the perfect friend's epistemological inaccessibility gives way to a problem of ontology. As will become clear in my reading of *El curioso impertinente*, the difficulty of the friend's unknowability in Cervantes is not that the friend inhabits a realm of transcendent perfection—one of the main points of Tito's long speech to Sofronia's family—but, rather, that the claim to transcendence is itself a fiction, or, in the language of the baroque, an *engaño*, that conceals the emptiness of any essentialist claim to virtue. Read in this way, the perfect friend is finally revealed as the residue of a fictional discourse that carries the indelible risk of signifying nothing. This reorientation from a problem of epistemology to a crisis of ontology is a driving force in the implosion of the ideal of perfect friendship in the final pages of "El curioso impertinente."

The framing of "El curioso impertinente" confirms the enhanced role of the public as arbiter of literary value in this Cervantine rewriting of the tale of two friends tradition. As the innkeeper explains, not only is the identity of the original author of the story a mystery, even the ownership of the physical text is left unresolved, a point that is underscored by the *ventero*'s insistence on his role as the story's temporary custodian.[16] Ignoring the question of authorship and deferring indefinitely the material problem of ownership—both for the innkeeper himself and for those guests who have asked to take the papers with them—the narrative instead emphasizes the more ephemeral experience of reception by the many readers for whom "El curioso impertinente" has been a source of pleasure.

In fact, this emphasis on the pleasures of fiction operates as something of a theme throughout the chapter that leads up to the public reading of "El curioso impertinente" before the assembled guests at the inn.[17] In an extended discussion of the merits of chivalric fiction between the priest, on the one side, and the innkeeper, his wife, daughter, and the servant, Maritornes, on the other, Cervantes explores the literary preferences of a series of humble characters who may be said to exemplify the aesthetic sensibilities of the *vulgo*, that is, of an emerging popular audience for these fantastic works of fiction. First to speak in defense of the *libros de caballerías* is the innkeeper, who offers a vivid account of what, in contemporary terms, might be conceived as literary consumerism: ". . . cuando es tiempo de la siega, se recogen aquí las fiestas muchos segadores, y siempre hay alguno que sabe leer, el cual coge uno destos libros en las manos, y rodeámonos dél más de treinta, y estámosles escuchando con tanto gusto que nos quita mil canas [for when it is harvest-time, the reapers flock here on holidays, and there is always one among them who can read and who takes up one of these books, and we gather round him, thirty or more of us, and stay listening to him with a delight that makes our grey hairs grow young again]."[18] What stands out most here is the innkeeper's validation of one of the most important elements of modern popular culture: the notion of entertainment as a legitimate and even privileged end of literary production.[19]

This defense of entertainment is echoed in various ways by the other characters from the inn. Still speaking of the chivalric novels, Maritornes, the somewhat less than perfectly chaste *criada*, declares her not surprising preference for romantic scenes of seduction, "cuando cuentan que se está la otra señora debajo de unos naranjos abrazada con su caballero [especially when they describe some lady or another in the arms of her knight under the orange trees]," with the jealous *dueña* serving as a look-out for this surreptitious lovemaking.[20] The more innocent innkeeper's daughter, on the other hand, insists that while she does not understand much of what happens in these books and dislikes "los golpes" that please her father, she is nevertheless brought to tears by sentimental displays of courtly love, in particular, "las lamentaciones que los caballeros hacen cuando están ausentes de sus señoras [the laments the knights utter when they are separated from their ladies]."[21] Finally, perhaps the most practical defense of the pleasures of chivalric fiction is voiced by the innkeeper's wife. Affirming her husband's opinion, she goes on to explain her reasoning in terms of the contribution of these texts to the family's domestic harmony: ". . . porque nunca tengo buen rato en mi casa sino aquel que vos estáis escuchando leer; que estáis tan embobado, que no os acordáis de reñir por entonces [. . . because I never have a quiet moment in my house except when you are listening to someone reading; for then you are so taken up that for the time being you forget to scold]."[22]

In his representation of these four characters, Cervantes posits the ascendancy of popular taste, an observation that is only accentuated by the scant attention that he gives to the other characters—drawn from the nobility—who are also present in this scene and who also form part of the audience for the priest's public reading of "El curioso impertinente."[23] In the end, only one of these other characters speaks, voicing an opinion that merely serves to affirm the value of entertainment as it relates to the priest's proposed reading material: "—Harto resposo será para mí—dijo

Dorotea—entretener el tiempo oyendo algún cuento . . ."[24] As with the innkeeper and his family's earlier defense of chivalric fiction, Dorotea prioritizes the entertainment value of "El curioso impertinente," which she describes in terms of an escape from her anticipated insomnia in the wake of her experiences earlier in the day.

The close association between popular taste and entertainment in the lead up to the priest's reading of "El curioso impertinente" is not, I would argue, coincidental. As will become evident in what follows, the reader's knowledge that the same representatives of the *vulgo*—the innkeeper and his family—play the role of audience for "El curioso impertinente" operates as a necessary precondition for understanding Cervantes's reinterpretation of the tale of two friends tradition. Despite self-conscious appeals to the language of moral exemplarity, there is an inescapable voyeuristic undercurrent in Cervantes's narrative that serves as a constant reminder of the presence of a witness, either the reader or some observer from within the context of the narrative itself. For this reason, friendship in "El curioso impertinente," in contrast to the Aristotelian model of the intrinsically good friend, is reconstituted as discourse or— what is essentially the same thing in this instance—performance, that is, in terms that deprive it of any intrinsic claim to meaning beyond that which is ascribed to it by an audience.

The first few pages of "El curioso impertinente" open up a polemic with the traditional tale of perfect friendship that largely determines the later evolution of the story. From the very first paragraph, one observes a subtle but fundamental reworking of key elements of that tradition:

> En Florencia, ciudad rica y famosa de Italia, en la provincia que llaman Toscana, vivían Anselmo y Lotario, dos caballeros ricos y principales, y tan amigos, que por excelencia y antonomasia, de todos los que los conocían *los dos amigos* eran llamados. Eran solteros, mozos de una misma edad y de unas mismas costumbres; todo lo cual era bastante causa a que los dos con recíproca amistad se correspondiesen. Bien es verdad que el Anselmo era algo más inclinado a los pasatiempos amorosos que el Lotario, al cual llevaban tras sí los de la caza; pero, cuando se ofrecía, dejaba Anselmo de acudir a sus gustos por seguir los de Lotario, y Lotario dejaba los suyos por acudir a los de Anselmo; y, de esta manera, andaban tan a una sus voluntades, que no había concertado reloj que así lo anduviese.[25]

> [In Florence, a rich and famous city of Italy in the province called Tuscany, there lived two gentlemen of wealth and quality, Anselmo and Lotario, such great friends that by way of distinction they were called by all that knew them "The Two Friends." They were unmarried, young, of the same age and

the same tastes, which was enough to account for the reciprocal friendship between them. Anselmo, it was true, was somewhat more inclined to seek pleasure in love than Lotario, for whom the pleasures of the chase had more attraction; but on occasion Anselmo would forego his own tastes to yield to those of Lotario, and Lotario would surrender his to fall in with those of Anselmo, and in this way their inclinations kept pace one with the other with a concord so perfect that the best regulated clock could not surpass it.]

Here, in the narrative's opening paragraph, we encounter an enhanced version of a formula that was first deployed at the outset of the story of Timbrio and Silerio in *La Galatea* as the narrator links the exemplarity of the friendship between Anselmo and Lotario—"que por excelencia y antonomasia"—to the public perception of that relationship—"eran llamados." The rhetorical term "antonomasia" is of particular significance as it transforms the defining moment of Anselmo and Lotario's friendship into the defining moment for friendship in general. The assertion is hyperbolic, but it is also, as the rest of the passage makes clear, based on very little practical evidence. The two friends are raised together and described as similar in their habits, but despite the somewhat abstract claim about the synchronization of their wills, no significant insight is provided into the underlying basis of their friendship.

The implications of the foregoing observations are somewhat ambiguous. On the one hand, the hyperbolic claim to exemplarity founded on popular acclaim recalls Cicero's account of the mythic friendship of Orestes and Pylades enacted as a public performance in the theater. The public that ratifies the status of Anselmo and Lotario as the embodiment of friendship "por antonomasia" remains at a distance, the very lack of detail in this opening paragraph serving, in this reading, to underscore the lofty status of a relationship that, in some sense, exists beyond the world of everyday life. As with Cicero's account, however, that distance, rather than undermine the claim to exemplarity, reveals it as a paradox of the two friends' inimitable perfection: Public admiration of the "two friends" recognizes in their idealized representation of friendship something worthy of praise even as it remains inaccessible to the mass of humanity.

On the other hand, Cervantes's deliberate exposition of the aesthetic tastes of the assembled characters from the inn in the preceding chapter tends to undermine a reading of the relationship between Anselmo and Lotario as the fulfillment of the Aristotelian exemplary ideal. To the extent that meaning depends on the audience's discretion, these characters arguably lack the cultural and intellectual awareness required to appreciate fully the Aristotelian ideal of perfect friendship. One is reminded in this regard of Tito's long speech to his in-laws from the *Decameron* and, in particular, his assertion of their essential inability to appreciate the claims to transcendence inherent in his friendship with Gisippo. Like Tito's in-laws, the innkeeper, his wife, daughter, and Maritornes—as characters drawn from everyday life—pertain to a world that is fundamentally alien to the exalted discourse of Aristotelian perfect friendship. Or, to take another example, compare the audience for the priest's reading of "El curioso impertinente" to the public that witnesses the dramatic representation of the tale of Orestes and Pylades in Cicero's anecdote from *De amicitia*. In place of the adulation of an informed audience that recognizes the unbreachable moral gulf separating mythic friendship from ordinary human relations, one confronts here a public motivated—as described above—primarily if not entirely by an interest in entertainment.

Considered from the perspective of the *vulgo* as audience, one may construct a very different account of the narrative's opening passage. While it is true that the lack of insight into the basis of Anselmo and Lotario's friendship tends to rarefy the representation of that relationship, the limited details that are provided, when reinterpreted without recourse to the Aristotelian paradigm, incline toward the opposite effect. Read more deliberately against the literary-historical context of the period, the two shared activities that are offered as evidence of the friendship between these two young men—hunting and amorous pursuits—appear almost trite in their conventionality and, for this reason, mitigate against any transcendent claims that might be made for their relationship.

Moreover, in undercutting the more traditional claims to transcendence through perfect friendship, Cervantes may be said to orient his discourse toward the concerns of everyday life. The local community within the narrative that dubs Anselmo and Lotario "los dos amigos" constitutes the collective opinion of neighbors and acquaintances, that is, of people who form the social context within which the characters themselves presumably live. This idea is reinforced in the next paragraph, which describes, in short order, how Anselmo falls in love with Camila and, with Lotario's blessing, marries. This rapid turn of events creates a conflict between the two friends that signals a rather stark deviation from what was observed in earlier texts from the tale of two friends tradition as Lotario, out of concern for his friend's honor, leaves off visiting Anselmo's home as had been his practice before his marriage.[26] In sharp contrast to the earliest narratives examined in this study, in which marriage provides the means toward resolving a major conflict between friends, it now serves as the source of ongoing discord as Anselmo's spousal ties to Camila introduce an unavoidable element of social difference between the two friends.[27] Where the narrator's insistence in the story's opening paragraph on the fundamental similarity between the two young men recalls the classical notion of the friend as a second self, this new development in Anselmo's personal life changes his social circumstances in ways that impede the harmony of what had been a perfect communion.

More importantly, this new impediment to the harmony of their exemplary friendship marks a radical revision in the depiction of the social practices of both friendship and marriage in the tale of two friends tradition. In Boccaccio, for example, marriage functions unproblematically within a symbolic language of exchange that is explicitly subservient to the exalted claims of perfect friendship. For this reason, marriage never presents a serious challenge to the pre-eminence of perfect friendship. Tito and Gisippo can remain friends in the wake of their marriage because, in the end, marriage is of little consequence beyond its symbolic function. In contrast, this passage exhibits a concept of marriage that is rooted far more firmly in the soil of social practices whose claims over the individual compete directly with those of friendship, an observation that Anselmo largely confirms in his own protestations against the changes in their former habits.[28] Where earlier texts from the tradition represent perfect friendship as somehow separate and superior to more ordinary social relations, one here encounters a far more domesticated and historically determined vision in which friendship is finally subordinated to the pressing concerns of honor within marriage.[29]

Of course, Cervantes is not the first to invoke the problem of social difference in the representation of perfect friendship. In particular, I have already shown at some length how the *Decameron* sets up a direct conflict between the elevated discourse of perfect friendship and the very significant social distinctions between the two perfect friends, Tito and Gisippo. In Boccaccio's narrative, however, the invocation of social difference never exceeds the bounds of a self-contained response to the mythic claims of perfect friendship. Thus, the parodic effect of Tito and Gisippo's failure to embody the ideal of Aristotelian perfect friendship never quite reaches the point of undercutting the ideal itself. Instead, that ideal retains its integrity to the extent that it is understood to lie beyond the realm of everyday life, in a mythic space that is contentious only to the extent that it is profoundly inaccessible. In contrast, in the opening paragraphs of "El curioso impertinente," Cervantes integrates the ideal of perfect friendship within the fabric of his representation of historically localized social practices.[30] Read in this way, Lotario's subordination of friendship to the demands of honor within marriage opens up the possibility of a critique of the Aristotelian ideal that might move beyond the self-contained space of Renaissance intertextuality and out into the world of early modern social relations, especially as encoded within the trope of honor.

The above analysis may be understood in another way as well. Both Lotario's decision to leave off visiting his now married friend and Anselmo's protestations against that decision raise a new and fundamental question that is largely excluded from the traditional Aristotelian discourse of friendship. What both men grapple with here at the very outset of the narrative—it is worth remembering that all of this occurs in the story's second and third paragraphs—is the problem of how to be a friend now that friendship itself has been forced down from a state of exalted transcendence and into the world of everyday life. This is, at its heart, an ethical question, one that forces a reckoning with the practical difficulty posed by competing social commitments. At this point in Cervantes's novella, one fails to detect even a hint of the self-assured insistence on the superiority of perfect friendship over all other human relations that pervades Tito's long speech to Sofronia's famila in the *Decameron*. From here on out, the two friends "por antonomasia" will be forced to struggle with practical concerns that deflate all such pretensions regarding the special status of friendship.

It is against this backdrop that Cervantes proceeds to introduce what will constitute the main conflict in "El curioso impertinente." Shortly after Lotario's reluctant accession to his friend's request that he resume visiting his home, Anselmo confesses what he eventually reveals as an irrepressible desire to test his wife's fidelity:

> . . . vivo yo el más despechado y el más desabrido hombre de todo el universo mundo; porque no sé de qué días a esta parte me fatiga y aprieta un deseo tan estraño y tan fuera del uso común de otros, que yo me maravillo de mí mismo, y me culpo y me riño a solas, y procuro callarlo y encubrirlo de mis proprios pensamientos; y así me ha sido posible salir con este secreto como si de industria procurara decillo a todo el mundo. Y, pues que, en efeto, él ha de salir a plaza, quiero que sea en la del archivo de tu secreto, confiado que, con él y con la diligencia que pondrás, como mi amigo verdadero, en remediarme, yo me veré presto libre de la angustia que me causa, y llegará mi alegría por tu solicitud, al grado que ha llegado mi descontento, por mi locura.[31]

> [". . . I am the most discontented and dissatisfied man in the whole world; for, I know not how long since, I have been harassed and oppressed by a desire so strange and so unusual, that I wonder at myself and blame and chide myself when I am alone, and strive to stifle it and hide it from my own thoughts, and with no better success than if I were endeavouring deliberately to publish it to all the world; and as, in short, it must come out, I would confide it to your safe keeping, feeling sure that by this means, and by your readiness as a true friend to afford me relief, I shall soon find myself freed from the distress it causes me, and that your care will give me happiness in the same degree as my own madness has caused me misery."]

Much has been written about "El curioso impertinente" and the tradition of "wife testing," with Ariosto as the most frequently mentioned source for this central theme in Cervantes's interpolated story.[32] From the perspective of my analysis in this study, however, what matters more are the specific details of Anselmo's speech and, in particular, the way in which his account of his strange desire frames Cervantes's rewriting of the tale of two friends. Anselmo insists both here and elsewhere that his impulse to test his wife—which he describes as a kind of madness in the passage above—is completely unmotivated. Squeezing him as if it were an external force—"me fatiga y me aprieta"—this strange desire undermines his self-control and leads him to engage in self-recriminations: "yo me maravillo de mí mismo, y me culpo y me riño a solas."

The significance of this initial presentation of Anselmo's desire is twofold. On the one hand, the reference to madness may be read as a challenge to any claim that Anselmo—or the reader, for that matter—might make as to his subjective autonomy. The victim of forces beyond his control, this lack of agency already compromises his ability to fulfill one of the basic requirements of friendship as a relationship of voluntary association between two individuals, a question about which I will have much more to say later. Beyond the matter of Anselmo's compromised agency, this unmotivated desire to test his wife's virtue may also be read to reflect the structural requirements of the tale of two friends narrative. As I have already indicated on various occasions previously in this study, the traditional tale of two friends privileges form over content leading almost invariably to plots riddled with improbable coincidences. In keeping with Cervantes's literary self-consciousness throughout *Don Quixote*, Anselmo's prolonged meditation on the *deus ex machina* of his strange desire lends itself to parodic interpretations that highlight this particular aspect of the tale of two friends tradition.

The role of Anselmo's strange desire as a structural driver in the narrative is confirmed in what follows as Anselmo goes on to describe the circumstances that will transform his impulse to test his wife's fidelity into what finally emerges as a test of his friendship with Lotario. Fearing that his secret may out—"pues que en efeto él ha de salir a plaza"— Anselmo hopes to exorcise his demons by enlisting the help of his friend to conduct a secret test of marital fidelity: ". . . ¡oh amigo Lotario!, que te dispongas a ser el instrumento que labre aquesta obra de mi gusto; que yo te daré lugar para que lo hagas, sin faltarte todo aquello que yo viere ser necesario para solicitar una mujer honesta, honrada, recogida y desinteresada [it is my desire, friend Lotario, that you should consent to become the instrument for effecting this purpose that I am bent upon, for I will afford you opportunities to that end, and nothing shall be wanting that I may think necessary for the pursuit of a virtuous, honourable, modest and high-minded woman]."³³ As with the initial presentation of Anselmo's strange desire, his entreaty to his *alter ego* seems almost wholly disconnected from any kind of rational motivation. It exists, one is tempted to conclude, as merely its own end, as if Lotario's willing submission to Anselmo's bizarre plan were in fact the only thing that mattered in this tale and, in this sense, provides one of the strongest points of contact between Cervantes's narrative and the earlier examples from Boccaccio and Alfonso.

And yet, unlike those earlier tales, Anselmo's direct appeal to his "friend, Lotario" combined with his astonishing pledge to provide Lotario with all that he needs to seduce Camila infuses this new test of friendship with an element of moral conflict that is unprecedented in the tale of two friends tradition and, for that reason, sets Cervantes's narrative apart. Lotario is the first to recognize the ethical significance of what he has been asked to do: "los buenos amigos han de probar a sus amigos y valerse de ellos, como dijo un poeta, 'usque ad aras'; que quiso decir que no se habían de valer de su amistad en cosas que fuesen contra Dios [True friends will prove their friends and make use of them, as a poet has said, *usque ad aras*; whereby he meant that they will not make use of their friendship in things that are contrary to God's will]."³⁴ With these words, Lotario not only underscores the immorality of Anselmo's request, more importantly, he subsumes friendship itself to the requirements of morality, here construed in terms of one's obligation to God. This idea would appear to rehabilitate the Aristotelian requirement of virtue as a prerequisite for perfect friendship. As Cicero speaking through Laelius puts it in *De amicitia*, "disagreements of a very serious nature, and usually justifiable, arise from a demand upon friends to do something that is wrong [Magna etiam discidia et plerumque iusta nasci, cum aliquid ab amicis quod rectum non esset postularetur]"³⁵ Lotario's reaction to Anselmo's request echoes this Ciceronian perspective and, in the process, infuses a new sense of moral urgency into their relationship.

The introduction of moral considerations into the narrative of perfect friendship thus arguably constitutes a reanimation of a more authentic, albeit modified Aristotelianism that might overcome the story's rather flat definition of Anselmo and Lotario as the embodiment of friendship "por antonomasia." By privileging his moral commitments, Lotario recognizes the importance of virtuous conduct within friendship, and by extension, the notion of virtue itself. With this idea, we return to the familiar terrain of perfect friendship as defined by an interest in the good. In place of the earlier reliance on appeals to superficial similarities or a somewhat loosely defined notion of public opinion, Lotario's objections to the immorality of his friend's request involve an explicit recognition of friendship's dependence on qualities that are intrinsic to the individual. This idea, I would argue, helps to illuminate the underlying significance of Lotario's words when he speaks in terms of a change in the identity of both men: "... el daño está en que yo pienso que no eres el Anselmo que solías, y tú debes de haber pensado que tampoco yo soy el Lotario que debía ser; porque las cosas que me has dicho, ni son de aquel Anselmo mi amigo, ni las que me pides se han de pedir a aquel Lotario que tú conoces ... [... the misfortune is, it seems to me, that you are not the Anselmo you were, and must have thought that I am not the Lotario I should be; for the things that you have said to me are not those of that Anselmo who was my friend, nor are those that you demand of me what should be asked of the Lotario you know ...]."[36] From an Aristotelian point of view, Anselmo's request necessarily implies a fundamental alteration in the essential identities of both men.

This apparent shift toward a renewed Aristotelianism, however, is not without complications. Where the Aristotelian notions of virtue and the good operate within a universalist paradigm that facilitates the kind of mythic exemplarity on display in Cicero's account of the story of Orestes and Pylades, Lotario's rebuke of the immorality of his friend's request that he attempt to seduce his wife is quickly assimilated in the now familiar terms of the historically localized discourse of honor. As Lotario puts it later in his long speech to his friend, "Tú me tienes por amigo, y quieres quitarme la honra, cosa que es contra toda amistad; y aun no sólo pretendes esto, sino que procuras que yo te la quite a ti [You do reckon me your friend, and you would rob me of honour, a thing wholly inconsistent with friendship; and not only do you aim at this, but you would have me rob you of it also]."[37] Through this invocation of honor, Lotario recasts the moral dimension of his predicament in language that is inextricably linked with the concrete historical circumstances of early modern Spain—the same circumstances, it is worth noting, that constitute the immediate social context for the audience assembled at the inn—and, in the process, necessarily contaminates the idealized notion of perfect Aristotelian virtue through its contact with a concept that is compromised by its function as a distinctly imperfect determinant of social value.

The contaminating influence of honor on the paradigm of ideal friendship is further evident in the pathology of Anselmo's obsession with testing his wife's virtue, as Lotario's other reaction to his friend's plan reveals:

> Mira que no hay joya en el mundo que tanto valga como la mujer casta y honrada, y que todo el honor de las mujeres consiste en la opinión buena que

dellas se tiene; y pues la de tu esposa es tal, que llega al estremo de bondad que sabes, ¿para qué quieres poner esta verdad en duda?[38]

["Remember there is no jewel in the world so precious as a chaste and virtuous woman, and that the whole honor of women consists in reputation; and since your wife's is of that high excellence that you know, why should you seek to call that truth in question?"]

The personal suffering that would attend Camila's possible infidelity is here presented in the public currency of her honor despite that fact that the "verdad" to which Lotario refers at the end of this passage exists as much in the hidden recesses of the human heart as in the public recognition of private virtue. In returning the focus of his discourse to the public dimension of Anselmo's possible dishonor, Lotario reveals the true character of his earlier appeal to virtue. As Lotario makes abundantly clear in the passage above, Camila's honor only matters, indeed, only exists to the extent that it is recognized in the public domain. Aristotelian notions of inherent virtue are thus displaced by a baroque obsession with appearances that challenges the idea itself of authentic moral feeling.[39]

At this point, I would return to the matter of Anselmo's madness, referenced earlier in my discussion. In his response to Lotario's long speech on the risks of Anselmo's proposed course of action, Anselmo himself introduces the topic for a second time:

—Con la atención que has visto he escuchado, Lotario amigo, cuanto has querido decirme, y en tus razones, ejemplos y comparaciones he visto la mucha discreción que tienes y el estremo de la verdadera amistad que alcanzas; y ansimesmo veo y confieso que si no sigo tu parecer y me voy tras el mío, voy huyendo del bien y corriendo tras el mal. Presupuesto esto, has de considerer que yo padezco ahora la enfermedad que suelen tener algunas mujeres, que se les antoja comer tierra, yeso, carbón y otras cosas peores, aun asquerosas para mirarse, cuanto más para comerse . . .[40]

["I have listened, Lotario, my friend, attentively, as you have seen, to what you have chosen to say to me, and in your arguments, examples, and comparisons I have seen that high intelligence you do possess, and the perfection of true friendship you have reached; and likewise I see and confess that if I am not guided by your opinion, but follow my own, I am flying from the good and pursuing the evil. This being so, you must remember that I am now labouring under that infirmity which women sometimes suffer from, when the craving seizes them to eat clay, plaster, charcoal, and things even worse, disgusting to look at, much more to eat . . ."]

In this passage, Anselmo rehearses an emphatic affirmation of Lotario's wisdom and dedication to their friendship and even insists on the error of his failure to follow Lotario's advice. Above all, Anselmo's confession constitutes a self-conscious acknowledgment of the irrationality of his request, of the fact that if he were in his right mind, the course of action that he should follow would be that dictated by Lotario's incontrovertible logic.

Earlier in this discussion, I suggested that Anselmo's insistence on the inscrutable, external origin of his desire to test his wife's fidelity undermines his claim to subjective autonomy. Here, Anselmo's self-reported awareness of the irrationality of that desire contributes to the production of that same effect. Indeed, the fact that Anselmo possesses sufficient self-awareness to recognize the logical integrity of Lotario's reasoning only heightens the sense that he is out of his mind, a conclusion that finds support in Anselmo's own assertion that he suffers, as Harry Sieber has argued, from a kind of mental illness.[41] Irrespective of the accuracy of any particular medical diagnosis, the underlying symptomatology is clear enough: Anselmo provides abundant evidence throughout these early pages of a fundamental breakdown in his rational faculties so that they remain impervious to Lotario's "razones, ejemplos y comparaciones."

With this last observation, an idea emerges that marks a further point of evolution beyond what was seen earlier in Boccaccio. From its origins in Aristotle, perfect friendship implies a robust assertion of subjective autonomy. This is perhaps most clear in Cicero, who speaks of the many requirements of friendship in a way that largely assumes the friend's ability to act in concordance with his will. In Boccaccio, this idea remains largely unchallenged even as the principle of perfect friendship is put to the test, as evident, for example, in the amicable way in which the two friends settle their dispute over their shared attraction to Sofronia. At no point in that dispute does amorous passion overwhelm the two friends' capacity to act rationally. In contrast, Anselmo is portrayed from the very outset as afflicted by a kind of madness that renders him absolutely indifferent to reason. Understood from this perspective, his desire to test his wife's fidelity is symptomatic of a stark loss of self-control. His will is emphatically not his own.

Anselmo's loss of subjective autonomy introduces a new and far more devastating problem for the paradigm of perfect friendship. It is not just that Anselmo's desire leads him to make a request that violates the principles of perfect friendship—the moral defect that was earlier identified with his failure to embody the Aristotelian "good"—but more fundamentally that the ultimate responsibility for that request can no longer be adequately attributed to Anselmo as a coherent subject. Previously in this chapter, I argued that Cervantes discards the essentialist concept of perfect friendship as defined through the friend's intrinsic claim to virtue through an appeal to a discursive understanding rooted in public opinion. Here, that argument discovers a complement in Cervantes's not-so-subtle destabilization of the ontological foundation for the Aristotelian model. Or, to put this same idea another way, the perfect friend is rendered unknowable because all subjects are, in the end, unknowable by definition. Thus, while not all friends suffer from madness in the sense that we observe it in Anselmo, one nevertheless observes as the narrative of "El curioso impertinente" develops an underlying skepticism about the ability of human beings to truly know one another. Madness, as soon becomes clear, is only the most extreme manifestation of this more general problem, for as Cervantes demonstrates repeatedly in the rest of the story, much of human behavior resists rational scrutiny, rendering the other fundamentally unknowable.

In fact, what follows from Lotario's decision to accede to his friend's peculiar request only serves to highlight the profound limits of human agency in Cervantes's fictional universe as the more rational of the two friends quickly runs up against the limits of his own inscrutable nature. For a time Lotario feigns to test Camila, insisting to Anselmo that his wife is the perfect image of virtue. Built on deception, however, Lotario's plan to protect Anselmo's honor is inherently in conflict with the most basic principles of perfect friendship. Anselmo, as might be expected, eventually uncovers the sham seduction and confronts his friend with his deception, to which Lotario responds with an invocation of his honor and a renewed commitment to the original scheme: "... casi como tomando por punto de honra el haber sido hallado en mentira, juró a Anselmo que desde aquel momento tomaba tan a su cargo el contentalle y no mentille... [... taking it as a point of honor to have been detected in a lie, he swore to Anselmo that he would from that moment work to satisfy him and not lie to him ...]"[42] Lotario's emotional reaction to having been caught out in his deception accentuates the fundamental circumstantial conflict that he faces and its impact on his ability to act in a way that might do justice to the claims of perfect friendship. Having expounded at length on the dangers inherent in Anselmo's original request, he nonetheless now insists that he will carry out the plan with absolute dedication. The narrator in this passage sets a new tone for Lotario's future actions: No longer a matter of friendship, which is not even mentioned at this point in the narrative, Lotario's insulted honor becomes the driving force behind his new resolve.

Lotario's concern for his honor in this instance, while understandable in terms of his social position, necessarily creates a rift between social values and the underlying ethical dilemma that he faces as the would-be suitor of his best friend's wife. Yet the greater significance of his decision to continue in his attempts to seduce Camila is not realized in ethical or moral terms. Rather, his renewed efforts in service to Anselmo's plan to test his wife lead Lotario into conflict with an external force that ultimately supplants the story's ethical dimension: "... y tenía lugar de contemplar, parte por parte, todos los estremos de bondad y de hermosura que Camila tenía, bastantes a enamorar una estatua de mármol, no que un corazón de carne [... and he had time to contemplate, one by one, all Camila's perfections, of mind and body—and they were enough to inspire love in a marble statue, let alone in a heart of flesh]."[43] Love, that eternal enemy of free will in the early modern period, robs the flesh-bound Lotario of his good sense so that while he contemplates the only true remedy to illicit love—"mil veces quiso ausentarse de la ciudad, y irse donde jamás Anselmo le viese a él, ni él viese a Camila [a thousand times he thought of withdrawing from the city and going where Anselmo should never see him nor he see Camila]"—he finally loses out to this more powerful foe.[44]

Incited by his passion, Lotario begins to pursue Camila in earnest and, shortly thereafter, the inevitable occurs. Invoking now familiar language, Camila, too, surrenders to the all-powerful enemy: "Rindióse Camila; Camila se rindió; pero, ¿qué mucho, si la amistad de Lotario no quedó en pie? Ejemplo que nos muestra que sólo se vence la pasión amorosa con huilla, y que nadie se ha de poner a brazos con tan poderoso enemigo, porque es menester fuerzas divinas para vencer las suyas humanas [Camila yielded, Camila fell; but what wonder if the friendship of Lotario could not stand firm? A clear proof to us that the passion of love is to be conquered only by fleeing from it, and that no one should engage in a struggle with an enemy so mighty; for divine strength is needed to overcome the human power of love]."[45] Once again referencing the overwhelming force of love, the narrator's description of this pivotal event is explicitly linked back to the arguably more fundamental question of friendship as Cervantes insists on Lotario's betrayal of his friend as the enabling act that facilitates Camila's own inevitable capitulation to the blind god. The association is not, I would argue, coincidental, but rather underscores the extent to which Lotario's affair with Camila is only significant as a manifestation of failed friendship. As if to confirm this point, the narrator now refers to Anselmo and Lotario for the first time, respectively, as "el impertinente y el traidor amigo," epithets that mark what might be described as the official demise of their ideal friendship.

At the same time, the representation of love as the enemy of both free will and friendship in the moment of Camila's seduction echoes the earlier scene of Lotario's own *enamoramiento* and, once again, foregrounds the lover's compromised agency. As with Lotario, whose thoughts of flight from this "poderoso enemigo" come to naught, Camila also finds the power of love irresistible. In a subtle play of concepts, love even displaces friendship as the new locus of exemplarity, here revealed not as a positive model for ideal human behavior, but as a force that through its capacity to undermine our very sense of self paradoxically reveals the limits of the aspiration itself toward exemplary conduct: "que nadie se ha de poner a brazos con tan poderoso enemigo. . . ." In place of the Ciceronian model of inimitable perfection, one now encounters a mode of negative exemplarity that functions as a far more practical warning on the limits of human agency.

From this point onward, Cervantes's skeptical view of human agency—especially as it relates to affairs of the heart—emerges as the driving force in the narrative's downward spiral toward its tragic conclusion. Suspecting that Camila has deceived him just as she earlier deceived Anselmo, a jealous Lotario rashly discloses the truth of his affair to Anselmo, only to quickly regret his hasty confession. Lotario's complete lack of self-discipline in this instance, so at odds with the deliberate rationality of his persona at the beginning of the tale, both confirms his complete undoing by love while also setting the conditions for what is arguably the narrative's climactic scene. Out of despair Lotario tells all to Camila, who at this point takes matters into her own hands. She instructs Lotario to arrange for Anselmo to hide the next day in her bedchamber, "porque ella pensaba sacar de su escondimiento comodidad para que desde allí en adelante los dos se gozasen sin sobresalto alguno [for she hoped from his concealment to obtain the means of their enjoying themselves for the future without any apprehension]."[46]

In the wake of the lover Lotario's inability to act rationally, the heretofore passive Camila suddenly emerges as the narrative's motive force. Unlike the pure will that characterizes ideal friendship, however, this new source of agency in the story is already marked as problematic, in this case through a reference to a negative gendered stereotype: "pero como naturalmente tiene la mujer ingenio presto para el bien y para el mal más que el varón, puesto que le va faltando cuando de propósito se pone a hacer discursos, luego al instante halló Camila el modo de remediar tan al parecer inremediable negocio . . . [but as woman has by nature a nimbler wit than man for good and for evil, though it is apt to fail when she sets herself deliberately to reason, Camila on the spur of the moment thought of a way to remedy what was to all appearance irremediable . . .]"[47] The narrator's overt misogyny in this passage, by challenging Camila's ability to reason deliberately, effectively calls into question the integrity of her will to act. The sense that the narrative lacks a trustworthy protagonist at this point, which is accentuated by Camila's unwillingness to let Lotario in on her plan, points once again to the final inscrutability of human agency. In other words, the earlier problem of self-control for a friend who is, in principle, an *alter ego* gives way to the much more complicated issue of the agency—and motivations—of those for whom no such special claim may be made.

Where initially the public reception of Lotario and Anselmo as "los dos amigos" gives rise to a discursive understanding of identity rooted in storytelling, the scene that follows reconfigures the underlying ontological problem of identity in terms of an analogous theatrical metaphor. With her husband hidden away—serving in this way as the literal audience for what is about to transpire—Camila and her maid, Leonela, enter the bedchamber, at which point Camila launches into a long defense of her honor against what she represents as Lotario's perfidious advances.[48] Her speech effectively rewinds the narrative to the moment before Camila's seduction, providing a theatrical do-over of the text's major plot line. At this point, the discursive move that equates honor and reputation yields within the space of performance to acting, understood in both senses of the word. Indeed, Camila herself makes this connection explicit as she moves from statements of honorable resistance to bold action, in this case conceived as performance in its purest form. After threatening to kill herself and Lotario for his impudence—"quiero matar muriendo"—she unsheathes Anselmo's dagger and lunges at her lover:

> Y diciendo estas razones, con una increíble fuerza y ligereza arremetió a Lotario con la daga desenvainada, con tales muestras de querer enclavársela en el pecho, que casi él estuvo en duda si aquellas demostraciones eran falsas o verdaderas, porque le fue forzoso valerse de su industria y de su fuerza para estorbar que Camila no le diese. La cual tan vivamente fingía aquel estraño embuste y falsedad que por dalle color de verdad, la quiso matizar con su misma sangre . . .[49]

> [As she uttered these words, with incredible energy and swiftness she flew upon Lotario with the naked dagger, so manifestly bent on burying it in his breast that he was almost uncertain whether these demonstrations were real or feigned, for he was obliged to have recourse to all his skill and strength to prevent her from striking him; and with such reality did she act this strange farce and mystification that, to give it a color of truth, she determined to stain it with her own blood . . .]

In this scene, actions not only speak more loudly than words, they would seem to possess an authenticity that transcends the problem of appearances. Camila's behavior is thus not merely an accompaniment to her earlier verbal defense of her honor. While her actions certainly accomplish her ostensible goal of convincing the hidden Anselmo of her virtue, they do so in a way that is independent of that claim to virtue. Surprised by the force of Camila's attack, Lotario momentarily doubts whether her "demostraciones eran falsas o verdaderas." Central to the deeper meaning of this scene, that momentary doubt illuminates a fundamental separation between action and intention. For that one moment of uncertainty, Lotario is forced to confront Camila's attack as a real act of violence against his person that he must fight off with his "industria" and "fuerza." For Lotario at this key moment in the narrative, the problem of Camila's true intentions is displaced by the reality of her violence as an independent fact in the world commanding respect on its own terms. Providing new insight into the Cervantine lemma that "cada uno es hijo de sus obras," Camila's violent attack against her lover hints at a mode of agency in which actions are finally the self-referential source of identity.[50]

In the end, however, the fact that Camila's actions in this scene are merely a mode of performance robs them of any claim to authenticity, a conclusion that is underscored by the narrator's use of the term "embuste" to describe what has transpired. And while Camila does ultimately achieve her goal of appeasing Anselmo's apprehensions and in the process facilitates her continued affair with Lotario, she suffers in the process a kind of ontological dislocation that risks reducing her to little more than a plot device or—what is essentially the same thing—the embodiment of desire understood as a kind of discursive abstraction. Furthermore, read in this way, Anselmo's renewed faith in his wife in the wake of this performance is finally revealed as the purest expression of *engaño*, not merely as a consequence of this particular scene, but as a fundamental condition of their relationship from the very beginning. In effect, Camila's deceit of her husband at this point in the story exposes the deeper significance of Lotario's original warning: What one witnesses here confirms the ultimate incommensurability of human nature with the expectations of idealized categories. In this instance, an *engaño* that previously took the form of an untested potential—that of Camila's impeccable virtue—is now made manifest through her willful deception of her husband. Lurking within this analysis is an analogy between the discourse of female virtue and the poetics of friendship: The untested ideal friendship between Lotario and Anselmo, as extolled in the story's opening paragraph, is itself also finally exposed as fundamentally incompatible with the practical reality of human affairs. Like idealized female virtue, perfect friendship is always already an *engaño*, a fact that

Lotario's willing participation in Camila's theatrical machinations only serves to confirm.[51]

As I have already indicated, following Avalle-Arce, the story of "El curioso impertinente" signals the exhaustion of perfect friendship within the tale of two friends tradition. Camila's ultimate betrayal by her maid, Leonela, in the final pages of the narrative serves as the catalyst for the tale's ending, leading first to a brief reaffirmation of public perception as the arbiter of a discursive model for friendship followed by the summary destruction of all three characters. There is in this two-step movement a final reckoning with the problem of identity as pure appearance but also, as will become clear, a glimpse of something new that might arise out of what otherwise reads as a kind of despondent nihilism.

Recognizing that Anselmo will soon learn the truth about her affair with Lotario—Leonela has promised to disclose all in a bid to conceal her own dalliances—Camila collects her jewels and flees to her lover. Striking in this section of the story is the swiftness with which the narrator recounts these events, as if the final tragic ending were a foregone conclusion, the fate of the characters having been sealed much earlier in the story. Distraught by the absence of his wife, and suspecting the true cause, Anselmo sets off in search of Lotario, at which point the narrative pauses to describe an encounter between the cuckolded husband and a stranger on the road from Florence. The embodiment of public opinion, this stranger delivers back to Anselmo the news of his own domestic misfortune:

> ... se dice públicamente que Lotario, aquel grande amigo de Anselmo el rico, que vivía a San Juan, se llevó esta noche a Camila, mujer de Anselmo, el cual tampoco parece ... En efeto, no sé puntualmente cómo pasó el negocio; sólo sé que toda la ciudad está admirada deste suceso, porque no se podía esperar tal hecho de la mucha y familiar amistad de los dos, que dicen que era tanta, que los llamaban *los dos amigos*.[52]

> ["... it is reported abroad that Lotario, the great friend of the wealthy Anselmo, who lived at San Giovanni, carried off last night Camila, the wife of Anselmo, who also has disappeared ... I know not indeed, precisely, how the affair came to pass; all I know is that the whole city is wondering at the occurrence, for no one could have expected a thing of this kind, seeing the great and intimate friendship that existed between them, so great, they say, that they were called 'The Two Friends.'"]

This speech reminds the reader of what has been true all along, namely, that in Cervantes's fictional universe ideal friendship only exists within the public domain of the friends' reputation. Repeating almost verbatim the words of the narrator from the very first paragraph of the story, the anonymous traveler explicitly confirms this link: "que los llamaban *los dos amigos*." In effect, the impact of Anselmo's private domestic troubles on the paradigm of perfect friendship only fully registers when those troubles percolate through public opinion, where they are finally reduced to the triviality of gossip.

This final revelation underscores the deeper problem with ideal friendship in Cervantes: its *a priori* separation from an originary basis in the Aristotelian concept of inherent goodness. The initial inkling in *La Galatea* of ideal friendship's dependence on public opinion here recognizes its fullest implications as a complete negation of the term's significance within private life. Anselmo and Lotario had long before given up any pretense of their friendship as somehow ideal, so that the public confirmation of that fact seems almost irrelevant as a judgment on their relationship *qua* relationship. Such an assessment only has meaning within the public sphere, at which point it is no longer truly a matter of friendship as a living bond between two individuals, but rather a symptom of the ultimate incommensurability of the ideal with Cervantes's poetic practice in "El curioso impertinente." That sense of incommensurability, however, is not a consequence of anything that occurs within the narrative. Neither Anselmo's obsessive drive to "test" Camila nor Lotario's ultimate submission to the forces of amorous desire may be said to cause the corruption of ideal friendship. Instead, the ideal is already compromised from the story's outset, a consequence of both the inscrutability of human motivations and the limits of human agency.

Very shortly after the encounter with the anonymous traveler, all three characters are dead. Lotario is killed in battle in Naples, the news of which provokes Camila's eventual demise at "las rigurosas manos de tristezas y melancolías [the cruel hands of sorrow and melancholy]."[53] In a sense, the two lovers remain true to each other after their initial betrayal of Anselmo, but in the moral calculus of the novella, this would seem to provide small comfort given their ultimate fate.[54] From the perspective of my earlier remarks on the paradigm of ideal friendship, however, the death of Anselmo is perhaps the more significant event in the narrative's final pages. Where Lotario and Camila are quickly dispatched in one short paragraph, the death of Anselmo is described in considerable detail. Racked by the news of his friend and wife's betrayal, he seeks refuge with an unnamed associate and retires to a guest room:

> ... Pidió luego Anselmo que le acostasen, y que le diesen aderezo de escribir. Hízose así, y dejáronle acostado y solo, porque él así lo quiso, y aun que le cerrasen la puerta ... Viendo el señor de casa que era ya tarde y que Anselmo no llamaba, acordó de entrar a saber si pasaba adelante su indisposición, y

hallóle tendido boca abajo, la mitad del cuerpo en la cama y la otra mitad sobre el bufete, sobre el cual estaba con el papel escrito y abierto, y él tenía aún la pluma en la mano. Llegóse el huésped a él, habiéndole llamado primero; y, trabándole por la mano, viendo que no le respondía, y hallándole frío, vio que estaba muerto.[55]

[... Anselmo at once begged to be allowed to retire to rest, and to be given writing materials. His wish was complied with and he was left lying down and alone, for he desired this, and even that the door should be locked ... The master of the house observing that it was now late and that Anselmo did not call, determined to go in and ascertain if his indisposition was increasing, and found him lying on his face, his body partly in the bed, partly on the writing-table, on which he lay with the written paper open and the pen still in his hand. Having first called to him without receiving any answer, his host approached him, and taking him by the hand, found that it was cold, and saw that he was dead.]

This description of Anselmo freezes the moment of his death into a vivid display of representational verisimilitude. The requirements of the narrative's plot, which elsewhere are advanced with a velocity that seemingly ignores descriptive precision, here give way to a detailed portrait of Anselmo's dead body. The scene is thus a kind of discursive tableau—appealing to a voyeuristic fascination with death—whose impact may be attributed to a kind of realism *avant la lettre*.

The enhanced verisimilitude of this depiction of the dead Anselmo underscores the larger significance of "El curioso impertinente" within the literary-historical development of the tale of two friends. Having already destroyed the ideal of friendship both from inside that relationship—the necessary consequence of betrayal—and from the outside space of public opinion, this vivid depiction of the lifeless Anselmo gives dramatic form to the final destruction of the literary paradigm for ideal friendship in the wake of new narrative procedures that favor the imitation of life over intertextuality and the representation of philosophical ideals, however conceived. Cervantes's focus on Anselmo's dead body at this point in the narrative confronts the reader with a vision of the world that is almost nihilistic in its unwillingness to attach meaning to human events. Even Anselmo's efforts to explain his predicament are finally truncated; he is, in the end, cut off in his attempt to write down his confession, as if to insist on the irrelevance of such considerations in the face of the material fact of death itself. Indeed, the point at which his written confession trails off—"y pues yo fui el fabricador de mi deshonra, no hay para qué ... [and since I have been the author of my own dishonor, there is no reason why ...]"—is itself the unwitting expression of that nihilistic principle, so much so that its composition happens, as it were, by accident.[56] In effect, Anselmo unwittingly gives voice to the meaninglessness of his own demise.[57]

The nihilistic undercurrent in this scene, however, is not tragic, despite the rather tragic end encountered by each of the characters that populate this interpolated fictional universe.[59] The hard-boiled realism that would depict cold corpses anticipates new modes of literary expression that both embrace this nihilistic tendency, in one form or another, and also discover alternative realms for human transcendence, not in the divine sense of a Platonic or Christian order, but through an exaltation of human potential within the limits of disenchantment, here understood, in the critical Spanish term *desengaño*. For Cervantes in particular, idealism as a divinely inspired reality gives way to fantasy, to the blurring of boundaries, and finally, to a poetics that reanimates the dream of something more even as it recognizes the futility of its own aspirations.

Notes

1. Venier, Review of *Cervantes y la melancolía*, p. 147.
2. Referring to the criticism of "El curioso impertinente" voiced by Sansón Carrasco in II.3, Wardropper, "The Pertinence of *El curioso impertinente*," p. 589, writes, "One of the charges that Cervantes does not seek to answer effectively is that the first part sinned with its episodes and interpolated stories. *El curioso impertinente* bears the brunt of this type of criticism. Why? Obviously because, as Cervantes admits, it is attached to the plot somewhat more loosely than the other tales. But is it not singled out for blame because the title suggests it is an irrelevance? While it is logically the inquisitive man who is described as 'impertinent,' a secondary meaning—that the tale of this *Curioso* is 'irrelevant'—echoes from the words. I suspect that this ambiguity is deliberate, a part of the process of confusing the reader."
3. *Don Quixote*, II.3. Spanish is adapted from the Rodríguez Marín edition. Except where noted, English translations are adapted from the Ormsby edition which I have selectively modernized and modified for readability and accuracy, especially with respect to pronouns.
4. Wardropper, "The pertinence of *El curioso impertinente*," p. 588.
5. As might be expected, there is a long critical tradition that would attempt to remediate the difficulties created by the presence of "El curioso impertinente" in terms of the novel's overall formal coherence. Américo Castro, *El pensamiento de Cervantes*, pp. 126–8, notes that criticism over the interpolated story of "El curioso impertinente" may be traced back to Cervantes's contemporaries and offers an overview of earlier critics on both sides of the issue. Wardropper's essay, cited above, also occupies a central place within this critical trajectory, setting the course for much of the later writing on

the topic. For additional perspectives in more contemporary criticism see, for example, Hahn, "*El curioso impertinente* and Don Quijote's Symbolic Struggle against *Curiositas*," pp. 128–40; El Saffar, *Distance and Control in Don Quixote: A Study in Narrative Technique*, pp. 71–2; Wilson, "'Passing the Love of Women': The Intertextuality of *El curioso impertinente*," pp. 9–28; Flores, "'El curioso impertinente' y 'El capitán cautivo,' novelas ni sueltas ni pegadizas," pp. 79–98; and Gerli, "Truth, Lies, and Representation: The Crux of 'El curioso impertinente,'" pp. 107–22.
6. Avalle-Arce, "Una tradición literaria: El cuento de los dos amigos," p. 22.
7. *Don Quixote*, II.3.
8. Ibid. I.Prologue.
9. Ibid. II.3. According to Rico's edition of *Don Quijote*, p. 652, n. 45, "*mezclar berzas con capachos es una frase hecha que vale por 'mezclar cosas heterogéneas, que no tienen que ver unas con otras.'*" Cohen's translation, p. 489, captures the idiomatic sense of this expression: "'I'll bet the son of a dog *has made a fine mix-up of everything*'" (my emphasis).
10. Ibid. II.3.
11. Ibid. II.3.
12. My reading of Don Quixote's remarks on "el pintor de Úbeda" expands on an idea first expressed in *Writers on the Market*, p. 208.
13. Ibid. II.3.
14. Maravall, *La cultura del barroco*, pp. 305–414. Maravall devotes several chapters to this notion of a "baroque world view."
15. Ibid. p. 393: "Conocer es descifrar el juego de las apariencias, «salvar las apariencias», conforme a la pretensión del moderno espíritu científico. Apariencia y manera no son falsedad, sino algo que de algún modo pertenece a las cosas. Apariencia y manera son la cara de un mundo que para nosotros es, en cualquier caso, un mundo fenoménico, respecto al cual nuestra relación es conocerlo empíricamente y utilizarlo."
16. In the words of the *ventero*, I.32: "—Pues bien puede leella su reverencia, porque le hago saber que a algunos huéspedes que aquí la han leído les ha contentado mucho, y me la han pedido con muchas veras; mas yo no se la ha querido dar, pensando volvérsela a quien aquí dejó esta maleta olvidada con estos libros y esos papeles; que bien puede ser que vuelva su dueño por aquí algún tiempo, y aunque sé que me han de hacer falta los libros, a fe que se los he de volver; que, aunque ventero, todavía soy cristiano."
17. Frenk, «Lectores y oidores», pp. 101–23, offers a detailed account of the role of oral delivery of literary texts in the Spanish early modern period, noting in passing, p. 108, Cervantes's representation of the public reading of "El curioso impertinente" before the characters assembled at the inn.
18. Cervantes, *Don Quixote*, I.32.
19. Riley's authoritative *Cervantes's Theory of the Novel* defends the importance of entertainment in *Don Quixote* in no uncertain terms. Referring to the dual imperative, as the Canon puts it "jointly to instruct and to delight"

(I.47), Riley, p. 84, writes, "Entertainment, however, came first. No one can have failed to notice the readiness of Cervantine characters to tell and to listen to tales. They are an agreeable pastime for the audiences in the novels as well as the reader. They afford mental relaxation, distraction, 'escape'. The pleasure of those who have listened to a story is repeatedly mentioned. Entertainment, Cervantes plainly implies, is the first duty of prose fiction."

20. Cervantes, *Don Quixote*, I.32.
21. Ibid. I.32.
22. Ibid. I.32. Writing about this same passage, Riley, *Cervantes's Theory of the Novel*, p. 100, notes the following: "Violence, eroticism, and sentimentality—Cervantes has fastened on the perennial worst qualities of literature written for a mass public." Setting aside Riley's value judgment as to the worthiness of the *vulgo's* presumption to judge, I would emphasize how the passage captures the heterogeneity of this emerging popular audience. Recognizing that heterogeneity and addressing himself to it in his own writing is one of Cervantes's singular achievements in *Don Quixote*.
23. These four characters arguably give concrete form to the abstract *vulgo* that Cervantes cites as the source of the success of the *libros de caballerías*. As his fictional friend puts it in the prologue to Part I, the purpose of *Don Quixote* is to "deshacer la autoridad y cabida que en el mundo y en el vulgo tienen los libros de caballerías." Riley, *Cervantes's Theory of the Novel*, p. 109, insists on the necessarily pejorative sense of the term *vulgo* not just in Cervantes but for Spanish writers in this period in general: "To the Golden-Age writer the *vulgo* was rather what the *bourgeois* was to that of the nineteenth century: a class distinction went with a general imputation of philistinism." Certainly, this reading of the term is consistent with its usage in works as dissimilar as Lope de Vega's "Arte nuevo de hacer comedias en este tiempo" and Mateo Alemán's picaresque novel, *Guzmán de Alfarache*. Notwithstanding the general disparagement of the *vulgo*, however, I would insist—as I have argued at length in *Writers on the Market*—that such attitudes also belie a recognition of the growing influence of a popular audience in the world of letters, especially for genres like the *comedia* and the novel that were increasingly subject to the pressures of the economic marketplace.
24. Cervantes, *Don Quixote*, I.33.
25. Ibid. I.33. The Ormsby translation renders Lotario's name as the anglicized "Lothario." I retain Cervantes's original spelling in all translated passages from *Don Quixote*.
26. I.33: ". . . acabadas las bodas, y sosegada ya la frecuencia de las visitas y parabienes, comenzó Lotario a descuidarse con cuidado de las idas en casa de Anselmo, por parecerle a él (como es razón que parezca a todos los que fueren discretos) que no se han de visitar ni continuar las casas de los amigos casados de la misma manera que cuando eran solteros; porque aunque la buena y verdadera amistad no puede ni debe ser sospechosa en nada, con todo esto, es tan delicada la honra del casado, que parece que se puede ofender aun de los mesmos hermanos, cuanto más de los amigos."

27. This reading is consistent with González Echevarría's suggestion in *Love and the Law in Cervantes*, p. 77, that the story's tragic ending is associated with the fact that "the main action . . . takes place after marriage."
28. I.33: "Notó Anselmo la remisión de Lotario, y formó de él quejas grandes diciéndole que si él supiera que el casarse había de ser parte para no comunicalle como solía, que jamás lo hubiera hecho . . ." Significantly, this passage ends with a reminder of the public status of Lotario and Anselmo's friendship: ". . . y que si, por la buena correspondencia que los dos tenían mientras él fue soltero, habían alcanzado tan dulce nombre como el de ser llamados *los dos amigos*, que no permitiese, por querer hacer del circunspecto, sin otra ocasión alguna, que tan famoso y tan agradable nombre se perdiese . . ."
29. Hahn, "*El curioso impertinente* and Don Quijote's Symbolic Struggle against *Curiositas*," pp. 130–1, is one of the few critics to address the historically determined function of honor in the play directly: "Let us consider another possible explanation for Anselmo's death: his loss of honour. In Golden-Age literature these two phenomena are considered inseparable, as may be judged from Lotario's remark, '¿no vengo a quedar deshonrado, y, por el mesmo consiguiente, sin vida?' (I.33). This concept expresses a custom of the time, a social code, whose violation entailed inescapable condemnation."
30. This idea is echoed by Castro, *El pensamiento de Cervantes*, p. 129: "Pero la novelita hace ver que un elemento esencial para la virtud femenina es la atmósfera que la cerca, uno de cuyos esenciales componentes es la conducta del esposo." In supporting this notion, Castro cites Petrarch ("Muchas veces, por cierto, el marido es guía y ejemplo de la deshonestidad de su mujer"), Mal Lara ("Ciertamente que en la necedad de muchos está la maldad de sus mujeres, y en el poco mirar por su honra"), and El Pinciano ("muchas de esas impertinencias son causadas de la poca prudencia de los maridos")—that is, he contextualizes it within contemporary theories of social practice.
31. Cervantes, *Don Quixote*, I.33. In addition to modernizing pronouns, I have substituted "madness" for "folly" in the final sentence of Ormsby's translation, as it captures an aspect of the original "locura" that is key to my analysis.
32. Ife, "Cervantes, Herodotus and the Eternal Triangle," p. 673, notes the long tradition of associating "El curioso impertinente" with "the numerous traditional tales of wife testing, of which a possible direct precedent can be found in Cantos 42 and 43 of Ariosto's *Orlando furioso*," an idea that he traces back "as least as early as Diego Clemencín." As Wilson, "'Passing the Love of Women,'" p. 16, points out, "When Cervantes' Lotario alludes to the 'test of the cup,' he is advertising the *Orlando furioso* as one of the subtexts of *El curioso*: 'la prueba del vaso'—the test rashly undertaken by Ariosto's 'simple doctor' Anselmo but refused by 'el prudente Reinaldos.'" It is worth noting,

however, that both Wilson and Ife offer multiple genealogies for "El curioso impertinente." Both critics, Ife apparently following Wilson to some extent on this point, also point to important source material from Herodotus, with Ife in particular privileging the Herodotean genealogy over the more traditional connection with Ariosto. As Ife describes it, p. 675, the story of Gyges and Candaules (from Herodotus) anticipates "El curioso impertinente" in depicting "an eternal triangle in which one man obliges another into intimacy with his wife, and is supplanted."
33. Cervantes, *Don Quixote*, I.33.
34. Ibid. I.33.
35. Cicero, *De amicitia*, X.35.
36. Cervantes, *Don Quixote*, I.33.
37. Ibid. I.33.
38. Ibid. I.33.
39. Explaining an often muddled distinction in the Spanish early modern conceptualization of honor, Lauer, "*Honor/Honra* Revisited," p. 84, cites Aquinas in arguing that "the opinions of others matter with respect to both *honor* and *honra*: for the former, God's judgment suffices for salvific purposes; for the latter, only the king's estimation is legally binding; for either one, public opinion may weigh in; for neither one, would a personal opinion or a matter of conscience matter." Two points are worth making here. First, Lauer's formulation recalls the subordination of human affairs to divine will that was first observed in Langer's analysis of perfect friendship as filtered through scholasticism. More to the point here, Lauer's commentary underscores the absolute absence of the kind of essentialist virtue that is a central feature of Aristotelian perfect friendship as even what Lauer describes, p. 83, as "a person's excelling goodness" is ultimately subject to God's judgment and is, therefore, not sufficient unto itself. Second, in linking even virtue before God with public opinion, Lauer recognizes the social context as the final frame of reference for all claims to virtue, whether they be spiritual or civil. In the end, God's will is unknowable, so that human beings are finally left with the far more immediate, and arguably more potent force of public opinion as the practical grounds upon which they will be judged honorable or not.
40. Cervantes, *Don Quixote*, I.33.
41. Sieber, "On Juan Huarte de San Juan and Anselmo's *Locura* in 'El curioso impertinente,'" p. 4, has argued that the gendered illness to which Anselmo refers is suggestive of a condition called pica, in which the disease process disrupts the patient's "entendimiento." Sieber comes to his diagnosis in consultation with the work of the Renaissance physician Juan Huarte de San Juan, whom he cites directly: "'... allí vemos juicios y composturas extrañas; los falsos argumentos y flacos hacen más fuerza que los fuertes y muy verdaderos, al buen argumento le hallan respuesta, y el malo los hace rendir.'"
42. Cervantes, *Don Quixote*, I.33. English translation of this passage is my own.

43. Ibid. I.33. The translation here is from Cohen, p. 298, whose rendition of this passage better captures the original than Ormsby. Here, as elsewhere, I adopt the Spanish spelling of "Camila" in preference over Ormsby and Cohen's use of "Camilla."
44. Ibid. I.33.
45. Ibid. I.34. English translation modified slightly from Ormsby's version for clarity.
46. Ibid. I.34.
47. Ibid. I.34.
48. Ibid. I.34. "Primero quiero saber qué es lo que vieron en mí los atrevidos y deshonestos ojos de Lotario que fuese causa de darle atrevimiento a descubrirme un tan mal deseo como es el que me ha descubierto, en desprecio de su amigo y en deshonra mía."
49. Ibid. I.34. The word "falsedad" appears in Francisco Rico's edition of *Don Quijote*, p. 411, as "fealdad," which he glosses as "acción indigna, villanía."
50. Much has been written about Camila's agency in this scene, particularly as this question relates to her gender. Wilson, "'Passing the Love of Women,'" p. 27, for example, writes, "The curious pertinence of Camila strikes us most forcibly during her improvisation, under pressure, of the storeroom drama—variously labeled in the text as Anselmo's *tragedy* ('la tragedia de la muerte de su honra') or his *anatomy* ('notomía de las entrañas de su honra'). Unlike all of *El curioso's* intertexts—*and in an implied debate with them*—Cervantes makes Camila into a 'maker.' Using theater as a means of resistance, Camila confronts her husband's 'hysterics' with her own histrionics. In record time, she produces, directs, and stars in her own agonistic imitation of the Roman myth of Lucrece—'aquella Lucrecia quien dice que se mató sin haber cometido error alguno.'" While she concludes that Camila at the end of the story "remains an object of exchange between the two men," Jehenson, "*Masochisma* versus *Machismo*," pp. 43–4, nevertheless recognizes a similar power of subjective agency in this scene: "Camila's performance succeeds in altering the very rules that have previously governed her signification . . . Camila has deftly usurped the cultural formations that had perpetuated the two friends' discourse of male domination and simply reinscribed them within her narrative of resistance. Her performance, and its reception, demonstrate how directly power and knowledge imply one another (Foucault, 27–8), and how easily gender assignations can be redeployed." Pérez, "Into the Dark Triangle of Desire," p. 102, however, adds an important corrective to these earlier assessments: "As witnesses to this scene, we also remain in radical uncertainty as to whether Camila really intends the dagger for the breast of Lotario . . . The absolute opacity of Camila's performance suggests that *all along* she has been more than they (or we) can know. And yet the content of the self that seems to exist beyond this triangle of desire cannot be expressed within it." Pérez's key insight is epistemological and reflects the fact that Camila's interior life is unknowable to either of the two friends

or, by extension, the reader. Thus, we are left with the ambiguous signs generated by her actions, of which the most we can say is that they point to a subjective presence that escapes rational analysis. Gerli, "Truth, Lies, and Representation," p. 115, arrives at a similar conclusion working from a somewhat different perspective. Focusing on Anselmo's obsession with knowing the "truth," he writes, "Anselmo's unfulfilled craving to know never ceases to afflict him . . . His incorrigible behavior is compelled by his own self-centered desire for absolute insight into the innermost recesses of Camila's mind. Her very otherness, however, the fact that she is not him, will doom to failure his epistemological inquisition and his quest for power through knowledge."

51. Wardropper, "The Pertinence of *El curioso impertinente*," p. 599, makes what is essentially the same point using different terms: "The initial truth from which the lie emerges in this spectacle is that Lotario is a good friend of Anselmo—'mi amigo verdadero' and that Camila is as good and faithful a wife as Anselmo thinks she is. Unnecessarily he submits these two truths—matters of honor, and therefore life and death—to a test, not realizing that certain truths, if tested, cease to be truths. This is the point at which belief enters the scale of assent." What Wardropper names as truth in this passage is the functional equivalent of an *engaño*, that is, a belief that functions in the world as truth. Gerli, "Truth, Lies, and Representation," p. 110, proffers another version of this idea: "In the world of 'El curioso impertinente,' truth is, as I shall argue, ultimately a question of faith and performance rather than of essential fact."

52. Cervantes, *Don Quixote*, I.35.

53. Ibid. I.35. The English follows Cohen, p. 324, whose translation here is closer to the original than Ormsby's.

54. Castro, *El pensamiento de Cervantes*, p. 353, notes that Camila does not die "por el pecado de su adulterio, sino por la pena que le produce la muerte de su amante . . ." Barbagallo, "Los dos amigos, *El curioso impertinente* y la literatura italiana," p. 218, echoes at least in part this exculpatory view by way of a comparison between Lotario and Camila with Dante's two lovers, Paolo and Francesca: "El caso de Lotario y Camila es semejante al de Paolo y Francesca del «Inferno» de Dante, no sólo por la ingenuidad y espontaneidad del enamoramiento, sino porque en ambas circunstancias el caso merece, si no perdón y disculpa, al menos simpatía y comprensión. Cuando Dante el peregrino se encuentra con Paolo y Francesca en el infierno, no puede por menos que sentir piedad y simpatía por ellos, así como Anselmo no puede por menos que disculpar y perdonar a Camila. En ambos casos, sin embargo, el Dante moralizador y poeta, y nuestro Cervantes, se muestran firmes e intransigentes, condenando las dos parejas de amantes a su triste fin. Si ellos no tuvieron la culpa de enamorarse, sin embargo tuvieron la culpa de no haber sabido huir de su pasión."

55. Cervantes, *Don Quixote*, I.35.

56. Ibid. I.35.

57. Hahn, "*El curioso impertinente* and Don Quijote's Symbolic Struggle against *Curiositas*," pp. 135–6, has argued that Anselmo's death is ultimately attributable to his curiosity. Citing both St Bernard and Ariosto, he describes "the problem of *curiositas*" as a "substituting of knowledge for faith." Writing more specifically about Anselmo, he continues: ". . . Anselmo's death is analogous to that of Adam, a punishment for his presumption; it is, therefore, a direct consequence of his curiosity. The circumstances of the death matter less than the fact that it was inevitable the moment the act of curiosity was carried out." Later, Hahn, p. 138, makes the moral subtext of this conclusion explicit: ". . . through his 'impertinent curiosity,'" Hahn writes, Anselmo "is committing the sin of Pride . . ." While I agree with much of Hahn's analysis, particularly as it relates to what might be described as Anselmo's epistemological failing, I believe he misconstrues the significance of the deathbed scene. Contrary to Hahn's view, I would argue that the "circumstances" of Anselmo's death matter a great deal, as they reflect a fundamental questioning of the narrative's claim to moral exemplarity as a matter of its formal structure.
58. Flores, "Formación del personaje femenino en *El curioso impertinente*," p. 346, offers one of the more robust defenses of the narrative's status as tragedy: "Me es imposible imaginar final más trágico que el que el narrador relata en *El curioso impertinente*. La muerte, una vez implementada, es el único castigo al que no se puede apelar; la vida, una vez perdida, el único bien que no se puede ni restituir ni recobrar." Jehenson, "*Masochisma* versus *Machismo*," p. 46, disputes such a reading: "The end of *El curioso*, then, is made to constitute the very 'stuff' of romance. It elides the elements necessary to make it either a tragedy or a morality tale. The reason is twofold. The 'traidor' Lotario (the narrator's label) dies as a hero and Camila, despite her brilliant tactics, remains an object of exchange between the two men. Unlike the women in Herodotus's *History* and in Ariosto's *Orlando Furioso*, Camila never learns (as they do) of her husband's and of her lover's scheming. She is unaware of the seduction scenes contrived in order to test her, and never learns of her lover's complicit part in them. Even more seriously, the text admits Lotario's betrayal of Anselmo and consequent remorse, but erases the gravity of Lotario's much more serious betrayal of Camila." In contrast, my own reading discovers in the dispassionate and highly objectified account of Anselmo's death a break with the conventions of both tragedy and romance, and more generally, with the notion that literary discourse attends upon the moral order of the universe.

Chapter 4

Staging Intimacy in Guillén de Castro

In an early scene from the first act of Guillén de Castro's dramatic reinterpretation of Cervantes's "El curioso impertinente," one of the secondary characters offers a brief meditation on the Spanish *comedia*.[1] Defending the genre's break with the classical precepts of Terence and Plautus, the Duke insists on the imperative of pleasing a broad, heterogeneous audience: "Y es su fin el procurer / que las oyga un pueblo entero, / dando al sabio y al grosero / que reír y que gustar . . . [and the goal of the *comedias* is that all people hear them, giving both the wise and the uneducated something that pleases and inspires laughter]."[2] As with Lope's famous treatise on the *comedia*, *El arte nuevo de hacer comedias en este tiempo*, Castro's protagonist voices here what Orozco Díaz describes as "la ley del nuevo arte dramático barroco [law of the new baroque dramatic art]" in which "lo *justo*" is that which responds to the "gusto" of this new expanded audience.[3] As I have argued elsewhere in the context of Lope's treatise, the Duke's words hint at a market-based understanding of the theater as an emerging mode of popular culture in which, not unlike the novel, the need to satisfy a diverse audience drives an aesthetics that lends increasing weight to entertainment as a legitimate end of literary production.[4]

I will have more to say about the genre of the novel later in this study. As for Guillén de Castro's theatrical reinterpretation of "El curioso impertinente," this recognition of the audience's role in the determination of aesthetic value is, I would argue, registered in a hybrid poetics that embraces the inherent hyperbolic potential of exemplary perfect friendship at the same time that it demonstrates a nascent interest at key moments in the power of representational verisimilitude to draw the audience into the intimate space of the characters' private lives. In other words, Castro's play appeals to its audience on two distinct levels, both through the spectacle of idealized representations of human behavior that bear little resemblance to everyday life and through a countervailing exploration of the idiosyncratic particularity of emotional life as experienced by imperfect individuals, an aspect of Castro's play that is most clearly on display in his representation of Camila.

The Duke's opening commentary on the *comedia* offers a hint of this hybrid poetics in his metacritical meditation on precisely how these early modern dramatic performances impact the audience:

> Representa un Español / un galán enamorado, / y parece en el tablado / como en el Oriente el Sol. / Haze un rey con tal afeto / que me parece al de España, / de suerte que a mí me engaña / y obliga a tener respeto.[5]

> [A Spaniard depicts a gallant lover and he appears on stage like the sun in the east. He represents a king with such effect that he seems to me to be the King of Spain and in such a way that I am deceived and must pay him proper respect.]

The Duke's laudatory remarks here effectively fuse what are, in fact, two very different modes of theatrical representation. Indeed, while both the "galán enamorado" who resembles the rising sun and the actor who plays his role "con tal afeto" that the audience mistakes him for the king may be said to leverage the power of theatrical representation as spectacle—the king in particular is as much a visual and rhetorical symbol of political power as its living embodiment—the means by which these two examples achieve their effect on the audience are, in fact, quite distinct. Where the theatrical depiction of a "galán enamorado" as the rising sun—especially to the extent that the visual image is accompanied by the playwright's deft use of metaphorical language—is necessarily hyperbolic and, in this sense, disconnected from the experience of everyday life, the actor's ability to deceive the audience into confusing the theatrical representation of the king with the living figure of royal authority depends, at least in part, on a poetics of representational verisimilitude.

Moving beyond the Duke's still somewhat ambiguous commentary, however, the distinction between theatrical hyperbole and representational verisimilitude becomes arguably even more relevant to the depiction of the interpersonal relationships that form Castro's primary focus. As already indicated, Castro draws a sharp contrast between the hyperbolic spectacle of exemplary perfect friendship and the depiction of other modes of human interaction that are drawn in such a way that they evoke the world beyond the stage. Key to this defining contrast in Castro's poetics is the figure of Camila, the contested lover whose honor serves as the fulcrum upon which both Cervantes's earlier narrative and

Castro's reinterpretation largely depend. However, unlike Cervantes, for whom Camila's subjectivity is largely subordinated to the plotting of Anselmo's obsessive quest to test her virtue, Castro's depiction of Camila exploits the theater's dependence on dialogue to amplify the complexity of her emotional predicament and, in the process, enhances her claim to agency. As the plot unfolds, Camila's relationship with Lotario in particular comes to exhibit symptoms of a mode of private intimacy that operates increasingly as a foil to the play's engagement with the long tradition of exemplary perfect friendship.[6] The result is a profound structural tension within the play's representation of both friends and lovers that reflects Castro's commitment to the longer tradition of writing perfect friendship as well as his interest in exploring the capacity of theatrical representation to capture some of the more subtle complexities of human relationships.

Some sense of this poetic hybridity is already apparent in the early scene in which Lotario describes his relationship with Anselmo. While Castro's initial depiction of the relationship between the play's two friends exhibits much of the exaggerated idealism that characterizes the tale of two friends tradition more generally, it also includes a level of detail that endows the story of their formative years with a greater sense of idiosyncratic particularity. Thus, where Cervantes's introduction of Anselmo and Lotario is limited to one short paragraph culminating in their apotheosis as the two friends "por antonomasia," Castro's much longer account of the protagonists' early years together combines elements of categorical idealization with an interest in creating a more textured backstory to account for their relationship. In a long speech to Torcato—a minor character whose role is largely extraneous to the play's main plot—Lotario first describes how he was taken in by Anselmo's father after the death of his own parents, establishing in this way a concrete account of the personal circumstances that prepare the way for his relationship with Anselmo.[7] Yet beyond providing an unprecedented level of detail in his account of the origins of his relationship with Anselmo, much of the rest of Lotario's speech is laden with inflated rhetoric that evokes many of the idealizing tropes of perfect friendship, especially the notion of the friend as an *alter ego*:

> Y fuymos Anselmo, y yo, / con una ygualdad estraña / nacidos en una cuna, / criados en una cama, / sola una ama nos dio leche, / que no quisimos tomalla / él ni yo, ¡prodigio grande! / de los pechos de otras amas. / Fuymos los dos a una escuela, / tuvimos los dos una alma, / aprendimos unas letras, / seguimos una esperança.[8]

[And Anselmo and I, born in the same crib, with a strange resemblance, were raised in the same bed; a single wet nurse gave us both her milk, and neither he nor I would take it from any other—What a marvel! We attended the same school, we had a single soul, we learned our letters, and followed the same hope.]

Here, specific details concerning their early life together—the fact, for example, that both boys were attached to the same wet nurse—are wedded to more abstract claims to their shared identity, an idea that is captured perhaps most succinctly in Lotario's assertion that he and Anselmo possessed a "single soul."

Beyond the complexity of Lotario's mixed appeal to idealized notions of exemplary perfect friendship and the more idiosyncratic features of his relationship with Anselmo, his speech also exhibits a subtle historizing impulse within his characterization of the Aristotelian ideal that—in a sense already observed in Cervantes's original—serves to further reorient the play's theoretical commitments within the specific social circumstances of early modern Spain:

> Entre él y mí no hay secreto, / y ninguno de importancia / se ha visto de nuestras bocas / en las lenguas de la fama. / No hay engaño entre nosotros, / porque entre nosotros anda / de ver la verdad desnuda, / la mentira avergonçada. / Nunca nos dimos disgusto, / por obra, ni por palabras, / ni aun por señas; y encontrados / en los gustos vezes varias, / jamás por mujer reñimos, / prueba de ser estremada / amistad, que una mujer / a deshacella no basta.[9]

[Between him and me there are no secrets, and none of importance have been heard from our mouths on the tongues of others. There is no deception between us because we strive to see the truth naked and the lie mortified. We never give displeasure in word or in deed, or even by signs; and frequently well met in our tastes, yet never have we fought over a woman, a proof indeed of our extraordinary friendship, that a woman is not sufficient to undo it.]

Lotario's depiction of his friendship with Anselmo here employs a language riddled with idealizing absolutes: Between these two friends there are no secrets of importance, nor deception, but only the "naked truth"; nor do they ever displease one another in deed or word, or even in signs; and, of special significance for my analysis here, they never dispute "por mujer," which Lotario editorializes as a "proof of our extraordinary friendship." There is in this passage, moreover, a curious progression as more abstract declarations of perfect harmony in friendship yield to an allusion to the primary source of conflict within the tale of two friends tradition, namely, the introduction of a contested lover. Not only does this final allusion presage events to come in Castro's play, it reveals the playwright's self-conscious positioning of his work within the established tradition of writing perfect friendship.

Despite such hyperbolic appeals to idealized categorical standards, however, a closer examination of the specific details of Lotario's account of perfect friendship reveals curious deviations from Aristotelian orthodoxy. Where the Aristotelian model of perfect friendship ultimately hinges on an essentialist belief in the good as the highest expression of virtue, Lotario's language here identifies the most exalted mode of friendship with notions of absolute honesty and transparency between friends, that is, with morally desirable attributes that nevertheless diverge somewhat from the classical model. Thus, it is not so much the Aristotelian idea of virtue that defines their perfect union, but a more particular emphasis on their embrace of "la verdad desnuda" and their rejection of "el engaño" and "la mentira."

In the last chapter, I discussed how Cervantes domesticates the idea of perfect friendship by absorbing it within the historically localized discourse of honor. Of special significance in my analysis was the role of public opinion in ascribing meaning within this complex code of conduct. As Cervantes repeatedly observes not just in "El curioso impertinente," but throughout *Don Quixote*, the possession of this central determinant of social value in the Spanish early modern period is dependent on one's public reputation as determined by the larger community. Cervantes's incorporation of perfect friendship within the discourse of the honor code thus creates an inevitable conflict, as the pretensions of Aristotelian virtue are degraded to a mere show of appearances. The result is an implosion within the very structural paradigm of perfect friendship, symbolically captured in the moral corruption and ultimate death of all three characters.

Lotario's insistence on transparency over virtue in the passage above may similarly be read in historical terms as containing a possible response to the difficulties posed by the Cervantine focus on honor. In contrast to Cervantes's insistence on honor as the external manifestation of one's public reputation and the defining attribute of perfect friendship, Lotario here posits the possibility of a shared private communion between two friends whose "secretos" are shielded from the corrupting effects of "las lenguas de la fama." Where Cervantes insists on the public nature of all social relations, even the intimate bond of friendship, Castro's Lotario appeals to an embryonic notion of private life and in this way creates a space for a notion of friendship that might somehow escape this Cervantine dynamic. According to this reading, what matters most for friendship is not the public display of virtue, but rather an explicitly drawn boundary between the personal fellowship of the two friends and the larger community.

Yet such allusions to the private nature of Lotario's relationship with Anselmo, even as they tend to historicize the play's treatment of the Aristotelian ideal of perfect friendship, inevitably run up against the powerful structural constraints of its formal setting within the tale of two friends tradition. As one of the two friends in Castro's reimagining of the tradition of writing perfect friendship, Lotario occupies a highly scripted role within a literary paradigm—and its associated poetics—that, as will become clear, ultimately impedes his ability to embody the more radical potential that remains largely latent in the passage above. In fact, Lotario's speech taken in its entirety arguably belies the idea of private intimacy between friends. Filled with hyperbolic rhetoric that seemingly begs for public acknowledgment, his monologue concludes with a statement of the public nature of their friendship that echoes the theatrical setting of the play itself. As he puts it in his concluding remarks, "En fin es nuestra amistad / tan grande, que en toda Italia / los conformes, los amigos / por excelencia nos llaman [In the end our friendship is so great that all of Italy is united in calling us the two friends *par excellence*.]"[10] Despite giving at least a nod to an arguably modern sense of private intimacy, Lotario finally retreats to the now familiar dependence of perfect friendship on its reception by a sympathetic public.

At the same time, this self-conscious embrace of the public's role as arbiter of value for Aristotelian perfect friendship takes on new meaning in the explicitly performative context of the theater. In particular, the dramatic staging of Lotario's pronouncements above recalls Cicero's exploration of the audience's reaction to Pacuvius's theatrical rendition of the mythic story of Orestes and Pylades: The hyperbolic insistence on a universal affirmation of Lotario and Anselmo as "los amigos por excelencia" serves to reconnect the exemplary function of perfect friendship with the concrete circumstances of reception, in this case, with the implied presence of a live audience whose own experience operates—especially in the context of the Spanish *comedia*—as a key point of reference for interpretation. In this way, Castro's theatrical interpretation of *El curioso impertinente* may be said to reanimate a dramatic potential that had been lurking within the tale of two friends tradition, the theatrical adaptation of Cervantes's interpolated tale marking a return of exemplary perfect friendship to its natural home.

The precise nature of that return, however, must be measured against the new imperatives of the early modern *comedia* as a genre that responds, as Lope puts it, to the "gusto" of the "vulgo." Where Cicero imagines an audience capable of recognizing the gulf between its own limited capacity for moral virtue and the mythic exemplarity of Pacuvius's mythic protagonists, Lope's *vulgo* as he describes it in the *Arte nuevo* is motivated largely by a desire for entertainment, often understood as an end in itself. Considered under this aspect and read in anticipation of the betrayals that will follow, Lotario's claim to public recognition as the embodiment of friendship "por excelencia" must be understood more as a manifestation of theatrical spectacle than as a reflection of authentic moral virtue. Thus, while the theatrical impulse inherent within exemplary perfect friendship described by Cicero may be said to re-emerge here at the end of Lotario's speech, the expression of that impulse is necessarily subject to the local historical forces at work in the growing popularity of the Spanish early modern *comedia*.

In comparison to the robust engagement with the public face of perfect friendship, Lotario's allusion to his private communion with his friend Anselmo remains both here and throughout the text underdeveloped. An almost latent impulse in Lotario's speech above, the notion that two individuals might share a secret confidence that would resist and even counter the pressures of what Lotario describes as "las lenguas de la fama," is instead redirected toward other relationships that display a quiet intimacy that more closely approximates the experience of private life in the world beyond the stage. The central expression of this alternative representational mode emerges with the transformation of Camila into an independent, speaking subject in Castro's adaptation of "El curioso impertinente." In Camila, representational verisimilitude finds expression through a voice that had been formerly suppressed, in this case, that of the wife whose agency is eclipsed by her traditional symbolic role as an object of exchange between perfect friends. A powerful foil to Lotario and Anselmo's rhetorical excess in the service of the Aristotelian ideal, Castro's Camila embodies a new set of poetic values that attempt, however incompletely, to hold up a mirror to nature.

Camila's special role as the primary vehicle for representational verisimilitude in Castro's play is closely tied to her gender, especially as it relates to the role of women in the tale of two friends tradition more generally. Unlike Anselmo and Lotario, who are essentially trapped by the rhetorical commitments inherent in their identity as the "two friends," Camila's subjectivity remains largely unexplored by the narrative tradition in which she figures so prominently. Even Cervantes, who at one point posits the possibility of Camila's autonomous agency, nevertheless denies the reader access to her interior life. In contrast, Castro leverages her release into the theatrical milieu in order to rewrite Camila as the voice of a verisimilitudinous expression of the self in direct contrast to the stultifying formalism of the perfect friend.

In practice, the expression of Camila's agency, as just indicated, is heavily influenced by her status as a woman. Unlike the two friends for whom self-expression is supported by a culture committed to male action, Camila's identity as a woman necessarily limits the scope of her newfound subjective presence in Castro's play. Yet it is precisely such constraints on her ability to act that help to explain her central role as the vehicle for a poetics of representational verisimilitude. Camila is forced by virtue of her social position to adopt a far more practical posture toward her circumstances, a contingency that influences nearly every aspect of her representation on stage and that imbues her character with a heightened sense of self-consciousness; she is, to borrow a term from Jonathan Thacker, acutely aware of the constraints implicit in her social "role-play."[11] Thus, unlike her male counterparts, who are given free range to indulge in hyperbolic expressions of both love and friendship, Camila is bound by an awareness of the oppressive demands of her social position. In giving voice to what it means to *not* be free to indulge in self-serving rhetorical excess, Camila comes to embody the implicit irony of the hyperbolic idealism of perfect friendship when juxtaposed against the far more limiting conditions of everyday life that constitute the practical reality of life for women in the Spanish early modern period.

In large part, Camila's role in the expression of a poetics of representational verisimilitude depends on Castro's innovative plotting, notably the backstory that he creates around Camila and Lotario. Where in Cervantes's narrative both Lotario and Anselmo meet Camila for the first time within the temporal framework of the tale's narrative present, Castro presents Lotario and Camila as secret lovers whose relationship precedes the play's opening.[12] This new element in the plot has three important implications. First, in depicting Camila and Lotario as clandestine lovers, indeed as betrothed in secret, Castro facilitates a re-enactment of the traditional gesture of self-sacrifice in the name of friendship when Anselmo, who is as of yet unaware of this pre-existing passion, asks for Lotario's help in wooing Camila for himself. The plotting here rehearses the orthodox tale of two friends paradigm as one friend sacrifices his lover for the sake of friendship—an element of the traditional narrative, it is worth noting, that is excised from Cervantes's interpolated story. Read from this perspective at least, Castro arguably demonstrates a clear interest in aligning his theatrical interpretation of "El curioso impertinente" even more closely with the longer narrative tradition of writing perfect friendship.

Yet despite this return to the origins of the tale of two friends tradition, the introduction of a pre-existing relationship between Camila and Lotario also has a new and critical function: Beyond its structural role, the relationship between Camila and Lotario serves to add unprecedented complexity to the circumstances of both her reluctant marriage to Anselmo and her subsequent affair with her former suitor. In fact, Castro endows the inner lives of both Camila and Lotario with a complexity that ultimately serves to disrupt the formal logic of self-sacrifice in the name of friendship that defines the play's commitment to the tale of two friends tradition. For Camila in particular, the transformation from object of exchange into a more fully formed subject challenges the ethical assumptions underlying the tradition of narrativizing perfect Aristotelian friendship. By encouraging the audience to contemplate Camila's treatment by the male protagonists in an entirely new way, Castro's play necessarily calls into question the moral claims of Aristotelian perfect friendship for a poetics that would take seriously the demands of representational verisimilitude.

Finally, the backstory of Camila's love affair with Lotario highlights the distinction between private and public life as a constitutive element of Camila's emergent subjectivity. When she first learns from the Duchess of her father's intention to marry her off, Camila responds with an allusion to the social constraints imposed by her gender: "Siendo mujer, / hija suya, y tu criada, / qué tengo que responder? / O qué voluntad tendré sin la vuestra? [As a woman, your daughter and servant, how else can I respond? Or, what will can I have without yours?]"[13] In its brevity, this passage captures with precision the full range of constraints on Camila's gendered identity; her will is not her own, but is rather subordinated, even subsumed into that of her social superiors—an assessment of her predicament, it is worth noting, to which the Duchess assents as if nothing could be truer in the world.

At the same time, concealed within this statement of submission to her social position lies the secret that sharpens the distinction between Camila's public and private lives: The Duchess expresses surprise when Camila fails to exhibit any interest in knowing the name of her intended, at which point we learn through an aside of the deeper logic informing Camila's behavior throughout this scene: "Ya sé que Lotario es, / a quien con el alma adoro [I already know that it is Lotario, whom I love with all my soul]."[14] As it turns out, Camila has come to believe that her father's plans accord with her own desires, a coincidence in the play's plotting that facilitates her exemplification of "virtue" that, as the Duchess puts it, "vence en quilates el oro [exceeds the perfection of gold]."[15] She can, in fact, play the public role of the perfect daughter and exemplary female royal subject with ease because her will is, as the dramatic irony of the scene finally reveals, identical to that of her social superiors.[16] In exposing the artifice of Camila's submission to the requirements of her public identity, this scene exposes her social role-playing while also encouraging the audience to experience her emotional attachment to Lotario as an authentic expression of sincerely held feelings.

Such signs of Camila's heightened agency as just described stand in stark contrast to Castro's depiction of perfect friendship in the scenes leading up to her arranged marriage with Anselmo. In these scenes, Castro falls back on all the essential elements of the orthodox story of self-sacrifice in the name of perfect friendship. Thus, before Lotario even has a chance to disclose the news of his proposed betrothal—secret information that, as we have already observed, is central to his private life—Anselmo catches a glimpse of Camila and is struck by Cupid's arrow. In a scene that pushes the dramatic action squarely back into the domain of rhetorical excess and hyperbolic exemplarity, Lotario immediately cedes to his friend's sudden lovesickness with a promise to help Anselmo achieve his heart's desire:

>   Lotario: Si tú gustas, de mi mano / quiero casarte con ella. / ¿No fiarás sin temor / que te la dé mi amistad, / que yguale a tu calidad, / y que diga con tu honor?
>   Anselmo: ¿En qué dudas? Bueno fuera / que esso de ti no fiara; / pues quando no me agradara / por tu gusto la quisiera.[17]
>
>   [Lotario: If you like, I will marry you to her by my own hand. Do you not have faith, without fear, that my friendship will give her to you, being equal to you and your honor?
>   Anselmo: What do you doubt? A proper thing indeed would it be if I did not have faith in you, for even if she did not appeal to me, I would love her just to please you.]

Lotario's rhetorical excesses here ironize what should be his defining moment of self-sacrifice while the absurd hyperbole of Anselmo's response throws the entire scene very nearly into the register of farce.

Or consider, for example, the monologue, in the form of a sonnet, that Lotario recites immediately after promising to help Anselmo arrange his marriage to Camila:

> ¡Ay, amistad, y amor! visible estrago,
> fogoso brío, movimiento lerdo,
> que me encoge dudando en lo que acuerdo
> y me anima pensando en lo que pago.
> ¿En no perder a Anselmo qué bien hago?
> ¿Y en perder a Camila qué bien pierdo?
> ¡Estraña competencia! loco y cuerdo,
> mil quimeras fabrico, y mil deshago.
> Pero perdona amor si me enemisto
> contigo, porque vença aunque me pese
> la amistad que en mi pecho se acrisola.
> Qué bien podrá sin mengua (quien se ha visto
> tantas vezes rendido al interese)
> rendirse a la amistad una vez sola.[18]

[Oh, friendship and love! Manifest destruction, burning spirit, dull torpor, that shrinks me in doubt about that which I should praise and incites me thinking about that which I will forfeit. In not losing Anselmo, what good do I do? And in losing Camila, what good do I give up? Strange competition! Both mad and sensible, I make and unmake a thousand imaginings. But love forgive me if I make you my enemy because, even though it pains me, the friendship that is purified in my breast is victorious. What an unmitigated good for he who has seen friendship so often yield to self-interest to at least once yield his own self-interest to friendship!]

The juxtaposition of two ideals here, love and friendship, exhibits all the hyperbolic fervor that the poet can muster. The "competencia" symbolically embodied in Camila and Anselmo, taken in isolation, provides the basis for an exaggerated lyricism in this monologue that freezes the action of the play into a moment of melodramatic angst.[19] In this sense, this sonnet-monologue embodies the moment of perfect theatrical hyperbole, that is, of theater that is most at home in its own performativity. And yet, beyond all the rhetorical fireworks, the dubious representational content of this highly irregular dramatic situation raises important questions: What do we expect from theatrical representation? Is lyricism married to hyperbole sufficient to carry the weight of the play's commitment to the ideal of exemplary perfect friendship? The risk of absurdity—even when it is not fully realized, or even rejected through deft directing—nonetheless persists as the potential unmasking of the underlying incommensurability between theatrical spectacle and the world beyond the stage. This is the essence of exemplarity as an ideal signifying nothing beyond itself.

In my discussion of Cervantes's novella, I focused extensively on Anselmo's confession of his irrepressible desire to test his wife and the long discussion with Lotario that this confession provokes. In what is arguably one of the less inspired scenes of Castro's retelling, Anselmo and Lotario rehearse many of the same arguments that arise in Cervantes's original: Anselmo describes his will to test his wife as a "locura" that has taken possession of his free will and, when Lotario balks at his proposal, he threatens to find someone else to do the job, even at the risk of his honor. Lotario, for his part, in initially rejecting Anselmo's request, as in Cervantes's original, suggests that such a test can only damage Camila's reputation, noting that even if she survives unscathed, her virtue will not be increased: "Quando salgan en tu esposa / finísimas esas pruevas; / no sé yo qué entonces, más / que tiene agora, tengas [When your wife comes out of these tests unblemished, I do not know what more than you have now you will have then]."[20] Faced with Anselmo's obstinacy, however, Lotario finally accedes to Anselmo's ill-advised plan, setting in motion the series of events that will drive the action of the play through to its conclusion.

Far more consequential than his largely derivative depiction of Anselmo's confession and the ensuing discussion is Castro's handling of Camila's seduction, a reflection, I would argue, of her heightened agency and, in particular, her central role in the play's response to the longer tradition of writing perfect friendship. As in Cervantes's original, Lotario's attempt at seducing his friend's wife only begins in earnest after Anselmo learns that, in deference to their long-standing friendship, Lotario has not been pursuing the agreed-upon plan with due diligence:

> Anselmo: A Lotario, quien creyera / al cabo de tantos años, / que yo seguro de engaños / en tu amistad no estuviera. / Ya he visto lo que ha pasado / . . . / Y del retrete á la puerta / me puse, donde he podido / ver en tu pecho dormido / quedar mi esperança muerta. / Mal mi amistad has pagado.[21]
>
> [Anselmo: Oh, Lotario! After so many years, who would believe that in your friendship I would not be safe from deception. I saw what happened . . . I hid behind the door to this interior room, where I could see my hopes die in your sleeping breast. How poorly you have requited my friendship.]

The staging of this speech parallels Cervantes's novella almost exactly as Anselmo, having spied on Lotario and Camila, rebukes his friend for failing to fulfill his promise to seduce his wife. Even more than his Cervantine model, however, Castro's language here amplifies the irony of Anselmo's complaint as the repeated references to friendship—which are completely absent in Cervantes's text—underscore Anselmo's absolute failure to understand the extent to which his own actions constitute a betrayal of his relationship with Lotario.[22] Similarly, Anselmo's accusation that Lotario has deceived him completely ignores the corrosive effects of his own admitted spying on his friend. If, as Lotario insists in the first act, the key to modern friendship is to be found in private confidences, this scene enacts the wholesale unraveling of that aspect of his relationship with Anselmo.

It may be that the promise of absolute transparency between two friends raises the bar for private friendship too high, that complete honesty between friends, while appealing as an ideal, is simply an unrealistic standard for any relationship. Lotario's deception, as suggested in my discussion of Cervantes in the last chapter, is well intentioned, even if it leads to the ultimate destruction of his friendship with Anselmo. Later in this study, I will explore how the main narrative of *Don Quixote* attempts to overcome this problem through an appeal to what I will call an aspirational model for friendship that dispenses with ideal categories altogether in favor of a clear-eyed focus on the practical reality of everyday life. Here, however, the pressures of the tradition of perfect friendship are such that no accommodation with these practical considerations is even possible. One ideal—the Aristotelian notion of the good—is necessarily replaced by another—the insistence on absolute transparency between friends—so that imperfect characters responding to ambiguous moral dilemmas are necessarily doomed to failure as measured by the exacting standards of perfect friendship, however defined.

At the same time, Lotario's ethical difficulties in this scene are framed in terms that recall the play's formal commitment to theatrical hyperbole. Anselmo's repeated references to friendship here serve to pull the reader away from the specific details of his predicament and toward the overarching claims of idealized ideological categories, a tendency that intensifies throughout the dialogue as Lotario renews his promise to seduce Anselmo's wife in the name of friendship:

Lotario: (*aparte* Hase visto tal exeso?) / Anselmo, yo te confieso / que estoy corrido, y turbado. / Aunque puedo, por la fé / de nuestra amistad, jurarte / que el atreverme a engañarte / por desengañarte fue. / Pero pues culpado estoy / de tu pensamiento estraño, / de servirte sin engaño / de hoy más palabra te doy. /

Anselmo: Mil vezes me has de abraçar, / tanto, tanto, amigo mío, / de nuestra amistad confío, / que por darte más lugar / de conquistar a mi esposa, / fingiré cierta partida / de Florencia . . .[23]

[Lotario: (*Ap.* Have you ever seen such excess?) Anselmo, I confess that I am embarrassed and confused, even though I could swear by the faith of our friendship that I only dared to deceive you in order to undeceive you. But since I am blamed by your strange imaginings, I give you my word from this day forward to serve you without deception.

Anselmo: You must embrace me a thousand times. So, so much my friend, I trust in our friendship, and in order to give you more space to conquer my wife, I will feign my departure from Florence.]

A few details here merit specific comment. First, Lotario's opening aside—"¿Háse visto tal exceso?"—provides perhaps the strongest evidence of a scene shift back to the register of theatrical hyperbole: With these words Lotario offers a metacritical recognition that the stakes of his conversation with Anselmo are about to change. Having crossed this signpost of recognition, Lotario sets aside his earlier ethical qualms and redoubles his commitment to friendship, here redefined in categorical terms as loyalty to one's friend whatever the potential consequences. Moreover, Anselmo's response to Lotario's protestations of friendship push the exaggerated rhetoric of their dialogue to the point where, once again, it runs up against the limits of absurdity. Thus, the thousand "embraces" with which he greets Lotario's renewed dedication to his plan transitions into the astonishing declaration that in recognition of their friendship Anselmo will depart from Florence so that Lotario might have more room to "conquer my wife." With this open invitation to his wife's infidelity and his own cuckoldry, Anselmo's rant in the name of ideal friendship exposes its own absurdity as the play's plotting again tracks in the direction of farce.

This backdrop of rhetorical excess provides a powerful and, one suspects, quite deliberate contrast to the more intimate space of representational verisimilitude that follows in the pivotal scene of Camila's seduction, now transported to the space of a long dialogue between the two former lovers. Indeed, the importance of dialogue to this process cannot be overstated, as revealed through a comparison with Cervantes's original version of *El curioso impertinente*: the earlier prose narrative skims over the specific details of this climactic moment, as if its structural function were all that mattered.[24] Thus, Cervantes's narrator reports how Lotario "lloró, rogó, ofreció, aduló, porfió y fingió ... con tantos sentimientos, con muestras de tantas veras, que dio al través con el recato de Camila y vino a triunfar de lo que menos se pensaba y más deseaba," which is to say, he did everything that might be expected of a typical Renaissance lover in such circumstances. One detects in these lines an acute awareness of the banality of the formula for Camila's seduction as if even the master storyteller of the Spanish early modern period finds it impossible to escape the influence of ossified literary conventions.

The contrast between Cervantes's truncated account of Camila's surrender to her feelings for Lotario and Castro's reformulation of this same scene in dialogue is striking. In particular, where Cervantes merely reports in summary narration, Castro stages the scene in two extended encounters between Lotario and Camila in the second act. Even more significant, in contrast to Cervantes's narrative, in which Lotario initially demonstrates no particular interest in his friend's wife, the two scenes that lead up to Camila's seduction in Castro's play operate as an extension of the backstory of Lotario and Camila's original love affair. Where Cervantes depicts the hapless Lotario as a victim of the capricious forces of love, Castro's dialogue references their earlier attachment explicitly, suggesting as a matter of course, that the embers of their former love still smolder beneath the surface of their mutual sacrifice in the name of exemplary friendship. Thus, while there are moments in these encounters in which Lotario speaks in the extravagant language that we have come to expect from early modern lovers, the emotional force of the dialogue arguably derives more from a profound awareness of the passage of time: ". . . que soñé / que atrás el tiempo volvía, / y gozava el mismo día / que en tus ojos me abrasé [. . . that I dreamt that I had returned to former times and rejoiced in that same day when my love was kindled in your eyes]."[25] Recollecting an earlier time in his love affair with Camila, Lotario infuses this scene with a powerful sense of nostalgia and loss that is completely alien to Castro's Cervantine model.

The full significance of this temporal awareness, however, is not unambiguous, as becomes clear in Camila's initial response to Lotario's renewed protestations of love:

Camila: ¡Ay, cuytada! Ya esso pasa / el límite a la razón. / ¿Son burlas essas quimeras? /
Lotario: Burlando las comencé, / pero ya muero, y no sé / si son burlas, o son veras. /
Camila: Lotario, corrida estoy / de que haverme conocido / tan de atrás, no haya servido / para que sepas quien soy. / No sé qué sienta, o qué diga / de tu infame proceder; / dísteme para muger / y búscasme para amiga.[26]

[Camila: Ah, miserable me! This now passes the limits of reason. Are these fantasies merely playing tricks?
Lotario: I began with trickery, but now I am dying and do not know if they are true or false.

Camila: Lotario, I am ashamed that having known me from so long ago has not served to inform you of who I am. I do not know what to feel or say about your vile conduct; you gave me as wife and now you seek me as a lover.]

In this exchange, Camila conveys an acute recognition of the complexity of her predicament that contrasts starkly with Lotario's singular devotion to his passion. Here, however, it is the long temporal arc of her relationship with Lotario that animates the bitterness of her rebuke, the fact that despite their long history Lotario would now have the temerity to seek her out "para amiga."[27] Yet perhaps the most notable feature of this dialogue lies in Camila's reference to her identity and her subsequent accusation against her former lover that he does not truly know her: "Lotario, corrida estoy de que haverme conocido tan de atrás, no haya servido para que sepas quien soy." With these words, the complexity of their former secret love affair is tied to a model of identity based on private intimacy. In place of a notion of the self founded on public reputation—as in Lotario's affirmation that "toda Italia . . . los amigos por excelencia nos llaman"—Camila asserts the possibility of knowing the other as a function of private life exclusively: To truly know Camila is to share an intimacy with her that is defined through an explicit exclusion of the larger community.

From a structural point of view, Camila's words in this speech recall the analysis in my introductory chapter of the alternative trajectory for friendship that flows from Cicero to Petrarch's letters and finally to the articulation of a new poetics of friendship in *Don Quixote*. Camila's intervention, while ostensibly focused on matters of love, rehearses a vision of mutual understanding between lovers that possesses many of the characteristics of that alternative model for friendship: In contrast to the unknowable perfect Aristotelian friend, Camila posits a vision of personal intimacy that, while it aspires to absolute knowledge of the other, recognizes the inherent limits of human perfectibility, here realized in terms of the inexorable influence of time over human affairs. At this point in her relationship with Lotario, however, the rehearsal of this alternative, far more human understanding of intimacy is largely negative. All Camila can do now is lament Lotario's failure to fulfill his earlier promises, the fact that his commitments to their love have not survived the test of time. In the end, amorous passion proves inadequate to the expression of a positive, aspirational understanding of intimacy.

Nevertheless, Camila's role in giving voice to a new model of personal intimacy both in this passage and elsewhere in Castro's play is not without interest for a study of the poetics of early modern friendship. In claiming that Lotario does not know her as he should, Camila applies the principle of representational verisimilitude to an assessment of the one character within the play with whom she can claim to share a bond that is fundamentally private. In other words, Castro reveals the *poetic* principle of representational verisimilitude to be inextricably tied to a way of thinking about human relationships in general. Read from this perspective, our modern notion of private, personal intimacy is exposed as an intrinsically aesthetic concept.

This last observation helps to explain the development of the rest of this important scene. The return to representational verisimilitude in the passage above extends throughout the remainder of the dialogue, so that when Camila finally gives in to her rekindled love for Lotario, the audience is already fully activated for the reception of this turn in the plot as somehow true in a way that much of the rest of the performance is not. Of particular interest in the final moments leading up to Camila's surrender are Lotario's increasingly long speeches in which he attempts to explain his treacherous behavior in originally facilitating Anselmo's marriage to the woman he himself had promised to marry:

> Demás de esto, quando engaños / en mi pudieran caber, / ¿pudiéraslos esconder / de tus ojos tantos años? / Pierde essa injusta sospecha, / y en lo demás de mi vida, / aunque te dexe ofendida, / te dexara satisfecha. / Camila, Anselmo te vio, / y en fin por mi desventura, / quedó muerto en tu hermosura; / y como lo supe yo, / quize con una amistad / esforçar una violencia, / prové después con la ausencia, / a curar la voluntad. / Y entendí volver con vida, / pero al verte luego vi / que estava, señora, en mí / sobresanada la herida.[28]

> [In addition, even if I were capable of such deception, could I possibly hide it from your eyes for so many years? Give up these unjust suspicions, and for the rest of my life, even if I have offended you in some way, I will leave you satisfied. Camila, Anselmo saw you and to my misfortune, in the end, he perished in your beauty; and when I discovered this, I wished with friendship to impose an act of violence; I attempted to cure my feelings through absence and believed that I had returned with life; but upon seeing you, I realized that the wound, *señora*, was only superficially healed.]

Unlike the rhetorical posturing that characterizes so much of the lovemaking of other characters in the play, Lotario's language here stands out for its emphasis on storytelling, on recounting the narrative events that have led him and Camila to their current state. In describing their long history together, Lotario appeals to Camila's sense of their shared private intimacy, in direct contrast to her far more superficial relationship with Anselmo, which is based exclusively on the objectifying power of visual apprehension—"Anselmo te vio, / y en fin, por mi desventura, / quedó muerto en tu hermosura."[29] Even Lotario's original self-sacrifice in giving way to Anselmo's passion for Camila comes under review here so that what was depicted originally in the play as proof of his commitment to perfect friendship is now described as a kind of forced violence. While the assertion is clearly self-serving, it nonetheless underscores the complex nature of communications between Lotario and Camila when compared to Lotario's hyperbolic declarations on the topic of friendship earlier in the play.

Further supporting the idea of shared intimacy in this passage, moreover, is Lotario's insistence on the impossibility of deception (*engaño*) between himself and his former lover. The explicit exclusion of deception from their relationship marks a further contrast between Lotario and his friend Anselmo, whose relationship with his wife is represented almost wholly in terms of his obsession with testing her fidelity, that is, in terms of an underlying fear that he does not know her. In asserting deception as impossible between himself and Camila, Lotario redirects language that he had initially used to describe his relationship with Anselmo to affirm the private intimacy underlying his love affair with Camila. Similarly, with his metaphorical reference to the "herida" that is merely "sobresanada," Lotario alludes to the longer arc of their love affair, suggesting the primacy of his feelings for his former lover despite his earlier act sacrificing his relationship with Camila to the demands of his friendship with Anselmo. Here again, Lotario emphasizes the longevity of his sentimental attachment as a truer sign of his love.

Despite such indications of genuine sentiment, however, there are also hints throughout this scene that what is about to happen between Lotario and Camila constitutes a fundamental corruption of their earlier love affair. This becomes glaringly evident in the precise moment of Camila's capitulation to her renewed passion for her old lover, a key turn in the plot that is first announced in an aside as a private confession not to her lover, but to the audience:

> Camila: (*Aparte:* ¿Es hechizo, o es locura / que siento? ¿Que se me antoja? / ¿Quien me detiene y me arroja, / me amenaça y me asegura? / Mal resisto esta terneza, / pero para no moverme, / con ella pudiera hazerme / de bronze naturaleza. / ¿Yo soy quien era? ¡Ay de mí! / Pero ya mía no soy; / resuelta, resuelta estoy, / para Lotario nací.)
> Lotario: ¿No me respondes? Temblando / me miras, cruel estás.[30]

[Camila: (*Ap.* Is this enchantment or madness? What is this I feel? What is this that I desire? Who holds me back or throws me forward, who threatens me or gives me comfort? Poorly do I resist this sweetness: but in order to resist, nature would have to remake me in bronze. Am I who I was? Woe is me! But alas now I am no longer my own. I am resolved, resolved: For Lotario was I born.)
Lotario: You don't answer me? Trembling you look at me; what cruelty.]

At the outset of the play, Camila's love affair with Lotario derives much of its force from their shared private intimacy. In this exchange, however, the fact that Camila excludes Lotario from her confession that she has fallen in love again suggests that something is different this time around. Referring to herself as afflicted by madness or a magic spell—"hechizo"—Camila conjures up the familiar tradition of love as a powerful external force that negates individual autonomy, a conventional idea that now takes on new significance in relation to this female voice who, for so much of the play, has demonstrated a powerful ability to set her own course in life. Echoing language that was first encountered in Cervantes's interpolated story, Camila resigns herself to the power of love, which she claims only a being made of bronze could resist. Nor is she completely unaware of the change. Questioning her identity—"¿Yo soy quien era?"—she admits that she is no longer her own person: "Pero ya mía no soy." This collapse of her autonomy is finally resolved into a kind of subjugation—"para Lotario nací"—that is far removed from the more balanced exchanges witnessed earlier in the play.[31]

Equally striking is Lotario's response to this speech that he cannot hear. As if to underscore the fact that he is not privy to this confessional monologue, Lotario complains of Camila's silence, describing it as a kind of cruelty. If previously their love had been marked by a profound *knowing*, Lotario's short intervention at this point signals an erosion in that key aspect of their relationship. Moreover, when Camila does finally respond directly to Lotario's query, her speech is filled with language that evokes the metaphor of love as a kind of mortal combat: "Mi desdicha fue forçosa, / venciste, yo estoy rendida; / de agravios me vi ofendida, / celos me hizieron curiosa [My misfortune was inevitable; you defeated me, I have surrendered; I saw myself offended by insults, (but) jealousy made me curious]."[32] This is not a love born of admiration or deep sentiment, but a surrender to far less admirable aspects of her character—jealousy and curiosity—with the second suggesting that Anselmo is not the only "curioso impertinente" in this play.

While this scene may be said to signal the end of a more heroic vision of Camila as a fount of independent agency, her surrender to Lotario is not necessarily incompatible with her role in promoting the poetics of representational verisimilitude. In particular, the explicit reference to her essential loss of identity in the passage above signals self-awareness concerning what has happened to her. Such self-awareness is suggestive of how for even the strongest-willed individual there comes a point at which the capriciousness of forces beyond one's control are finally incontestable.

Camila's response to Lotario ends, appropriately enough, with an appeal to her honor: ". . . dudé, recelé, temí, / prové, resolvíme, y di / con el honor al través."[33] The accelerated pacing reminds us of the conventionality of the plotting here—not unlike what was observed earlier in Cervantes's original—while her evocation of her honor underscores the socially difficult situation into which she has been cast.[34] In an echo of Cervantes's original tale, idealized notions of female virtue, like perfect friendship, break down under the pressure of representational verisimilitude as a poetic mode that privileges the practical circumstances of human experience over abstract categorical ideals. From this point of view, the inherent dualism of the *comedia*'s poetics may be said to have already worked its transformation over the tale of two friends tradition so that Camila's return to her first love becomes not so much the sign of her failed virtue or even, for that matter, of Anselmo's corruption of ideal friendship, as of a scaling down of the play's earlier exalted expectations.

The ascendance of representational verisimilitude in the scene of Camila's seduction constitutes an aestheticization of intimacy as notions of emotional authenticity and sincerity are imposed upon the self-consciously duplicitous space of the baroque stage. Through representations of private life that seem real, the audience is encouraged to participate in the lie of fiction, displacing the earlier claims of rhetorical hyperbole in favor of a poetics that offers a compelling opportunity for self-identification. At the heart of this new aesthetics is the promise of finally knowing the other if only imperfectly, of an understanding of the dynamics of intimacy, as it were, from the inside. Herein lies the embryo of an entirely new framework for representing interpersonal relations.

Within the more confined space of the early modern Spanish stage, however, the larger implications of this aestheticization of intimacy for the discourse of friendship are obscured by the easy alignment between the Aristotelian ideal and the irrepressible hyperbole that is the other defining impulse of the Spanish *comedia*. In the play's final act, the conventional discourse of perfect friendship re-establishes a kind of poetic hegemony as the slow dialogic expression of personal intimacy gives way to an accelerated rush toward a spectacular ending in which the pretense of verisimilitude is roughly cast aside. Culminating in the death of Anselmo at the hands of his former friend, Lotario, the play's ending is precipitated by a heated encounter between Camila and her maid over the latter's own amorous dalliances. Seeking revenge, Leonela reveals her mistress's secret to Anselmo, leading him shortly thereafter to confront Lotario about these new accusations. A duel ensues between the two men in which Anselmo is mortally wounded.

There is very little dialogue in the moments leading up to the duel, which, it is worth noting, takes place off stage. Rather, the audience hears Anselmo's two-line accusation of treason against his friend and adultery against his wife—"¡Amigo alevoso, / y tú, adúltera insolente! [Traitorous friend, and you, insolent adulterer!]"—followed in short order by Lotario's equally brief self-defense—"Anselmo, tente. / El defenderme es forçoso [Anselmo, hold back. I must defend myself]."[35] Then, after a brief monologue in which Camila frets over the possibility of an escape, Lotario and the mortally wounded Anselmo re-emerge on stage, at which point something remarkable occurs: Anselmo not only confesses his guilt for his untimely end, he goes on to make the extraordinary claim that his death at the hands of his friend constitutes the greatest gift of friendship—"fue siempre mi grande amigo, / y el darme agora la muerte / fue la mayor amistad / que en su vida pudo hazerme [He was always my great friend and that he would now give me death is the greatest favor that he could do for me in his life]."[36] Stricken with remorse for his impertinent curiosity, the dying Anselmo concludes his last speech in the play with a request to the Duke that he pardon Lotario and authorize his former friend's marriage to his widow: "Es señor, que de mi muerte / alcance perdón Lotario, / para que después hereden / él y Camila casados, / como mis gustos, mis bienes [Let Lotario be pardoned for my death so that afterward he and Camila, married, may inherit my goods with my pleasures]."[37]

Having initially set out to kill Lotario in a duel, Anselmo's exaggerated claims of self-sacrifice here in the name of friendship far exceed the bounds of credulity, recalling the absurdity that is a central feature of theatrical hyperbole throughout Castro's play.[38] As a result, not only does Anselmo's final speech offer very little that might be apprehended through the lens of self-identification, it introduces serious doubts as to the adequacy of the moral calculus with which the play settles accounts.[39] In fact, Anselmo's confession of guilt, the moral weight of which is heightened by his impending death, imposes an ethical clarity where, in fact, none exists, a complexity that the play itself has already implicitly acknowledged in the representation of Camila's recriminations against her first lover: Does not Lotario himself bear responsibility for the surrender of his betrothed to his friend's whim? Moreover, after witnessing Anselmo's capricious nature—a presumed defect that Aristotelian friendship in its purest form would normally disallow—one cannot help but question Lotario's decision to continue to support him in his morally dubious quest to test his wife. Anselmo is a profoundly troubled figure, but Lotario himself suffers from a failure to recognize his friend's limitations, suggesting that the ideal friendship celebrated in the play's opening scene is already deeply flawed by a lack of mutual understanding between these two men.

Of course, in the original tradition of the tale of two friends, the very idea of defending the priority of friendship over other ethical considerations would be largely unintelligible. Gisippo and Tito, Timbrio and Silerio, these are pairings in which friendship is pure performance without the complicating local effects that an emerging interest in representational verisimilitude necessarily generates. The notion of an ongoing and evolving relationship between these characters is alien to the structural imperative of a narrative form that demands perfection in word and deed—even as it occasionally calls that imperative into question. Read within the framework of this longer tradition of writing perfect friendship, the utter rejection of representational verisimilitude in this final scene signals a definitive reassertion of the structural requirements of the orthodox tale of two friends. Understood in this way, the gaping moral problem at the heart of Anselmo's speech evaporates into rhetorical hot air. In his claim to reanimate the ideal of friendship, Anselmo's absurd statement about his impending death realizes its full significance in precisely that absurdity. Like all pure claims of perfect friendship, what he asserts here necessarily exceeds the limits of observable human conduct in the world beyond the stage.[40]

At the same time, however, Anselmo's words also reveal the extent to which the narrative friendship tradition has become unmoored from its Aristotelian origins: To argue for one's murder at the hands of one's friend as the highest gift of friendship radically upends the classical model of the virtuous perfect friend. In the play's concluding scene, both friends return to occupy a state of exalted unknowability, here conceived not as a sign of their moral superiority, but rather as a manifestation of the demands of a resurgent poetic order that exists as an end in itself. The inherently moral discourse of perfect friendship and its ultimate basis in an idealized notion of the good gives way to an idealization that exists only along the pure surface of theatrical representation. Having relinquished any claim to practical exemplarity, the apotheosis of the two friends at the end of Castro's play confirms the final alignment of perfect friendship with the formal claims of theatrical hyperbole as an independent locus of poetic meaning. And yet the ascendancy of a theatrical model for perfect friendship in the final scene of Castro's play does not necessarily negate the new poetics of personal intimacy that emerge in the earlier encounter between the former lovers Lotario and Camila. Rather, the assertion of representational verisimilitude as the formal framework for a more recognizably modern mode of personal intimacy persists in Castro's text not merely as a counterbalance to the robust assertion of theatrical hyperbole at the play's end, but more essentially as a critical element in holding the attention of a modern audience whose appetite for spectacle coexists with a craving for personal self-identification with the characters who populate the stage.

Notes

1. Faliu-Lacourt and Lobato, *El curioso impertinente*, p. 3, suggest that Castro wrote his play shortly after the publication of the first part of *Don Quixote* in 1605. The recent bibliographical investigations of Jurado Santos, *Obras teatrales derivadas de las novelas cervantinas*, provide extensive information on the Valencian playwright's extensive interest in Cervantes's writings.
2. Guillén de Castro, *El curioso impertinente*, p. 5. All citations from *El curioso impertinente* are taken from the Martínez y Martínez edition with some updated accentuation following the edition of Faliu-Lacourt and Lobato. Additional changes in orthography and punctuation following Faliu-Lacourt and Lobato's edition are registered in the notes. English translations are my own. Ignacio Arellano, "Del relato al teatro," p. 80, argues that the Duke's opening remarks on the *comedia* serve as an indicator to the audience of what will follow: "Aunque *El curioso impertinente* no sea exactamente una comedia lúdica, el marco de referencias y por tanto el horizonte de expectativas del público ha sido fijado en estos primeros momentos del acto I, y se aleja de la versión trágica cervantina." Read in this way, the Duke's commentary constitutes a concession to the important role of the audience in assigning value to Castro's text.
3. Orozco Díaz, *¿Qué es el «Arte nuevo» de Lope de Vega*, p. 25. Orozco Díaz is, of course, responding to Lope's original verses which he replicates in his study, p. 24: "Y escribo por el arte que inventaron / los que el vulgar aplauso pretendieron, / porque, como las paga el vulgo, es justo / hablarle en necio para darle gusto." In the introductory essay to their contemporary edition of Castro's play, Faliu-Lacourt and Lobato, p. 10, argue that "la alusión a Lope de Vega . . . refleja de modo interesante las relaciones entre los dos dramaturgos con la afirmación pública, de parte del valenciano, de su admiración por el Fénix de los ingenios."
4. In *Writers on the Market*, pp. 23–40, I provide a more extensive analysis of the economic basis of this new role for the audience in helping to define the poetics of the early modern *comedia*.
5. Guillén de Castro, *El curioso impertinente*, pp. 5–6.

6. Egginton, *How the World Became a Stage*, pp. 89–91, traces this interest in representational verisimilitude to both the Italian theatrical tradition and to the renewed interest in classical theories among early modern Spanish *preceptistas*, especially as exemplified in the early modern commentators on Aristotle's *Poetics*. Of particular interest in this history is the classical notion of decorum, which requires in the context of the Spanish *comedia*, as Bayliss, *The Discourse of Courtly Love*, pp. 106–7, puts it, "that the audience must be able to recognize the differences between a king and a peasant, a lady and a gentleman, or an aristocrat and a lackey." Both Egginton and Bayliss's analysis are in keeping with a long tradition of writing about the *comedia*. Thus, in a study of Lope de Vega's poetics produced over a generation ago, Pérez and Sánchez Escribano, *Afirmaciones de Lope de Vega*, pp. 175–88, explore the Aristotelian origin of Lope de Vega's interest in verisimilitude and its link with the Horatian notion of decorum. Writing around the same time about the Spanish *comedia* more generally, Aubrun, *La comedia española*, p. 281, insists that the character that inhabits this genre—which he describes as a mode of "tragicomedia"—is, in fact, "el *alter ego* del hombre real," a notion that highlights the imitative basis of the poetics of representational verisimilitude. On the other hand, it is much more difficult to find antecedents to my proposition here about the role of theatrical hyperbole in the *comedia*. While one encounters frequent references to the spectacle of the theater, I have discovered very little on the question of how the rhetorical manifestation of that spectacular impulse might embody an alternative poetic mode that is distinct from and in tension with the discourse of representational verisimilitude.
7. Faliu-Lacourt and Lobato's description of Torcato, p. 13, is instructive: "¿Quién es pues este Torcato? Una creación de Castro que desempeña, durante la ausencia de Anselmo, el papel de amigo y confidente, de protegido que depende de Lotario como éste, aunque en menor grado, queda deudor, moralmente sobretodo [sic], del padre de Anselmo en un curioso reflejo de las situaciones de apuro financiero pintadas en otros textos (*Pretender con pobreza*)." Arellano, "Del relato al teatro," p. 82, suggests that Torcato "ilustra una modalidad corrompida de amistad, ligándose así a uno de los temas centrales, y sirve de obstáculo a la amistad de los protagonistas." While I agree with Arellano's assessment, the practical significance of this secondary character is never really developed in a way that impinges on the love triangle that emerges as Castro's primary interest.
8. Guillén de Castro, *El curioso impertinente*, p. 12.
9. Ibid. p. 12–13. I have followed Faliu-Lacourt and Lobato's punctuation in combining the last two sentences in Martínez y Martínez's edition into the single sentence that appears here, and in rendering "entre nosotros" as two words.
10. Ibid. p. 13.
11. The idea of role-play here comes from Thacker's reinterpretation of Abel's theory of metatheatre. Specifically, Thacker's insight, *Role-Play and the*

World as Stage in the Comedia, p. 3, into "a sociological model for interpreting life lived in a group, known as role-theory," helps to illuminate the self-consciousness of a female character like Camila, who, as will become clear in my analysis below, is forced to reckon with the social role into which she has been cast as a function of her gender and social position.
12. In the first act, p. 10, Lotario claims that their love affair has been going on for three years, but also suggests that it has never been formally acknowledged even by the lovers themselves; for Camila, according to Lotario, has consistently treated him with "desdén," which he paradoxically insists "muestra que me quiere bien." Understood in the context of the play as a whole, the fact of their previous involvement—however defined—is arguably more important than the specifics of that involvement prior to the play's opening. García Martín, *Cervantes y la comedia española en el siglo XVII*, p. 72, notes this important innovation in his comparison of Guillén de Castro's play with its Cervantine source.
13. Guillén de Castro, *El curioso impertinente*, p. 15.
14. Ibid. p. 15.
15. Ibid. p. 15. The text here follows Faliu-Lacourt and Labato with the substitution of "quilates" for "quintales" in Martínez y Martínez's edition.
16. Thacker's thesis, p. 47, offers a more general conceptualization of what I am attempting to describe here: "This study examines several works by Golden-Age dramatists in an attempt to show that, despite the constraints put upon certain individuals by patriarchy, they are able to express their desires, not necessarily by riding roughshod over the expectations of patriarchy, by finding a way to escape to a parallel society, but rather by commandeering other social roles from within those available within their society, and deceitfully (and metatheatrically) presenting them as their own. Self-expression, it will be seen, occurs through imaginative role-play, metatheatre, which becomes a strategy for refusing to play the appropriate social role, and by extension, in a 'real' world dependent on role-play for its sense of order, a means by which patriarchy's demands can be at least modified."
17. Guillén de Castro, *El curioso impertinente*, p. 32.
18. Ibid. p. 33.
19. With reference to Lope, Aubrun, *La comedia española*, p. 218, notes the importance of the sonnet to the representation of the peculiar psychology of the *comedia*: "Tanto por su origen como por su contenido, el soneto expresa la introspección a la manera de Petrarca. «El soneto está bien que en los que aguardan», dice Lope, y eso significa de hecho: el soneto conviene a los que reflexionan o se miran en el espejo de su alma." The link between poetic form and historical function that Aubrun observes here is undeniable. The history of the sonnet in Spain, however, hardly sustains the purity of Aubrun's claim for unimpeded self-reflection. If that history demonstrates anything, it is the progressive imposition of rhetorical artifice, that is, of a poetic language that revels in its own cleverness. Understood in this way, the sonnet may be said to provide the ideal formal device for

conveying the kind of exaggerated rhetorical claims that are on display in this passage from *El curioso impertinente*.
20. Guillén de Castro, *El curioso impertinente*, p. 49.
21. Ibid. p. 54.
22. Compare the dialogue from Castro's play with Anselmo's words at the same point in *Don Quixote*, I.33: "¡Ah—dijo Anselmo—, Lotario, Lotario, y cuán mal correspondes a lo que me debes y a lo mucho que de ti confío! Ahora te he estado mirando por el lugar que concede la entrada desta llave y he visto que no has dicho palabra a Camila; por donde me doy a entender, que aun las primeras le tienes por decir; y si esto es así, como sin duda lo es, ¿para qué me engañas, o por qué quieres quitarme con tu industria los medios que yo podría hallar para conseguir mi deseo?" Castro replaces the oblique "cuán mal correspondes a lo que me debes" with two explicit references to Anselmo and Lotario's "amistad."
23. Ibid. pp. 54–5.
24. Faliu-Lacourt, "Formas vicariantes de un tema recurrente," p. 174, underscores the central importance of dialogue in Castro's reimagining of Cervantes's novella, arguing at one point, "Los personajes de la comedia no son sino lo que dicen o dicen de ellos los demás personajes, sin intervención del autor-plasmador que concibió sus papeles."
25. Guillén de Castro, *El curioso impertinente*, pp. 61–2. The text here follows Faliu-Lacourt and Lobato rendering "bolvía" as "volvía."
26. Ibid. p. 62.
27. Faliu-Lacourt, "Formas vicariantes de un tema recurrent," p. 176 discovers in this remark a sign of the play's "estructura en 'espiral'" in which "las secuencias remiten a situaciones pasadas."
28. Guillén de Castro, *El curioso impertinente*, p. 79.
29. Faliu-Lacourt and Lobato, *El curioso impertinente*, p. 16, make a similar distinction between the two friends and their relationship with Camila: "Aparece entonces muy claramente que la relación de los dos recién casados es una relación de posesión y amor propio opuesta al verdadero amor que une a Camila y Lotario aunque, como en la literatura caballeresca, se haya retrasado la unión de los amantes."
30. Guillén de Castro, *El curioso impertinente*, p. 81.
31. Faliu-Lacourt and Lobato, *El curioso impertinente*, p. 29, suggest that Camila's eventual seduction as reflected in her words here—"Para Lotario nací"—confirms something that had been inevitable from the play's very beginning. Such a reading, however, minimizes Camila's agency and impedes an understanding of her role in the play's enactment of an alternative poetics of personal intimacy.
32. Guillén de Castro, *El curioso impertinente*, p. 81.
33. Ibid. p. 81.
34. Arellano, "Del relato al teatro," p. 85, suggests that Camila is more concerned with her honor than her "homónima cervantina" and cites several passages in which she makes direct reference to this important measure

of social value. I would tend to read this difference as reflecting Camila's enhanced agency in Castro's play as well as her awareness of the constraints of her social position.
35. Guillén de Castro, *El curioso impertinente*, p. 107.
36. Ibid. p. 108.
37. Ibid. p. 109.
38. García Martín, *Cervantes y la comedia española*, p. 78, writes about this scene: "Nos encontramos en una situación en la que la venganza de honor es obligada. Anselmo tiene que morir o matar. Guillén une a esta lógica postura de esposo ultrajado la comprensión y el reconocimiento reflejados en Cervantes. En el momento de morir, Anselmo recobra su consciencia y perdona." Significantly, García Martín makes no attempt to explain Anselmo's abrupt change of heart, an omission that supports my main point here, namely, that Anselmo's actions and words at the end of this scene are completely unmotivated.
39. An earlier generation of critics was troubled by the moral ambiguity of the play's ending, which was felt to involve a loosening of Castro's adherence to the demands of the honor code, one of the defining principles of what Weiger, "Sobre la originalidad e independencia de Guillén de Castro," p. 8, describes as "la convención lopesca." Weiger, pp. 11–12, provides a concise summary of this critical debate: "«La huella del punto de vista cervantino se descubre aquí en el triunfo de los adúlteros contra los principios del honor en la drama», observa Américo Castro. Esmeralda Gijón también menciona el «desenlace tan inusitado en la literatura de la época», agregando que en *El curioso impertinente* «resplandece su independencia [de Castro] frente al criterio usual del honor que campeaba en el vulgo y una no menos libre concepción de la justicia, al solucionar el conflicto dramático con la muerte del marido por Lotario y la salvación de los amantes . . .». De una manera semejante señala Valbuena Prat la independecia de Castro, considerándola una característica de la producción dramática de don Guillén: «La independencia de este drama frente al concepto usual del honor en el teatro, no hay que buscarla sólo en la oriundez cervantina, sino que se explica por una predisposición de gran parte de la dramática de Guillén a una más liberal idea de la honra y de la moral de la justicia, sin temer las situaciones más difíciles y escabrosas»."
40. My interpretation of the ending to *El curioso impertinente* may be productively understood through the lens of Regueiro's analysis in "Textual Discontinuities and the Problems of Closure in the Spanish Drama of the Golden Age," p. 43: "Closure, the 'sense of appropriate cessation,' that 'feeling of finality, completion, and composure,' of which Herrnstein Smith speaks, may be much more difficult to achieve in many *comedias* when they are freed from a universality of 'order disturbed to order restored.'" The ending to *El curioso impertinente* corroborates Regueiro's thesis on at least two different levels. First, the moral ambiguity that attends Anselmo's dying wish imposes a burden on the play's harmonious ending that necessarily

corrodes the efficacy of the more general theatrical principle that Rugueiro critiques here. It is in this sense that the ending of Castro's play may be described as unavoidably ironic. Second, the ascendancy of friendship in the concluding scene raises a fundamental question of priorities: Does the reaffirmation of the ideal of perfect friendship represent a point of continuity with the principle of the harmonious ending, or is it imposed despite the requirements of such an ending? In affirming the latter, my analysis here underscores a fundamental subordination of the apparatus of the *comedia* to the imperatives of the tradition of writing perfect friendship in Castro's play.

Chapter 5

María de Zayas's Good Friends

Guillén de Castro's dramatic rewriting of *El curioso impertinente* highlights an important gendered element in the *comedia*'s hybrid poetics that also reflects back on the tale of two friends tradition more generally. Not only does Castro's Camila find her voice and, in the process, contest the woman's traditional role as object of exchange between perfect friends, her representation on stage embodies a poetics grounded in verisimilitude that challenges the rhetorical excess that, as outlined in the previous chapter, is a defining feature of both the Spanish *comedia* and the tale of two friends tradition more generally. Casting Lotario and Camila as troubled lovers with a long and complex personal history, Castro crafts dialogue between the two that enhances the audience's sense of their private intimacy in direct contrast to the hyperbolic claims that are made throughout the play in the name of perfect friendship.

As the primary focus of this new poetic interest in personal intimacy, however, Camila's gendered role as the contested lover within what is essentially still a tale of perfect male friendship necessarily constrains the representation of her personal life to relationships that are invariably defined in the language of love. The new discourse of personal intimacy to which she gives voice is thus never extended to the realm of friendship for the simple reason that while Camila may have more than one lover, she is—by definition—friendless. In Castro's play, friendship as a distinct category of human relationship remains imprisoned in the conventional discourse of the tale of two friends tradition as an exclusively male domain.

Given this background, it is perhaps not surprising that one of the first significant dramatic expressions of this new mode of personal intimacy *within* the discourse of friendship occurs in a play that challenges the gendered basis of the longer narrative tradition more directly. Inverting the gender roles that are a defining characteristic of that tradition, María de Zayas's *La traición en la amistad* undertakes a radical reconceptualization of the friendship narrative by placing a male love interest at the center of a complicated rivalry between female friends.[1] This essential structural shift facilitates an exploration of female agency within friendship that disrupts the ossified hyperbolic poetics that define so much of the tale of two friends tradition.

From Boccaccio onwards, the tale of two friends invariably leverages the debilitated social status of women in the service of the extraordinary claims of ideal male friendship. Even Castro, who demonstrates a genuine interest in the question of female subjectivity, ultimately abandons Camila to a fate that reflects the prejudices of the play's larger social context. In contrast, María de Zayas's exclusive focus on friendship between women in her one and only dramatic work privileges female subjectivity as an end in itself.[2] Thus, while *La traición en la amistad* draws heavily on the tropes of earlier writings on male friendship, it necessarily adapts those tropes to the very different social circumstances that attend the play's inversion of conventional gender roles in the narrative friendship tradition.

While the radically altered premise upon which María de Zayas constructs her dramatic interpretation of the tale of two friends is clear enough, the implications of her innovations for the larger tradition of writing perfect friendship are complicated and, considered in strictly poetic terms, somewhat ambiguous. There are scenes, especially in the play's second act, in which Zayas's discourse of personal intimacy fulfills its expressive potential in the representation of female friendship. In particular, the depiction of the relationship between Marcia and Laura employs the poetics of representational verisimilitude in support of a model of friendship in which the inherent dynamism of narrative storytelling lends a semblance of real-world authenticity to the intimacy that grows up around the two women. At the same time, however, there are also many instances in which the conventional poetics of theatrical hyperbole overwhelm the play's ability to fully realize this new modality for friendship. This is evident above all in Zayas's introduction of Fenisa as a kind of female Don Juan who embodies the exaggerated essence of the "bad" friend.[3] While Fenisa functions principally as a foil to the play's positive depictions of personal intimacy, the naturalized moralism that defines her as inherently evil ultimately contaminates the entire play so that by the end of the third act even the "good" friends—in particular Laura and Marcia—find themselves overwhelmed by a demand for poetic justice based on an essentialist moral logic.

Robert Bayliss has argued forcefully for the importance of reading *La traición en la amistad* through the filter of genre.[4] In fact, Zayas's inversion of gender roles in the tale of two friends may be said to advance the poetics of modern friendship up to the point at which the theatrical milieu, with its hybrid representational structure, once again forces the plotting back toward the expected trajectory of both the Spanish *comedia* and the narrative tradition of writing perfect friendship, that is, to a conventionalized happy ending based in the dual rhetorical imperatives of moral clarity and an exaltation of the ideal of perfect friendship. In this sense, her focus on female friendship illustrates both the potential and the limits of the Spanish early modern theater in representing a new, modern idea of personal intimacy.

La traición en la amistad opens with a scene that invites comparisons with earlier texts from the tale of two friends tradition as the anxious lover Marcia appears on stage to confess her affection for the handsome Liseo to her skeptical friend Fenisa. Admiring the fine qualities of her beloved—"¿por qué ha de ser milagro / que yo ame, si me obliga / toda la gala que he visto? [If the gallantry I see obliges me, why is it a wonder that I would love?]"—Marcia shows her friend a "naipe" depicting the image of this man in whom "se cifran / todas las gracias del mundo [are inscribed all the world's graces]," at which point Fenisa falls headlong into the trope of love at first sight, generating in the process the archetypal conflict of narrative perfect friendship:[5]

Fenisa: (*Aparte:* ¡Ay, Dios! ¿Qué he visto? / ¿Qué miras, alma, qué miras? / ¿Qué amor es éste? / ¡Oh, qué hechizo! / Tente, loca fantasía. / ¡Qué máquina, qué ilusión! / Marcia y yo somos amigas; / fuerza es morir . . .)[6]

[Fenisa: (*Aside:* My God! What is this I have seen? My soul, my soul, what do you behold? What love is this? Oh, what bewitchment! Stay, my mad imagination. What artifice, what illusion! Marcia and I are friends; death is my destiny . . .)]

As evidenced in this passage, Fenisa's emotional turmoil in the face of Liseo's portrait quickly transitions to a familiar internal struggle over the competing obligations of love and friendship, and even includes a final hyperbolic gesture toward death as the only solution to the crushing angst generated by this very conventional conflict. Here, then, barely 100 lines into the first act, Zayas establishes a clear genealogical link between her play and the long tradition of writing friendship.

This initial set-up, however, is merely a point of departure for what will be quickly revealed as a radical revision of the traditional plotting. For not only will Fenisa emerge from this scene to inhabit an entirely unprecedented role within the tale of two friends tradition, that of the categorical "bad" friend, the realization of this new identity will be forged initially through an embrace of what may be best described as the negative potential of representational verisimilitude. Evidence for this new trajectory is already on display in this early dialogue between Marcia and Fenisa. As indicated above, Fenisa expresses her newly kindled passion in an aside, that is, in a speech from which her interlocutor is explicitly excluded, an element in the staging of this scene to which Marcia makes explicit reference as she observes her dumbfounded friend: "Suspensa estás. ¿Qué imaginas? / Fenisa ¿no me respondes? / ¿no hablas? [You seem bewildered. What are you thinking? Fenisa, why do you not answer? Why do you not speak?]"[7] This initial breakdown in communication between Fenisa and Marcia signals an early but definitive change in the evolution in the familiar plot of the perfect friendship narrative; despite her explicit allusion to her duties to friendship—"Marcia y yo somos amigas; / fuerza es morir"—the woman who suddenly and impetuously falls in love with her friend's lover decides to keep this astonishing new development to herself. Instead of the expected impulse to confession and self-sacrifice in the name of friendship, from this point forward deception and manipulation become Fenisa's defining attributes as she makes clear her intention to deceive her friend so that she might more easily pursue her own selfish desires.[8]

As if to underscore this shift from silence to deception, Fenisa—still speaking to Marcia—wastes no time in formulating a plan to sate her newly inspired passion:

Fenisa: (*Aparte:* Perdida / estoy por Liseo. ¡Ay, Dios! / Fuerza será que le diga / mal dél, porque le aborrezca.) / ¿Cuidado de tantos días / como el del galán Gerardo / por el que hoy empieza, olvidas? / Demás de aqueste, puede, / fingiendo amor, cortesía, / estimación y finezas, / burlarte. Y es más justicia / estimar a quien te quiere / más que a quien quieres.[9]

[Fenisa: (*Aside:* I am lovesick for Liseo. My God! I must speak ill of him to provoke her disdain.) Would you truly forsake the long-suffering gallant Gerardo for that which begins this very day? Moreover, courtesy, rank and graces, feigning love, may deceive you. And, it is certainly more just to love the one who loves you more than the one you love.]

Here again an aside serves to mark off Fenisa's internal musings as Zayas's "bad" friend signals to the audience her premeditated intent to deceive. When she finally returns to address Marcia directly, Fenisa censors any mention of her own amorous feelings and, instead, invokes a series of arguments designed to discourage Marcia from pursuing her love for Liseo: the foolishness of discarding a truly faithful suitor, Gerardo, in favor of a new infatuation; the risk that this new lover might himself be untrue; and finally the wisdom of favoring the one who loves you over the one you love. These are practical arguments that appeal to Marcia's social position as a woman who, in pursuing amorous passion over the safer course of a secure marriage, runs the risk of dishonor.[10] As such, they are necessarily aligned with a poetics based in verisimilitude; they speak, in other words, a language that is reflective of the lived experience of women of a certain social status in the world beyond the text.

This last observation reveals the underlying aesthetic basis of Fenisa's attempt to dissuade her friend from pursuing Liseo as the efficacy of her rhetoric is inextricably linked to the successful fulfillment of the principles of representational verisimilitude. Expressed in more concrete terms, her reasoning to Marcia will only work to the extent that it makes practical sense as determined by an audience for whom the ultimate basis of all such assessments is the experience of everyday life. In a deliberate exploitation of the problematic "lie of fiction," the more Fenisa's words to Marcia convince, the more they expose the danger inherent in fictions that would feign the truth of the everyday experience of the world.

In the end, there is something profoundly subversive in this recasting of Fenisa as the "bad" friend. Where friends in earlier texts from the friendship tradition may fail to live up to the standards of the Aristotelian model, Fenisa offers the first example of a friend who actively conspires to undermine the ideal. By first following and then punctuating the expectations of the long tradition of writing perfect friendship, Fenisa contaminates the ideal with a damaging dose of cynicism from which the play arguably never recovers. And yet, even as she corrodes the ideal of perfect friendship, her strong sense of individual purpose—the fact that she acts for herself and not in the service of externally imposed social norms—marks her as the harbinger of a new kind of subjectivity.[11] As Margaret E. Boyle eloquently puts it, Fenisa "refuses discretion," asserting in the process a right to private motives that are, in the end, impervious to the will of that public voice that in so many of the other texts that have been considered in this study serves as the final arbiter of identity.[12] Indeed, pushing the logic of private intimacy to an exclusionary logical extreme, she embraces a radically alienated vision of subjectivity in which all that matters is the self.

At the same time, the radical alienation that compresses private life into a series of monologues and asides also necessarily exiles all other relationships to the public domain. For her so-called friends, Fenisa's identity is reduced to nothing more than her public reputation, that is, to a play of appearances that renders her fundamentally unknowable. In contrast to the Aristotelian tradition, in which unknowability signals the perfect friends' shared transcendence, here Fenisa's withdrawal into an almost solipsistic egoism is finally revealed as a symptom of the prosaic circumstances of her social isolation. Indeed, if there is a deeper meaning in Fenisa's predicament, it is to be found not in the categorical thinking of the Aristotelian ideal of perfect friendship but rather in Zayas's attempt to grapple with the darker corners of the human psyche. Beyond the rejection of any meaningful communal private life, there lies the deeper problem of desire, the underlying motivating force that drives an ambition for amorous conquest that knows no limits. "Tantos quiero cuantos miro [I desire all upon whom I gaze]," Fenisa declares in one of the play's more significant revelations: With these words Fenisa affords the audience a brief glimpse into the inscrutable engine that drives her forward, the paradox of the strong subject whose claim to agency is built on the enigmatic foundation of human desire.[13]

While Fenisa's egoistic isolation exposes the dangers of drawing too tight a circle around the experience of subjectivity, it does not negate the possibility of other, more generous interpretations of the discourse of private intimacy. In fact, within the play's overall plotting, Fenisa soon reveals her structural role as the negative exemplar against which Zayas sets up a modern alternative to the tired discourse of perfect Aristotelian friendship.[14] With Fenisa cast as the categorical "bad" friend, other women in Zayas's play give voice to a mode of friendship based, perhaps too innocently, on confessional storytelling that aspires to the ideal of sincerity. Extending the more optimistic potential for personal intimacy encountered previously in Castro's depiction of Camila in *El curioso impertinente*, the two new friends, Marcia and Laura, reanimate the ancient emphasis on a common understanding between friends, not in the classical sense as an abstract marker of perfect friendship, but rather as an aspirational objective that is rooted in a vigorous assertion of subjective self-control.

The second act wastes no time in introducing this alternative model for modern friendship as Marcia, the forlorn lover from the first act, receives an unexpected visit. The caller, as it turns out, is Liseo's first lover, Laura. After the two exchange platitudes, with each woman lauding the beauty of the other, Laura turns to the main business of her visit, which is twofold: first, to inform Marcia of her prior claim to Liseo's affections and second, to expose Fenisa's designs on the object of the shared object of their affection. As in the previous dialogue between Fenisa and Marcia, the audience is witness to a conflict over matters of the heart, but in this case without the scaffolding of an established friendship; these are two women whose initial presentation is defined exclusively in terms of a seemingly irreconcilable rivalry.

Yet it is precisely this lack of a prior friendship—or any relationship, for that matter—between the two women that creates the circumstances for what is arguably the play's the most important innovation. As Laura makes quite clear early on in her visit, her purpose is less confrontational than confessional. In fact, Laura's operative rhetorical mode throughout the scene is narrative storytelling as she serves up for her interlocutor an extended account of the private details of her life up to the point of her abandonment by an unnamed scoundrel:

Laura: Quedé niña, sola y rica, / con un noble caballero / que tuvo gusto en criarme / por ser de mi madre deudo. / Puso los ojos en mí / un generoso mancebo, / tan galán como alevoso, / desleal y lisonjero. / Como mi esposo, alcanzó / los favores con que pienso / que si tuve algún valor, / sin honra y sin valor quedo. / Cuando entendí que mi amante / trataba de casamiento, / trató, Marcia, de emplearse / en otros cuidados nuevos.[15]

[Laura: I was left a young girl, alone and wealthy, with a noble gentleman relative of my mother who took me in and raised me. Later a generous youth set his eyes on me, as gallant as treacherous, disloyal and flattering. With a promise to be my husband, he took those favors of me so that I believe that if I once had valor, I am now left with neither valor nor honor. At which point I came to understand that my lover planned to marry, that he was engaging in new affairs.]

The story she tells is not terribly original, and Liseo—who at this point remains unnamed—comes off looking like the typical philanderer who, by this point, has become something of a stock character in the literature of the period. More significant, however, is how this rather long narrative speech segues into a climactic moment of confession and intimacy. Comparing her former lover to the cruel Roman emperor, Nero, Laura speaks right up to the point of revealing in one fell swoop both Liseo's identity and, with it, the fact of Marcia's unwitting involvement in this sordid affair: "A pocos lances, hallé / que este mi tirano dueño, / Nerón cruel, que a mi alma / puso como a Roma incendio, / ¡Ay, Marcia! Supe . . . [I soon discovered that this, my tyrannical master, who as Nero to Rome, set fire to my soul. Ah, Marcia, I discovered . . .]"[16] She breaks down in tears at this point, generating a dramatic tension that extends for a good fifteen lines or so, until she finally exposes the truth that forms the core of her conflict with Marcia: "Supe, Marcia, que Liseo, / que éste, el traidor ingrato, / que en tal ocasión me ha puesto, / te adora a ti. Ésta es / la causa porque temiendo / estaba de declararme [I discovered, Marcia, that Liseo—this ungrateful traitor, who has put me in my current state—adores you. This is the reason why I feared revealing myself to you]."[17] The effect of Laura's narrative account of her life story followed by the heightened suspense of her final admission accentuates the confessional tone of the proceedings, intensifying the sense of intimacy between the two women precisely at the moment at which she acknowledges that they are, in fact, rivals.

The link between confession and personal intimacy finds confirmation in Marcia's response to the story she has just heard. Even though she is implicated by Laura as her rival, the rhetorical force of Laura's account of her predicament is finally designed to evoke compassion and, in the end, solidarity in a new mode of friendship:

Marcia: Laura, si tu sentimiento / es ése, puedo jurate / que no le he dado a Liseo / favor que no pueda al punto / quitársele. Yo confieso / que le tengo voluntad; / mas, Laura hermosa, sabiendo / que te tiene obligación, / desde aquí de amar le dejo. / En mi vida le veré. / ¿Eso temes? Ten por cierto / que soy mujer principal / y que aqueste engaño siento.[18]

[Marcia: Laura, if these are your feelings, I can swear to you that I have given no favor to Liseo that I cannot rescind. I confess that my will tends in his direction; but, beautiful Laura, knowing now his obligation to you, from this moment on I leave off loving him, nor will I see him again in my life. Is this what you fear? Understand that I am a noble woman and that I feel this deception.]

Of particular note here is Marcia's prompt readiness to sacrifice her own amorous ambitions in favor of a brand-new friend. Not only is Marcia's rejection of Liseo at this point absolute and unwavering, her words assert an unabashed sincerity that will be later confirmed through actions.[19] Unlike Fenisa, who remains intentionally silent after the ignition of her own amorous passions, Marcia's confession to Laura of her love for Liseo—"Yo confieso que le tengo voluntad"—functions here as a precondition for all that will follow in this new, very different friendship.

The newfound intimacy between two women who should be rivals is closely associated with a sense of self-control that operates in direct opposition to the discourse of uncontrolled desire that circulates around Fenisa's lovemaking. Even the use of the word "voluntad" in this instance telegraphs a radically different sensibility, as if the fact of loving were somehow a choice that one makes. This interpretation fits well with the sense of absolute conviction that inhabits the rest of the speech: Unlike Fenisa, Marcia asserts an unprecedented degree of control over her will even to the point of defying that formidable enemy against whom, as Cervantes remarks, "es menester fuerzas divinas para vencer las suyas humanas."[20]

Without doubt, such an interpretation of Marcia's selflessness in this scene owes a lot to the tradition of ideal friendship and, in this sense, her relationship with Laura may be said to fit within the long tradition of writing perfect friendship. Nevertheless, in contrast with that tradition, the budding relationship that María de Zayas posits here between Marcia and Laura is already marred by the conflict between the two women that is also the point of its inception, a circumstance that would be completely out of place in a conventional story of ideal friendship. Where the typical tale of two friends invariably begins with the harmony between two individuals whose moral purity is guaranteed by narrative situations in which the distinctions between good and evil are always brightly illuminated, the largely accidental friendship between Marcia and Laura owes its very existence to the fact of moral complexity. Or, to consider this notion from a slightly different perspective, the fact that their friendship begins with an act of confession already underscores the problematic nature of their relationship; in effect, they have morally significant secrets from one another that must first be revealed and then finally assuaged through a commitment to do the right thing in the future. Certainly, Marcia's culpability is mitigated by her ignorance of Liseo's previous involvement with Laura. However, from the perspective of the formal requirements of the tale of two friends, the mere fact of moral complexity is sufficient to let the audience know that this is not a typical story of ideal friendship.

The significance of this distinction, however, is not merely a matter of plotting. Rather, the moral complexity that attends the founding of this new friendship between Marcia and Laura reflects the novel poetics that underlies their relationship. In more traditional narratives of Aristotelian perfect friendship, there is an inevitable impulse toward the allegorical so that the idealized figure of the perfect friend tends to suppress interest in the details of storytelling in favor of an abstract exemplarity of dubious practical import. Moral clarity, in this context, is a reflection of an *a priori* commitment to philosophical ideals that tend to script the narrative from beneath the surface of the plot. In contrast, the conflict between Laura and Marcia derives from poetic principles of representational verisimilitude that, at least initially, inform their construction as literary personae. In this view, moral complexity in Zayas's text is reflective of an underlying commitment to capturing, at least to some degree, the moral complexity of the world.

This fundamentally aesthetic distinction helps to clarify another important area of apparent similarity between Zayas and her predecessors in the tale of two friends tradition. The notion of choosing one's friends has a prestigious classical pedigree and constitutes one of the common features of nearly all narratives of perfect friendship. However, in the classical view, this sense of unfettered volition must finally be read, as I have argued previously in this study, as an extension of the categorical idealization of the Aristotelian perfect friend. By definition, that Aristotelian concept only functions to the extent that the perfect friend may be said to possess absolute free will, lest the friendship itself become subordinated to some other secondary interest. In contrast, Marcia's expression of her will to sacrifice her interest in Liseo to Laura's pre-existing and therefore more compelling claims must be judged against the very different expectations of a poetics that embraces the flawed practical reality of everyday life. Examined from this perspective, Marcia's vigorous profession of her subjective autonomy is revealed as more meaningful—especially if analyzed in terms of the discourse of exemplarity—but also more problematic, since declarations of the will, in the context of a poetics of verisimilitude, are more often than not contaminated by the pressures of contingent circumstances.

Mercedes Maroto Camino notes that much of María de Zayas's play is set in "an interior feminine space made public." With this choice, "Zayas literally turns the theatrical space inward by making it a domestic, interior space where women dominate and control the action."[21] This observation highlights the peculiar novelty of Zayas's engagement with the tradition of perfect friendship, the way in which she may be said to redirect the public milieu of the theater toward a new and unprecedented interest in the discourse of personal intimacy.[22] At the same time, however, this formulation also reveals the inherent limitations of this new poetics. There is, in the end, a fundamental tension between the play's representation of the new private friendship between Marcia and Laura and the broader context of theatrical representation. Thus, even as Laura's confession and Marcia's selfless affirmation of friendship foreground this emerging discourse of personal intimacy, the scene's participation in the spectacle of the theater can never be fully effaced. Indeed, contemplated from the perspective of theatrical form, a pure retreat to the private space of personal intimacy is unsustainable, an observation that finds confirmation in the third act in which the *comedia*'s hybrid poetics shifts back toward the hyperbolic moralism that so frequently signals the drive to a happy ending.

At this point, the figure of Fenisa asserts herself once again, the moral reductionism that guarantees her role as the incorrigible bad friend revealing its larger structural purpose: The negative exemplar of bad friendship pulls the play's other friends—most notably Marcia and Laura—back into the universe of categorical abstractions; under Fenisa's tutelage these two women cede their affinity with the experience of everyday life to the structural demands of a moral abstraction—that of the "good" friend. Thus, even as Zayas initially inverts the gendered basis of the traditional tale of two friends and even as she opens a space for a new, modern understanding of the poetics of friendship, her play's final act nevertheless withdraws much of its earlier promise of something radically new in favor of a reconstitution of the arguably more powerful affinity between dramatic hyperbole, moral reductionism, and the problematic exemplarity of the traditional tale of two friends.

Signs of this shift back to a more conventional theatrical poetics abound in the third act. It is evident in the hackneyed lovemaking between Gerardo and Marcia in the act's opening scene, presumably in anticipation of the happy ending that awaits all the play's "good" friends. It is visible in the increasingly amplified depiction of Fenisa's extravagant desire to love all men and her repudiation by nearly all the other characters in the play. And finally, it is on display in contorted plotting that seems designed—as if by reverse engineering—to bring the storyline back into compliance with the expectations of the narrative tradition of writing perfect friendship.

The first two items above arguably set the stage for the third. The renewed courtship between Marcia and Gerard serves as confirmation of Marcia's commitment to yield to Laura's previous claims over Liseo. Here, however, what begins as a robust assertion of individual autonomy in a murky context of moral conflict is now reconstituted in the conventionalized language of courtly love, that is, in a discourse that necessarily undermines Marcia's claim to subjective independence. In place of an earlier appeal to a poetics of verisimilitude that aspires to capture the idiosyncrasies of the particular circumstances of the friendship between Marcia and Laura, the play reverts to expansive displays of dramatic hyperbole that reduce Marcia to the theatrical stock character of the besotted lover:

Marcia: Para sólo mirarte / quisiera de Argos los volantes ojos.
Gerardo: Yo para regalarte / y darte de riquezas mil despojos, / ya que tal bien poseo, / que el oro fuera igual a mi deseo.
Marcia: Pues yo ser sol quisiera / para darte los rayos de mi esfera, / de todo ser señora / para hacerte de todo rico dueño, / por recrearte aurora.
Gerardo: Yo para darte gusto mi fe empeño, / dulce amor, que quisiera / ser la fértil y hermosa primavera, / tierra para tenerte / y cielo para siempre poseerte.[23]

[Marcia: Let me have the flying eyes of Argos only to see you.
Gerardo: Oh that gold were equal to my desire so that I might give you a thousand spoils of wealth.
Marcia: Well, I would wish to be the sun so that I might give you the rays from my orb and be the mistress of the whole world in order to make you the owner of it all, transforming you into the dawn.
Gerardo: I pledge my faith to please you, my sweet love, that I would wish to be the fertile and beautiful springtime, the earth to hold you and the heavens to possess you always.]

The metaphorical excess of this final exchange, in exalting and idealizing Marcia and Gerardo's renewed lovemaking, necessarily empties it of any credible claim to verisimilitude. With their self-depiction alternatively as Argos, "the sun," the "fertile and beautiful springtime," the "earth ... and the heavens," Marcia and Gerardo essentially unmoor their relationship from any association with the practical circumstances of living in the world.[24] Indeed, to the extent that his love remains at all tethered to the experience of everyday life, that connection is limited to the superficial association between visual perception and desire captured in Marcia's reference to Argos: "Para sólo mirarte / quisiera de Argos los volantes ojos." There is a subtext to this metaphor that hints at a critique of this new love as merely another version of what was already observed in the opening scene in which the "bad" friend Fenisa falls in love with Liseo based on a single encounter with his visual representation.

As a complement to Marcia and Gerardo's overstated embrace of their renewed love, Fenisa also emerges in the final act to fulfill her role as the quintessentially "bad" friend. In keeping with the spectacularly abstract mode of her representation, her identity at the end of the play is inextricably linked with her growing public reputation and, more specifically, with the fact of her repudiation by nearly every other character in the play. Significantly, the unanimity of that condemnation makes no distinction between action and identity. With nearly all the other characters on stage, Marcia announces Fenisa's culpability to the assembled cast: "Las amigas desleales / y que hacen estas tretas / pocos son estos castigos [For disloyal friends that engage in such ruses, this is indeed small punishment]."[25] A reminder of the play's primary interest in friendship, Marcia's words transform the act of betrayal into the essential defining characteristic of Fenisa's identity; she becomes from this moment on the "amiga desleal," as Cervantes might describe it, "por antonomasia." In this way, she confirms her status as the embodiment of an abstraction, her reduction to what is finally a singular attribute beyond which no other claims about her identity may be made. She becomes, in other words, the antithesis of the conventional perfect friend, evincing a negative exemplarity of no practical bearing on the real lives of the play's audience.

Taken together, the renewed emphasis on Fenisa's categorical role as the "bad" friend and Marcia's sublimation into the rarefied discourse of Renaissance courtly love are symptomatic of a significant realignment in the play's poetic priorities. Nowhere is this realignment more evident than in the convoluted plotting of the final act. Through a series of largely inexplicable twists and turns, the play works its way back into conformity with the central defining elements of the long narrative tradition of writing perfect friendship. Beyond the theatrical preoccupation with poetic justice and the correct attribution of husbands and wives, the final scenes of *La traición en la amistad* demonstrate a particular interest in dramatizing the narrative requirement of self-sacrifice in the name of friendship, as Marcia works explicitly to restore Laura's claims over Liseo. In fact, much of the clunky plotting of the final act may be explained in terms of this deeper structural logic.

Consider, as a point of departure, the long balcony scene in which Laura pretends to be Marcia in an extended dialogue with Liseo—with Marcia in attendance playing the supporting role of Belisa. The staging evokes the kind of ritualistic lovemaking that is a staple of the literature of the period as Liseo presents himself beneath Marcia's window as a supplicant to his beloved. Yet the scene arguably makes little sense in terms of the play's overall plotting. Liseo argues his case as Marcia's suitor, but Laura-speaking-as-Marcia denounces Liseo's dalliances with Fenisa and dismisses him as a duplicitous traitor. Despite her rejection, however, Liseo, who believes that Laura has taken refuge in the religious vocation of a convent, is not deterred in his pursuit of his new love-interest and, if anything, the rebuff he experiences in this scene spurs him on to even greater amorous fervor. The economy of lovers is thus largely unchanged by the end of this long scene.

Viewed as a reflection on the discourse of perfect friendship, however, the scene reveals a very different aspect. First, there is the ruse by which Laura takes on Marcia's identity, a gesture that in its seeming superfluity points to its symbolic function within the very different structural logic of the tradition of writing perfect friendship: The confusion between the two women gives dramatic form to the ancient notion of the friend as an *alter ego*, while the conspicuous placement of Liseo at the base of the window under the gaze of both Marcia and Laura evokes in spatial terms the love triangle that lies at the heart of nearly every narrative of perfect friendship. In this way, what registers at the level of plot as confusion signifies in visual terms a reanimation of the play's interest in providing dramatic form for a much more traditional narrative of Aristotelian friendship.[26]

Such a reading is bolstered in a somewhat different manner at the end of the scene. After Laura (still playing the role of Marcia) exits, Marcia (still playing the role of her cousin Belisa) steps in to offer Liseo a solution to his problems: She agrees to intercede on Liseo's behalf in his pursuit of the elusive Marcia if only he will agree to sign a statement promising marriage:

> Promete ser su esposo / y amansarás su rostro desdeñoso, / en un papel firmado / en que diga, "Prometo yo, Liseo, / por dejar confirmado / con mi amor y firmeza mi deseo, / ser, señora, tu esposo, / pena de que me llamen alevoso," / con que podré segura / hacer por ti lo que amor procura.[27]

> [Promise to be her husband and you will tame her scornful countenance, in a signed letter that says, "I, Liseo, in confirmation of my love and strong desire, promise to be, *señora*, your husband, under pain of being called treacherous," and with this I will be able to make certain for you that to which your love aspires.]

Later in the third act, Liseo hands over the requested document to the real Belisa, who upon his departure announces the fulfillment of the *engaño* by which Liseo will be forced—"a tu pesar"—to acknowledge his marriage to Laura.[28] It is then only a matter of waiting for Laura to reappear on stage with the letter in hand, at which point Liseo meekly confesses his authorship of the missive: ". . . aunque negarla quiera, / es Belisa buen testigo, / pues ella me mandó hacerla [. . . although I would wish to deny it, Belisa is an apt witness for she made me write it]."[29]

Measured against any standard of verisimilitude, Marcia's ruse is deeply unsatisfying. That Liseo would omit to mention the name of his beloved—i.e. Marcia—in his original letter and then fail to contest the itinerary by which it suddenly materializes in Laura's possession defies credulity. Beyond the rather forced plotting, however, the deeper problem lies in the absolute denial of Liseo's subjective autonomy. Belisa's triumphant claim that Liseo will recognize Laura as his wife "a tu pesar" hints at this difficulty; at no point does she even contemplate the possibility that Liseo might resist such an attempt to push him into an unwanted marriage. Even more striking is Liseo's utter passivity in the face of Laura's claim to be the intended recipient. Indeed, the entire scene only works to the extent that Liseo abandons his will to that of the women around him.[30]

As with the window scene, however, the awkward plotting that leads to Liseo's passive acceptance of his marriage to Laura reveals Zayas's continued interest in the long narrative tradition of writing perfect friendship. For one thing, Marcia's direct intervention here to restore to Laura her rightful husband, in direct opposition to her own amorous inclinations, recalls the expansive gestures of self-sacrifice that constitute a defining element of that tradition. The legalistic language of the letter only serves to underscore this point as the emotional subtext of the entire play is suspended in the interest of the practical commitments of ideal friendship and marriage, both of which are revealed as essentially contractual obligations that fulfill the demands of social propriety and, finally, literary form. The "trick" that entraps Liseo in a marriage commitment to Laura is the formal equivalent of the deception by which Sofronia unknowingly consummates her marriage to Tito. And like Sofronia, Liseo's passivity is finally revealed not as some kind of defect in his character but rather as a symptom of his singular purpose: He exists at this point in the play only to serve as the means to Marcia's fulfillment of her role as the selfless friend.

From here on, the play veers toward an awkward formalism that signals a retreat to generic expectations that are typical of early modern Spanish theater from this period. The "good" friends in the play—Marcia, Laura, and Belisa—are all rewarded with marriage while the "bad" friend is literally ostracized from the social milieu of the play to be offered, in what Catherine Larson describes as a "metaphorical public branding," to the men in the audience—"Si alguno la quiere, avise / para que su casa sepa."[31] The final fate of each character—and here Zayas again focuses almost exclusively on the women in the play—explicitly fuses poetics with morality, with happy and unhappy endings meted out accordingly. The play thus re-establishes the primacy of grand theatrical gestures, simplified ethics, and hyperbolic rhetoric over representational verisimilitude, even as it insists, in a revelation of the deeply conflicted nature of early modern exemplarity, that the "historia" just witnessed is "tan verdadera / que no ha un año que en la corte / sucedió como se cuenta [so true that it has not even been a year since these events occurred in the court as recounted here]."[32]

The ludicrous claim that what has just played out on stage is a true story suffers from the same internal logical conflict that finally leads to Cervantes's rejection of the tale of two friends paradigm in *Don Quixote*. Unlike Cervantes's own playful engagement with the epistemological categories of truth and fiction, however, María de Zayas's play never quite reaches a level of ironic awareness that would fully recognize the intrinsic conflict between exaggerated claims to exemplarity and representational verisimilitude. Such awareness never arrives not because of a lack of poetic sophistication but rather, quite the opposite, because of a recognition that the fundamental theatrical trope of audience identification is itself constructed on the basis of an inclination toward self-deception. The facile moral judgment passed on Fenisa and the three "good" friends in Zayas's play finally reflects a need to cater to the audience's sense of moral superiority. Claims to the truth of the story only feed that self-indulgent whim, encouraging each spectator to an inflated sense of righteousness.[33]

In the end, moral exemplarity and ideal friendship are domesticated in *La traición en la amistad* in what constitutes a fundamental departure from the Aristotelian ideal. Where the Aristotelian tradition—and its narrative expression in friends like Tito and Gisippo—posits ideal friendship as something distinctly uncommon, even divinely inspired, the final scenes of *La traición en la amistad* project the possibility of idealism as a matter of moral virtue to which all may aspire. By positing an exemplarity that flatters the audience into the false belief in easily attained but nevertheless ideal standards of morality, the play brings the allure of sweeping hyperbolic statements about human experience to a level that would seem accessible to all. Ideal friendship, so rigidly defended as the privileged domain of the few in the classical tradition, is seemingly made available to the many.

As a response to the problem of exemplarity in the narrative tradition of ideal friendship, Zayas uses the fiction of identification with the characters on stage—an attenuated version of the illusion that breaks down the fourth wall and transforms those characters into part of the audience's real-world experience—to mend the rupture between the public claims of ideal friendship—"los dos amigos eran llamados," as Cervantes's narrator puts it—and the private space in which such friendships necessarily exist by virtue of their superior, even divine nature. In fact, perfect friendship is no more accessible to the seventeenth-century theatergoer than it is to the solitary reader of Boccaccio in the past or the present. Yet Zayas's *comedia*, with its invitation to transcend the limitations of reality while simultaneously pursuing the illusion of representational verisimilitude, effaces that fundamental distinction between the lived experience of personal intimacy and the long tradition of idealized friendship.

The greater significance of María de Zayas's play for a study of early modern representations of friendship, however, lies in the poetic implications of her incisive reordering of the gendered logic of the tale of two friends tradition. In writing a play about female friendship, Zayas not only challenges the conventions of friendship as an exclusively male domain, she opens a space within the hyperbolic excess of theatrical performance for private intimacy conceived as mutual understanding from within the concrete circumstances of everyday life. Read in this way, the friendship that emerges between Marcia and Laura becomes all the more meaningful for its contextualization within the oppressive constraints of the Spanish early modern honor code. For it is precisely because they recognize each other as women living *in* the world—as opposed to beyond it—that Zayas's protagonists are able to claim a sense of mutual understanding that is, in the modern sense of the word, personal.

Notes

1. As Hegstrom, *La tración en la Amistad*, p. 16, notes, there is some uncertainty as to when *La traición en la amistad* was written: "Melloni believes, based on some verses of the play, that it was written between 1618 and 1620. Yet in what may be a reference to *La traición*, Pérez de Montalbán mentions that Zayas had a finished *comedia* in 1632. Based on Montalbán's wording, Paun de García deduces that Zayas must have finished the play closer to 1632 than Melloni proposes."
2. Many critics have noted that there is currently no evidence that *La traición en la amistad* was ever performed. See for example Bayliss, "Feminism and María de Zayas's Exemplary Comedy," pp. 2–3.
3. The notion of Fenisa as a female Don Juan—or "Doña Juana" as Stroud describes her in "Love, Friendship, and Deceit in *La traición en la amistad*," p. 543—is well established. See also, Vollendorf, "Desire Unbound: Women's Theater of Spain's Golden Age," pp. 277–8. Bayliss, "Feminism and María de Zayas's Exemplary Comedy," p. 9, citing the antecedents of Gwyn Campbell, Catherine Larson, and Stroud, notes how all three critics "have pointed to Fenisa as a feminized Don Juan, reading her performance as a form of gender-bending negative exemplarity . . ." For a more extensive comparison of *La traición en la amistad* with Tirso de Molina's *El burlador de Sevilla*, see Larson, "Gender, Reading, and Intertextuality," pp. 129–38. Hegstrom, *La traición en la amistad*, pp. 16–19, who describes Fenisa as a

"mujer varonil," also explores the similarities between Zayas's antagonist and Tirso's Don Juan in the introduction to her modern English-language edition of the play.
4. In his analysis of María de Zayas's *comedia*, Bayliss, "Feminism and María de Zayas's Exemplary Comedy," p. 6, focuses primarily on how a full appreciation of genre impacts feminist readings of the play: "I would argue that the feminist exemplarity we have found encoded in Zayas's *novelas* has impacted our reception of *La traición en la amistad* in a way that has displaced critical focus on the codes and social context of seventeenth-century Spanish theater."
5. María de Zayas, *La traición en la amistad*, pp. 28–9. English translations are mine. Contextualized appropriately, this scene anticipates the play's engagement with Fenisa as the embodiment of unbridled desire as an end in itself. The trope of love at first sight harks back to a Platonic meeting of souls through the window of the eyes, that is, to an understanding of love that is inextricably linked to the lover's essential being, however defined. See especially Plato, *Phaedrus*, 255b–d. In contrast, Fenisa falls in love with a pictorial representation of Liseo, that is, with the pure surface of a visual image that, by definition, lacks a soul.
6. María de Zayas, *La traición en la amistad*, p. 29.
7. Ibid. p. 29.
8. Of the male friends examined so far in this study, only Cervantes's Lotario from "El curioso impertinente" violates this confessional imperative, an observation that underscores the interpolated story's formal disruptiveness.
9. Zayas, *La traición en la amistad*, p. 30.
10. There is a meaningful similarity between Fenisa's logic here and Lotario's reasoning in his attempt to dissuade Anselmo from his ill-omened project to test Camila's fidelity. Read in the light of my analysis here, the arguments that Lotario marshals to dissuade Anselmo from his plan to test his wife may be said to share a similar aesthetic sensibility, grounded as they are in a practical assessment of the moral conventions of seventeenth-century Spanish society.
11. Boyle, *Unruly Women*, p. 67, provides a good sense of the larger implications of Fenisa's claim to free will: "Radically departing from the idealized image of women proposed by the Renaissance humanist tradition, Fenisa acts according to her own free will, and aggressively pursues a number of men, encouraging others to follow her example, ignoring the wishes of her female friends, and using deception 'the wrong way' by prioritizing personal desire without respect to women's community. In doing so, she exposes a double standard, not only between men and women, but also among women."
12. Boyle, *Unruly Women*, p. 68.
13. Zayas, *La traición en la amistad*, p. 41.
14. Bayliss, "Feminism and María de Zayas's Exemplary Comedy," p. 9, identifies a long critical tradition that has viewed Fenisa in terms of "negative exemplarity": "Gwyn Campbell, Matthew Stroud, Catherine Larson,

and others have pointed to Fenisa as a feminized Don Juan, reading her performance as a form of gender-bending negative exemplarity . . ." What arguably distinguishes my analysis here from this tradition is a particular emphasis on Fenisa's role in upending the traditional notion of the Aristotelian perfect friend.
15. Zayas, *La traición en la amistad*, p. 60.
16. Ibid. p. 61.
17. Ibid. p. 61.
18. Ibid. pp. 61–2.
19. Commenting on this passage, Larson, "Gender, Reading, and Intertextuality," p. 132, writes, "A sense of sisterly solidarity joins with a moral consideration of what is right, leading these female characters to sacrifice personal satisfaction for the support and fellowship of other women. To accomplish their goals, the women metamorphose from passive objects to active subjects; they begin to act with authority, and they consequently assume greater control and power over the male suitors of the play." See also n. 30 below.
20. The quote from Cervantes, of course, comes from "El curioso impertinente" and, in this sense, serves as a reminder of how far María de Zayas has departed from the more traditional representation of love within the tale of two friends tradition.
21. Maroto Camino, "María de Zayas and Ana Caro," p. 9.
22. Contextualizing the play in sociopolitical terms, Gorfkle, "Female Communities, Female Friendships and Social Control," p. 618, affirms Zayas's interest in representations of personal intimacy: "The spectator becomes engaged with the communal model as she is invited to peer into the intimate circle of the group, and respond to its values, those of reason and good counsel . . . In a calculated, reflective and rational gesture, Marcia pushes Liseo out of her soul and Gerardo back in . . . Marcia forfeits desire to the demands of society. Her gesture is ostensibly conservative, since by relinquishing her passions, she submits to the ideological ends prescribed by her culture for the social control of women." Significantly, Gorfkle identifies intimacy with a "communal model" that operates within the norms of the larger social context.
23. Zayas, *La traición en la amistad*, p. 95.
24. Boyle, *Unruly Women*, p. 73, argues that Marcia accepts the "unloved" Gerardo in order to conform with expected social norms: "And as Marcia comes to understand in act 3, she must take Gerardo as her husband for the sake of protecting the norms of the community." Similarly, Hegstrom, *La traición en la amistad*, p. 17, writing about a more general sense of "gender solidarity when questions of honor are concerned" among the play's "good" friends, goes on to argue that "love is clearly secondary to the recuperation of lost honor for these women characters." And yet, as my analysis of the passage reproduced here indicates, the language that Marcia uses in her dialogue with Gerardo displays a level of rhetorical excess that far exceeds what one might expect were her relationship with

her long-suffering suitor based exclusively on social necessity or the need to preserve her honor. The point, however, is not to question or affirm the sincerity of Marcia's feelings for her future husband, but rather to recognize how the scene's hyperbolic poetics necessarily undermines any meaningful practical assessment of her motives.
25. Zayas, *La traición en la amistad*, p. 128.
26. This sense of the two women's shared identity is enhanced by the content of Laura's intervention: read out of context, her complaint against Liseo's unfaithfulness to Marcia just as easily describes her own predicament as Liseo's spurned lover.
27. Zayas, *La traición en la amistad*, p. 100.
28. Ibid. pp. 106–7.
29. Ibid. p. 126.
30. Hegstrom, *La traición en la amistad*, p. 20, notes the passivity of all three of the primary male characters by the play's end, which she contrasts with the more active role taken by the women in the play: ". . . if in the beginning most of the male characters (Juan and Liseo) control their female partners through deception and only Gerardo passively accepts a feminine, devoted stance, all three of these male characters find themselves controlled by their female counterparts at the end of the comedy. Zayas restores order in *La traición* by the imposition of feminine active dominance at the conclusion of the play."
31. Zayas, *La traición en la amistad*, p. 128. Larson, "Gender, Reading, and Intertextuality," p. 133. Soufas, *Dramas of Distinction: A Study of Plays by Golden Age Women*, p. 145, offers a markedly different reading of the play's ending that preserves Fenisa's role as the embodiment of a radical expression of free will: "There is no conventional social space for Fenisa to occupy; she has been excluded by both the female and male members of her depicted society. Yet even though she both fails in her attempt to prolong indefinitely her amorous games and also loses Liseo, she does maintain her freedom after all the other women are matched with their respective husbands. She thus escapes patriarchal control and enclosure . . ."
32. Zayas, *La traición en la amistad*, p. 128. Bayliss, "Feminism and María de Zayas's Exemplary Comedy," p. 10, writes persuasively about how generic expectations influence reactions to the play's ending. Contrasting *La traición en la amistad* against what he describes as Zayas's "novelistic feminism" in her prose fiction, he argues that "we run the risk of applying similar expectations to her comedy; to this I would attribute the dissatisfaction of some critics, such as Soufas and Stroud, with the play's resolution, in which Liseo is duped into marrying Laura in order to restore the honor that his seduction and subsequent abandonment had taken from her. Would a contemporary audience in the habit of seeing popular comedies that end with betrothal, even an exclusively female audience, have been so dissatisfied? Is the play's conclusion a concession of some sort to the aesthetically and ideologically determined conventions of the *comedia*?"

33. It must be emphasized that this sense of moral self-righteousness, as is frequently the case with the *comedia*, depends on the use of hyperbole in the service of concrete, historically determined social norms, an observation that helps to explain, at least in part, the facile moral logic that sorts out the good and bad actors at the end of the play. What it means to interrogate the ending in ways that exceed the ideological limits of the conventional *comedia* is, perhaps, less clear. As Larson, "Gender, Reading, and Intertextuality," p. 133, observes, "It could further be argued that in order to establish their authority and control, the women have only repeated the stereotypically negative female behaviors of manipulation and deceit, and that the female characters of Zayas's play ultimately merely reiterate the male gaze, the representations of women as seen by men. Clearly, the multiple marriages that take place at the end of the comedy leave the reader/spectator with questions regarding the play beyond the ending. How will these independent women, who controlled their men so well in the course of this play, handle their new roles as married women? How will Laura's marriage turn out, given that she is marrying a known philanderer who only agrees to marry her after having been tricked—and who has previously stated, 'sus penas estimo en nada . . .'?" My analysis here does not pretend to answer such questions except to note their dependence on a heightened sense of verisimilitude that is perhaps at odds with the hyperbolic abstraction of the play's resolution of all dramatic and social conflicts. Or to put this idea another way, the play ends the way that it does—as do many plays from the period—precisely because it has little interest in addressing the kind of questions that Larson raises.

Chapter 6

Guzmán de Alfarache's "Otro yo"[1]

Just before jumping to his death in a fit of madness late in the second part of Mateo Alemán's picaresque novel, Guzmán de Alfarache's companion Sayavedra calls out in his delirium: "¡Yo soy la sombra de Guzmán de Alfarache! Su sombra soy, que voy por el mundo [I am the shadow of Guzmán de Alfarache! I am his shadow that travels through the world]."[2] Critics of *Guzmán de Alfarache* tend to identify the figure of Sayavedra with Juan Martí, the author of an apocryphal second part to Alemán's highly successful narrative, who wrote under the pseudonym Mateo Luján de Sayavedra.[3] As Edward Friedman notes, the "killing off" of Sayavedra constitutes an "ingenious, calculated, and effectively—and hyperbolically—vindictive" response to Martí's plagiarism.[4] Benito Brancaforte even describes the destruction of Sayavedra as a kind of literary necessity.[5] Considering the enormous popularity of Martí's work—"selling more copies than Alemán's sequel"—one can perhaps forgive Alemán the small consolation of this symbolic destruction of his rival.[6]

This traditional reading of Sayavedra as the plagiarist's *alter ego* does not, however, exhaust the interpretative potential of this important episode in the narrative. In particular, while this reading illuminates the significant external forces at work in Alemán's text, it completely overlooks the internal context for Sayavedra's emergence into the narrative: The entire episode is framed as a meditation on the nature of friendship in the picaresque, first through an extensive theoretical discussion of the topic, and then, with the appearance of Sayavedra himself, through a kind of practical case study. From this other perspective, Sayavedra's identification with Guzmán at the moment of his death constitutes a symbolic deformation of the Aristotelian ideal of the friend as a second self as well as the narrative's final verdict on the possibility of friendship in the picaresque.[7] In killing off Sayavedra, the narrative dramatically terminates the text's one significant experiment with this highest order of friendship.

The groundwork for this other interpretation is prepared by Guzmán himself in his extensive musings on friendship immediately prior to Sayavedra's introduction into the narrative. The influence of classical models is evident from the outset, as Guzmán argues that true friends are like quicksilver and gold that when mixed into a single substance may only be separated by the "fire" of death: "tal el verdadero amigo, hecho ya otro él, nada pueda ser parte para que aquella unión se deshaga, sino con sólo el fuego de la muerte sola [such is the true friend, rendered a second self, that nothing can unmake this union, only with the fire of death]."[8] Even here, however, the pressures of the picaresque quickly rise up to the surface and Guzmán's exaltation of true friendship soon gives way to a lament on the practical difficulties of finding such relationships: "En todos cuantos traté, fueron pocos los que hallé que no caminasen al norte de su interese proprio y al paso de su gusto, con deseo de engañar, sin amistad que lo fuese, sin caridad, sin verdad ni vergüenza . . . Siempre me dejaron el corazón amargo [Among all those that I met, there were few whom I found who did not follow their own self-interest and pleasure, with a desire to deceive, without true friendship, without charity, without truth or shame . . . They always left me with a bitter heart]."[9] Reflecting the "soledad" that José Antonio Maravall defines as a core principle of picaresque existence, Guzmán's contemplation of his own experiences leads to the pessimistic recognition of the difficulties of this kind of friendship in a world populated by tricksters, thieves, and charlatans.[10] More to the point here, these comments at the beginning help set the expectations for what will follow, namely, a tale of friendship that ultimately goes bad.

Guzmán's grudging acknowledgment of self-interest as the only basis for interpersonal relations in the picaresque implies a radical reordering of the classical schema for friendship in which utilitarianism is the mark of an inferior form of companionship.[11] While a practical necessity at times, these inferior relationships are tolerable because they do not impede the final goal of a higher, selfless form of perfect friendship. Guzmán's "bitter heart," the result of his own personal disappointment with friendship, on the other hand, signals an emotional capitulation before the collapse of the ideal. Gone is the classical optimism that might allow one to suffer false friendships born of necessity, here replaced with despair in the face of the realization that one's second self may not, in fact, exist.

With the introduction of Sayavedra in the subsequent chapters, however, the narrative moves beyond the abject pessimism of Guzmán's abstract musing and provides the reader with a dramatic representation of a new model for picaresque friendship based on shared stories, common experiences, and above all self-identification. The narrative basis of Guzmán's one significant attempt at friendship reflects a break with the hierarchy of Aristotelian categories and, more importantly, a clear rupture with the tale of two friends tradition that has informed—in one way or another—every work examined in this study so far. In what is perhaps the most significant departure for the archetypal narrative of perfect friendship, Alemán allows the reader to witness Guzmán's one attempt at true friendship as it comes into being. Where the underlying friendship between such exemplary friends as Tito and Gisippo is presented as a categorical absolute, the more purely discursive model for personal intimacy on display in the *Guzmán* rewrites the Aristotelian notion of the friend as a second self, replacing the categorical ideal with a dynamic, inherently modern vision of friendship as a complex emotional relationship subject to continuous renegotiation and at constant risk of dissolution. Understood in this way, Sayavedra's untimely end comes to reflect less the impossibility of picaresque friendship than its inherent fragility. Perhaps more than in any other genre of the period, the ruthless deceptiveness of picaresque existence in the public sphere relentlessly threatens to undermine the benevolent impulses that make stories of private friendship possible.

Throughout the chapters that describe Guzmán's relationship with Sayavedra, the novel never strays far from the central problem of friendship in a fictional world populated by compulsive liars. This relationship begins auspiciously enough after Sayavedra intervenes to defend the outnumbered Guzmán in a street brawl. At this point, however, the narrative displays little interest in the interpersonal dimension of this new association. Sayavedra eventually informs Guzmán of the most superficial details of his own background, and then provides the impetus for the latter's departure from Rome, suggesting that in this way he might escape his present difficulties. Acceding to Sayavedra's advice, Guzmán sends most of his possessions ahead of him to Florence. Shortly thereafter, however, Sayavedra inexplicably disappears and a few pages later the reader learns that Guzmán's new acquaintance, acting in league with a criminal gang, has in fact conspired to steal all of his belongings.[12]

Yet contrary to what one might expect, this initial act of betrayal quickly gives way to a reconciliation between the two picaros. When Sayavedra is detained by the authorities for his presumed involvement in the plot, Guzmán refuses to denounce him, and, in a later chapter, when the two meet again by chance, he even expresses compassion for his companion's predicament in one of the most emotional scenes of the entire novel:

No me bastó el ánimo, en conociéndolo, a dejar de compadecerme dél y saludarlo, poniendo los ojos, no en el mal que me hizo, sino en el daño de que alguna vez me libró, conociendo por de más precio el bien, que allí entonces dél recibí, que pudo importar lo que me llevó ... No pude resistirme sin hablarle con amor ni él de recebirme con lágrimas, que vertiéndolas por todo el rostro se vino a mis pies, abrazándose con el estribo y pidiéndome perdón de su yerro, dándome gracias de que nunca, estando preso, lo quise acusar y satisfaciones de no haberme visitado luego que salió de la cárcel.[13]

[Upon recognizing him, I didn't have the heart not to feel for him and greet him focusing my gaze not on the evil he did to me, but on the injury from which at one point he had liberated me, considering more valuable the good he did then than that which he stole from me ... I couldn't help talking to him with love, nor he from receiving me with tears, and with these flowing all over his face he came to my feet, and embracing my stirrups and asking for forgiveness for his error, and thanking me for never having denounced him when he was detained, he explained to my satisfaction why he didn't visit me upon his release from prison.]

Significantly, this first account of the two picaros' reunion is completely at odds with the general spirit of Guzmán's narrative. Completely ignoring his apparent self-interest, Guzmán's active participation in this spontaneous show of emotion transcends the hardened utilitarianism that characterizes nearly everything else he does in the novel. Clearly moved by his companion's tears, Guzmán's behavior in this scene arguably reveals a desire for interpersonal commiseration that is more typically repressed by the social alienation of the picaro's existence.

Beyond such unexpected displays of emotion, however, the narrative's more pessimistic worldview is never far from the surface. Despite the emotional intensity evoked in the passage above, Guzmán's relationship with Sayavedra quickly falls back into compliance with the rhetorical norms of the picaresque, as Sayavedra's pleading for forgiveness gives way to abject submissiveness: "empero que para en cuenta y parte de pago de su deuda quería como un esclavo servirme toda su vida [however, in order to pay the bill of his debt he wanted to serve me all my life like a slave]."[14] Remarkably, Guzmán fails to register the troubling nature of Sayavedra's pledge and instead responds to his new companion according to the instrumentalist logic that is far more typical of the genre: "Parecióme que, si de alguno quisiera servirme, habiendo pocos mozos buenos, que aqueste sería menos malo ... pues dél sabía ya ser necesario guardarme y con otro, pareciéndome fiel, me pudiera descuidar y dejarme a la luna [It seemed to me that if someone wanted to serve me, there being so few good young men, that this one would be the least bad ... for I already knew that I needed to protect myself from him, and with someone else, seeming to be faithful, I might not take care, and leave myself on the moon]."[15] From a classical point of view, Guzmán's characterization of his relationship with Sayavedra at this point already recognizes the futility of the higher forms of friendship in the picaresque world; in place of the ideal friend as second self, Guzmán settles for the lesser evil of a friend who might be useful if only because—and here the cynicism of the passage reaches its full crescendo—his potential for betrayal has already been exposed.

The reassertion of utilitarianism in Guzmán's final explanation of his reconciliation with Sayavedra highlights the conflicted nature of their relationship. After the emotional intensity of their original reunion, the cold calculating logic of Guzmán's decision to accept Sayavedra into his service sounds forced, highlighting a dissonance in the protagonist's attitude toward his companion that his remarks do little to dissipate. On a formal level, the relationship between the two picaros is indeed extremely hierarchical throughout the rest of their time together. Sayavedra consistently maintains a pronounced formality in his conversations with his new master, and while he does not shy away from offering advice, he always defers to Guzmán in the end. At the same time, however, underneath such formalities, the complicity of the two in the subsequent chapters creates a powerful bond that finds expression in Guzmán's ever-growing confidence in his servant. Through their constant companionship and collusion in all manner of schemes, the two develop a relationship that defies the static categories of classical models for friendship in favor of a fluid, evolving partnership that creates a provisional space of intimacy and trust in a world otherwise defined by trickery and deception.

The conflicted nature of the relationship between Guzmán and Sayavedra is augmented by the narrative's repeated recourse to the classical ideal of the friend as a second self—this despite Guzmán's earlier despair of ever finding such a friend. "Soy un pobre mozo como tú," insists Sayavedra before launching into an extensive account of his own life story. The story that he tells does indeed mirror in important ways the sordid tale of Guzmán's own frustrated ambitions, but, more importantly, the very act of narration itself redefines the relationship between the two picaros, as dramatized in Guzmán's response to his companion's story:

> Decía yo entre mí: Si a este este Sayavedra, como dice, le dejó tan rico su padre, ¿cómo ha dado en ser ladrón y huelga más de andar afrentado, que vivir tenido y respetado? ...
> Luego revolvía sobre mí en su disculpa, diciendo: Saldríase huyendo muchacho, como yo. Representáronme con su relación mis proprios pasos; mas volvía,

diciendo: Ya que todo eso así es, ¿por qué no volvió la hoja, cuando tuvo uso de razón y llegó a ser hombre, haciéndose soldado?

También me respondía en su favor: ¿Y por qué no lo soy yo? Veo la paja en el ojo ajeno y no la viga en el mío.[16]

[I said to myself: "If this Sayavedra, as he says, was left so rich by his father, why has he become a thief, and why does it please him to live offending others rather than to be held in respect?" . . .

Then I turned my thoughts to his defense, saying: "He must have been fleeing as a boy, like me." With his story he portrayed my own steps; but I turned my mind again, saying: "And if all of this is as he says, why didn't he turn the page and use his head, and become a man, enlisting as a soldier?"

And again, I responded to myself in his favor: "And why am I not one? I see the speck in his eye, and not the plank in my own."]

The dramatization of Guzmán's ambivalence in this passage underscores the inherent barriers to commiseration in the picaresque world. Accustomed as he is to distrust the motives of everyone he meets, Guzmán's clear desire to sympathize with his companion's narrative runs up against the practical experience of picaresque deceit and deception, both in his previous dealings with Sayavedra and as a defining characteristic of the genre. From this perspective, the reference to Matthew 7:3 with which the passage ends provides a powerful biblical inflection to Guzmán's earlier lament over the lack of true friends, in this case, through a version of the same mirroring process that defines the classical idea of the friend as a second self. Jesus's admonition in the Sermon on the Mount serves to underscore the key moral problem of compassion that is at the heart of the modern practice of private friendship.

Despite such difficulties, however, the overall tone of the passage is, in fact, optimistic, suggesting the possibility of sympathetic commiseration even in the corrupt world of the picaresque. Echoing Sayavedra's own claim that "I am a poor boy like you," Guzmán returns repeatedly to contemplate the parallels between their two lives, leading him at one point to efface completely the differences between them: "With his story he portrayed my own steps." Here, the unrealistic expectations of the idealized classical model of the friend as a second self, arguably the source of Guzmán's own bitter heart, finds compensation in the possibility of a different mode of identification between friends based on a shared personal narrative.

Guzmán's ambivalence in the passage above effectively dramatizes the process through which his companion's life story is made to fit his own. Unlike the static ideal of classical friendship, Guzmán's identification with his companion's predicament involves an active molding of his self-image to the requirements of a sympathetic reading of Sayavedra's narrative.

The ideal of the friend as a second self is thus reanimated as an act of good will between two very imperfect individuals.

The efficacy of this new model for friendship reflects a more general desire for recognition that might compensate Guzmán's abject social marginalization and the accompanying tendency to obscure any sense of his concrete, individual identity. In this sense, this emphasis on mutual recognition in the passage above suggests an important evolution beyond the view of Alemán's protagonist as either purely "protean"—that is, marked by a never-ending series of mutations—or as the reified object of "a process of typification."[17] Guzmán's ability to identify with his new friend underscores the potential of private friendship as a bulwark against the crushing anonymity of public life in the picaresque.[18] Constructed in opposition to the larger social context, Guzmán's new friendship with Sayavedra provides him, as Johnson notes, "with the opportunity as well as the necessity to demonstrate his own uniqueness."[19]

Finally, the tension between private friendship and public anonymity that emerges in Guzmán's one true friendship also intersects with the poetic structure of the picaresque. I have argued elsewhere that the poetics of the picaresque, with its emphasis on the deceptiveness of experience, involves an essential inversion of the principle of representational verisimilitude.[20] In place of the ideal of an aesthetics that might render the world as it is, the picaresque presents a physical and moral universe in which things are never what they seem. Guzmán's "bitter heart" in the face of false friendships may be understood as one aspect of this fundamental principle of the picaresque. In effect, the failings of Guzmán's friends provide a moral analogue to what is, in the first instance, a problem of poetics. From this perspective, Guzmán's role as sympathetic listener may be taken to involve a reassertion of the optimistic potential inherent in an imitative poetics founded in verisimilitude. In Guzmán's attempt to read his own life story into Sayavedra's autobiography—to literally self-identify with his companion—the narrative implicitly aligns private friendship with a mode of imitation that embraces the ideal of representational transparency based in what is essentially an act of good will on the part of both characters. Or to put this same idea in other terms, it holds out the possibility that Guzmán and Sayavedra may come to truly know each other.

The strong correlation here between the poetics of verisimilitude and the rise of private friendship as an alternative to the abject loneliness of life in the picaresque also throws light onto the underlying structure of a more recognizably modern understanding of friendship. Unlike the classical ideal, the notion of the friend as a second self that emerges in Guzmán's relationship with Sayavedra is grounded in a representational procedure that eschews the very possibility of an idealized teleology such as may be discovered in the *Disciplina clericalis* or the *Decameron*. This is already evident in Guzmán's struggle to come to terms with Sayavedra's story. The product of a self-conscious act of good will, the identification between the two picaros that provides the foundation for their friendship can never be taken for granted but must be constantly reaffirmed in a discursive process whose end marks, as I will show in the discussion that follows, the end of picaresque friendship.

In the sordid world of picaresque fiction, friendship is subject to pressures unknown in the classical discourse on the topic. Where the classical ideal realizes its highest expression in a process of mutual purification involving a rejection of the corrupting influences of everyday life, Guzmán's friendship with Sayavedra cannot escape the pressures of an impoverished material existence on the margins of society. In particular, while Sayavedra does show himself to be Guzmán de Alfarache's one true friend, the proof of his devotion is invariably cast in terms of morally dubious propositions and outright criminal schemes that provide a stark manifestation of what Michel Cavillac describes as "el irreductible divorcio entre la verdad subjetiva del hombre y su experiencia del individuo degradado por la realidad objetiva de las relaciones sociales [the irreducible divorce between man's subjective truth and his experience as an individual degraded by the objective reality of social relations]."[21] Despite the questionable moral foundation of their relationship, however, Sayavedra shows himself to be intensely loyal to his new master, leading Guzmán to ever greater displays of familiarity, from his first casual use of the epithet "amigo" to his final acknowledgment of Sayavedra as his "otro yo." In the inverted logic of the picaresque, solidarity in crime becomes, or so it would seem, the ultimate measure of friendship.

At the same time, the bond that grows between Guzmán and Sayavedra through their various criminal plans helps to delineate a clear barrier between their private relationship and society at large. Unlike Guzmán's abstract musings on friendship in an earlier chapter, this division between private and public life emerges through a series of encounters with other characters who collectively provide the foil against which Guzmán's new friendship comes to claim its privileged status. Three of these minor personages stand out in particular for their representative value: (1) a greedy Milanese merchant; (2) Guzmán's malevolent Genoese uncle; and (3) another would-be friend whose protestations of loyalty are seemingly as sincere as those of Sayavedra himself. Each of these three men helps to delineate the external world against which Guzmán's relationship with Sayavedra is defined. Thus, Guzmán's ruthless scheme to swindle his uncle as payback for earlier mistreatment creates a sharp contrast between the breakdown of the ostensibly natural bonds of family life and the solidarity of his constructed criminal association with Sayavedra. Similarly, Guzmán's collaboration with Sayavedra in an elaborate plan to frame the Milanese merchant may be read metaphorically to represent the clear distinction between their very unique friendship and the irremediable deceptiveness of the larger society. Finally, the appearance in the narrative of the merchant captain and would-be friend, Favelo, exposes the arbitrary nature of friendship in the picaresque and in the process calls into question the very possibility of amicable sincerity. Taken together, these three examples underscore the stunted nature of private life in the picaresque so that Guzmán's special relationship with Sayavedra is finally revealed as the truly unusual case, the exception that confirms the more general rule of cruelty and marginalization that is far more typical of the genre.

In helping to solidify the relationship between Guzmán and his companion, the first encounter with the greedy Milanese merchant plays a formative role in establishing the boundaries between the ruthless competitiveness of public life and the growing solidarity of loyal friendship. Significantly, the episode begins with a scene that quashes the last vestige of Guzmán's former distrust of his friend. Having recently arrived in Milan, Guzmán spies Sayavedra deep in conversation with someone he has never seen before. Later when they reunite for a meal and Sayavedra fails to mention his secret meeting, Guzmán can hardly control his consternation: "Que la sospecha es terrible gusano del corazón [For suspicion is a terrible worm in the heart]."[22] No longer able to contain himself, Guzmán finally confronts Sayavedra about the meeting. In the exchange that follows, Sayavedra's innocence becomes quickly apparent as the unknown man is revealed to be an old friend who seeks Sayavedra's—and later Guzmán's—help in a plot to swindle his master, that is, the greedy merchant who shortly thereafter becomes the central interest of the narrative. While Guzmán does not explicitly acknowledge it, the revelation of Sayavedra's innocence marks a watershed moment in their relationship. From this point on, Guzmán displays nothing but absolute confidence in the loyalty of his friend.

In contrast to the growing bond between Guzmán and Sayavedra, the plan to rob the greedy merchant is represented from the very outset as a contest of wits in which the two parties attempt to outmaneuver each other. As Guzmán himself puts it concisely, "Conformidad teníamos ambos en engañar [We were both intent on deception]."[23] Here, the metaphorical value of the episode comes into view as Guzmán's encounter with the greedy merchant provides a personified condensation of the picaresque social dynamic, a reading of the scene that is only accentuated by his explicit reference to the merchant's dodgy reputation at a key moment in the narrative:

> Eran en mi favor la voz común, las evidencias y experiencias vistas y su mala fama, que concluía, y decían todos: . . . No es nuevo en el bellaco logrero robar haciendas ajenas.[24]

> [In my favor were the common voice, the evidence and witnessed experiences, and his bad reputation, which concluded the affair, and everyone said: . . . "There's nothing new about this crooked swindler trying to steal other people's property."]

The tension in this passage between the merchant's local reputation and the fact that he is never mentioned by name transforms him into a social stereotype; his particular identity matters much less than what he represents to the "voz común," that is, to a public all too familiar with the picaresque discourse of deceit and deception. He embodies, in this sense, the purest expression of the Bakhtinian notion of the character as "ideologue," a "socially significant" representation of an ideologically determined "language" whose particular destiny is of secondary interest.[25] Furthermore, the anonymity of both public opinion and the avaricious merchant provides a powerful contrast with the discursive process through which Guzmán comes to identify Sayavedra's personal narrative with his own. Where the anonymity of social relations in the public sphere reflects an irredeemable condition of otherness, the personal friendship between Guzmán and Sayavedra depends on a process of active self-identification. Where the "voz común" speaks out in loud condemnation, Guzmán listens with quiet sympathy.

The significance of this final distinction becomes palpably clear at the end of the two friends' stay in Milan. Announcing to Sayavedra his plan to travel to Genoa to avenge the cruel treatment he had formerly received from his family there, Guzmán indicates that he and Sayavedra should exchange clothing in order to "desmentir espías [throw off spies]."[26] Sayavedra's hearty embrace of this idea, which goes far beyond the practical requirements of a ruse, underscores the intrinsic force of self-identification in the relationship between the two pícaros:

> Paréceme muy bien, dijo Sayavedra, y digo que quiero heredar el tuyo verdadero, con que poderte imitar y servir. Desde hoy me llamo Guzmán de Alfarache.[27]

> ["This seems very good to me," said Sayavedra, "and I declare that I want to inherit your true name, with which I can imitate and serve you. From today, I will be named Guzmán de Alfarache."]

Moving beyond the more practical considerations that motivate Guzmán's original proposal, Sayavedra parlays a simple picaresque trick into a more authentic sign of his self-identification with his companion. As a response to the anonymity of public social relations—so aptly captured in the previous episode of the Milanese merchant—Sayavedra's claim to Guzmán's name calls attention to the idiosyncratic nature of personal intimacy, while his expressed desire to imitate his companion reminds the reader of the underlying poetic structure of this alternative, arguably more modern mode of friendship. Once again, public deception provides the foundation for private solidarity between these two partners in crime.

The narrative extends this meditation on the underlying poetic structure of personal relationships in Guzmán's fateful meeting with the second key minor character from this section of the novel: his Genoese uncle. Guzmán's own drive for revenge in this episode provides the ostensible motivation for this reunion and recalls his earlier mistreatment by this same family member in the novel's first part. For my purposes here, however, the most striking moment in the episode arises with the uncle's unwitting acknowledgment that he had completely misrecognized his nephew in their previous encounter:

> Sabed, sobrino, que habrá como siete años, poco más o menos, que aquí llegó un mozuelo picarillo, al parecer ladrón o su ayudante . . . diciendo ser . . . mi sobrino. Tal venía y tal sospechamos dél, que, afrentados de su infamia, lo procuramos aventar de la ciudad . . . De la vuelta que le hice dar me acuerdo, que se dejó la cama toda llena de cera de trigo. Ella fue tal como buena, para que con el miedo de otra peor huyese y nos dejase. Y pues, quería engañarnos, me huelgo de lo hecho. Ni a él se le olvidará en su vida el hospedaje . . .²⁸

> ["Nephew, you should know that about seven years ago, more or less, a young picaro came here, looking like a thief or a thief's apprentice and saying that he was my nephew. Such was his appearance and such were our suspicions about him that, affronted by his infamy, we worked to throw him out of the city . . . Of the turn we gave him, I recall that he left his bed full of excrement: that was a good one, and for fear of another worse we hoped he would flee and leave us. In effect, he wanted to deceive us [*engañarnos*], and I'm happy about what was done. Nor will he in all the days of his life forget the lodging he received . . ."]

The uncle here aligns his earlier abuse of Guzmán with his nephew's impoverished outward material appearances: that Guzmán at that time looked "like a thief or a thief's apprentice" provides his uncle with sufficient cause to inflict all manner of suffering in an attempt to drive away an uninvited rogue. Unwilling to verify the claims of his visitor, the uncle presupposes Guzmán's true identity in the trappings of his poverty and, in the process, misrecognizes his own flesh and blood.

Despite the uncle's clear misrecognition of his nephew on a personal level, his assessment of what might be described as Guzmán's public condition is, in fact, quite accurate: Guzmán was and continues to be both a thief and an apprentice to thieves. Viewed from this perspective, the problem of recognition may be said to evince a certain indeterminacy that follows the same public/private divide that was observed previously in Guzmán's encounter with the Milanese merchant. Where his uncle sees only the archetypal criminal, that is, the personification of the social phenomenon of picaresque criminality, Guzmán recognizes in his uncle's words an excerpt from his own life story—"Yo pobre, como fui quien lo había padecido . . . [As I was the poor boy who had suffered it . . .]"[29] In effect, the uncle unwittingly repeats back to Guzmán a version of his own personal narrative in a manner that reveals the complete lack of communication between the two men. Despite their family ties, his uncle is incapable of relating to Guzmán in the language of sympathetic commiseration that characterizes friendship in private life. Unable to see beyond the social type of the generic picaro, the uncle's view comes to embody instead the same anonymous public opinion that, according to Johnson, consistently imposes its will on Alemán's protagonist throughout the novel.[30]

As this example demonstrates, the discursive nature of private life as well as its close association with a poetics of verisimilitude leads to inevitable conflicts with the dominant representational principles of the picaresque novel. In such a context, the "naturalized" category of family, as George Mariscal has observed for early modern society in general, provides a wholly inadequate measure of private life.[31] Such relationships are, to borrow a term from Timothy Reiss, wholly "embedded" in a larger social fabric that, in the case of the picaresque, embodies a kind of collective alienation with little room for meaningful self-expression.[32] In effect, family relationships as depicted in the genre are so closely integrated into the larger framework of picaresque social norms that they are unable to supply a meaningful escape from the oppressive isolation of picaresque existence. Friendship, on the other hand, precisely because it arises out of a self-conscious resistance to the genre's social and poetic norms, establishes a new framework for human interactions that offers at least the hope of individual self-expression as an antidote to the marginalization and misrecognition that characterizes Guzmán's autobiography up to this point.

Yet even friendship can never fully escape the pressures of the genre's representational logic, a fact that the narrative finally makes clear through the last character I will examine, a sea captain named Favelo whose enthusiastic but ultimately frustrated attempt to forge a friendship with Guzmán is repeatedly compared to Sayavedra's more perfect bond with the novel's protagonist. On first glance, the contrast between Favelo and Sayavedra would appear, once again, to reinforce the special quality of Guzmán's one true friendship, a point that Guzmán himself emphasizes shortly after meeting his new would-be friend:

> Siempre lo procuré conservar y obligar. Llevábame a su galera, traíame festejando por la marina, cultivándose tanto nuestro trato y amistad, que, si la mía fuera en seguimiento de la virtud, allí había hallado puerto; mas todo yo era embeleco ... Comunicábamonos muy particulares casos y secretos; empero, que de la camisa no pasasen adentro, porque los del alma sólo Sayavedra era dueño dellos.[33]

> [I also tried to preserve our friendship and win him over. He took me to his ship, and showed me around the fleet, cultivating our friendship so well that if mine had followed virtue, I would have found a harbor there; but I was nothing but deception ... We communicated particular cases and secrets; but they never entered beyond my shirt, because only Sayavedra was possessed of the secrets of my soul.]

Having offered both here and elsewhere a highly favorable account of Favelo's person, Guzmán nonetheless rejects the possibility of a deeper relationship. On its face, the hierarchy that relegates Favelo to an inferior kind of friendship appears quite arbitrary. Indeed, from an objective point of view, Favelo is arguably the better candidate for friendship: Unlike Sayavedra, he has no history of deception and his comportment throughout their relatively brief relationship is absolutely above reproach. This perhaps accounts for the slightly self-incriminating tone of the passage above—"But I was nothing but deception." With these words, Guzmán not only accepts responsibility for his unwillingness to engage this new friend, he also implicitly acknowledges the ascendancy of utilitarian values in his treatment of Favelo. As the reader soon learns, Guzmán cultivates this new friendship only so that Favelo might provide him passage to Spain once his plan to dupe his Genoese family has come to fruition.

Guzmán himself explains his disinterest in pursuing a true friendship with Favelo in a passage that, once again, highlights the moral ambiguity of picaresque private life: "Que no los amigos todos lo han de saber todo. Los llamados han de ser muchos; los escogidos pocos y uno solo el otro yo [Not all friends have to know all things. Those who are called are many; the chosen few, and only one the 'other self.']"[34] While ostensibly invoked to lend moral authority to his friendship with Sayavedra, Guzmán's reference to the biblical parable of the wedding feast has the practical effect of highlighting the moral relativism at work in their relationship. More specifically, the exclusivity of their communion reflects not the exemplary "goodness" of their character—as in the case of the classical ideal—but rather a practical accommodation to the picaresque's social and poetic reality; in a world where "all is deception," Guzmán can be true to Sayavedra only to the extent that he is free to deceive everyone else.

If Favelo's appearance in the narrative underscores the moral ambiguity of picaresque friendship, the end of Guzmán's relationship with Sayavedra calls into question the very viability of such associations. Shortly after making their escape from Genoa on board Favelo's ship, Sayavedra is struck with a fever, leading him, in a fit of madness, to call out the lines cited at the opening of this chapter: "I am the shadow of Guzmán de Alfarache! I am his shadow, that travels through the world." The play on the classical notion of the friend as a second self thus comes full circle as Sayavedra's earlier self-conscious assertion of his desire to "inherit" Guzmán's "true name" in order to "imitate" him is symbolically transformed into a madman's caprice. As Guzmán himself explains:

Con que me hacía reír y le temí muchas veces. Mas, aunque algo decía, ya lo vían estar loco y lo dejaban para tal.
    Pero no las llevaba conmigo todas, porque iba repitiendo mi vida, lo que della yo le había contado . . . Guisábame de mil maneras y lo más galano, aunque con lástima de verlo de aquella manera, de lo que más yo gustaba era que todo lo decía de sí mismo, como si realmente lo hubiera pasado.[35]

[With which he made me laugh, but also fear him on many occasions. But, although he was saying something, [the shipmates] saw him as crazy and left him as such. But he didn't convince me completely, because he kept repeating my life and all that I had told him . . . He cooked me up a thousand different ways, and made me look so gallant—even though it made me sad to see him that way—but what pleased me most was that he said it all about himself, as if he had really experienced it.]

The palpable ambiguity that runs through this paragraph reflects the fragile foundation of Guzmán's friendship. He laughs at Sayavedra's mad ravings, but then, realizing that he is retelling Guzmán's own life story, fears the public disclosure of his shady dealings. An ironic fulfillment of his earlier promise to imitate Guzmán's life, Sayavedra's behavior in this final scene of his life makes a sad mockery of the sympathetic storytelling that provided the original basis for their relationship. With Sayavedra's delusional mimicry of the stories that he has heard, the imitative poetics that previously offered the promise of a mode of private friendship that might resist the corrupting influence of picaresque *engaño* falls into disrepair.

The breakdown of the poetic and emotional framework of Guzmán's friendship presages the demise of his friend and the final triumph of the picaresque poetics. The passage above is immediately followed by a cursory account of Sayavedra's death and Guzmán's reaction to his one true friend's tragic end. Still suffering from his mad delusions, Sayavedra rises in the middle of the night and, as mentioned earlier, throws himself to a watery death. The entire scene is portrayed in three sentences and culminates with the account of Guzmán's response to his shipmates' offer of condolences: "y así se quedó el pobre sepultado, no con pequeña lástima de todos, que harto hacían en consolarme. Signifiqué sentirlo; mas sabe Dios la verdad [and thus, the poor man was entombed, with no small amount of sadness to everyone, who overwhelmed me with their offers of consolation. I showed that I felt it, but God knows the truth]."[36] Confronted with the death of his "other self," Guzmán retreats into the picaro's habit of deception while simultaneously negating to his reader any trace of his former friendship. After a couple more explicit statements confirming Guzmán's absolute indifference to Sayavedra's fate, the narrative quickly moves on to other matters, as if to underline the utter failure of this single picaresque experiment with friendship.

The close alignment between Guzmán's denial of any emotional attachment to his former friend and the reassertion of the discursive norm of *engaño* reflects, once again, the implicit poetic structure of the picaresque engagement with the emerging early modern split between public and private life. Perhaps more than any other literary mode of the period, the picaresque affirms the essential deceptiveness of public life against which any expression of sincere personal intimacy must constantly struggle to gain even merely transient recognition. In this sense, Guzmán's friendship with Sayavedra is doomed from the very beginning not because of any inherent personality defect in either picaro, but rather as an aesthetic requirement of the genre. Arguably the first comprehensive literary engagement with the new urban reality of the turn of the seventeenth century, the picaresque novel's unforgiving portrayal of public life sheds a harsh light on the difficulties of friendship in the modern world.

Notes

1. This chapter originally appeared as "Guzmán de Alfarache's 'Other Self': The Limits of Friendship in Spanish Picaresque Fiction" in *Discourses and Representations of Friendship in Early Modern Europe, 1500–1700*, and has been adapted for use here with permission from the publisher.
2. Alemán, *Guzmán de Alfarache*, vol. 2, p. 242. Spanish is adapted from the 1913 Cejador edition. All English translations are my own.
3. Luján, or Martí, penned his apocryphal continuation of the first part of *Guzmán de Alfarache* in 1602, that is, two years before the publication of Alemán's own second part in 1604.
4. Friedman, "Insincere Flattery: Imitation and the Growth of the Novel," p. 106.
5. Brancaforte, *Guzmán de Alfarache ¿Conversión o proceso de degradación?*, p. 97: "Sayavedra, 'sombra' de Guzmán, necesita ser completado. Alemán rehace el Guzmán apócrifo, por medio de Sayavedra, a imagen y semejanza de su Guzmán, para luego destruirlo. Es decir, el Guzmán apócrifo tiene que ser primero salvado como carácter novelístico, para luego ser aniquilado . . ." The connection between Sayavedra and the author of the spurious second part of *Guzmán de Alfarache* has also been made by McGrady, *Mateo Alemán*, pp. 122–4, and Kartchner, "Playing Doubles," pp. 16–23.
6. Friedman, "Insincere Flattery," p. 100.
7. On the ideal of the friend as "another self," Aristotle, *Nicomachean Ethics*, 1166a30, writes: "The decent person, then, has each of these features in relation to himself, and is related to his friend as he is to himself, since the friend is another self." Cicero, *De Amicitia*, XXI.80, continues this Aristotelian tradition in his own treatise on friendship: "Ipse enim se quisque diligit, non ut aliquam a se ipse mercedem exigat caritatis suae, sed quod per se quisque sibi carus est; quod nisi idem in amicitiam transferetur, verus amicus numquam reperietur: est enim is qui est tamquam alter idem [For everyone loves himself, not with a view of acquiring some profit for himself from his self-love, but because he is dear to himself on his own account; and unless this same feeling were transferred to friendship, the real friend would never be found; for he is, as it were, another self]."
8. Alemán, *Guzmán de Alfarache*, vol. 2, p. 120.
9. Ibid. vol. 2, p. 122.
10. Concerning the isolation of the picaro, Maravall, *La literatura picaresca desde la historia social*, p. 309, writes, "se mantienen en el fondo de su existencia singular apartados, no «a solas» reflexivamente, para dar lugar a una meditación sobre sí mismos y su entorno, sino en una radical soledad, algo así, diría, como existencialmente «solos». La soledad es el lugar moral de su emplazamiento."
11. As already discussed in the Introduction, this hierarchy is most clearly articulated in the *Nicomachean Ethics*, where Aristotle argues that friendships may be broken down into three categories based on utility, pleasure, and goodness.

12. Consistent with the reading of Sayavedra as a stand-in for Juan Martí, Friedman, "Insincere Flattery," p. 106, interprets the theft of Guzmán's possessions as a reference to Martí's plagiarism.
13. Alemán, *Guzmán de Alfarache*, vol. 2, pp. 124–5.
14. Ibid. vol. 2, p. 125.
15. Ibid. vol. 2, p. 125.
16. Ibid. vol. 2, p. 179.
17. Cros, *Protée et le Gueux*, is perhaps the first to view the pícaro as a protean figure, an idea that is picked up by various other critics, including Brancaforte, *Guzmán de Alfarache ¿Conversión o proceso de degradación?*. For the notion of the pícaro as "a process of typification," see Dunn, *Spanish Picaresque Fiction*, p. 187.
18. The distinction between private and public life that I use throughout this chapter was first inspired by the work of Ariès and Duby in their encyclopedic *A History of Private Life*.
19. Johnson, *Inside Guzmán de Alfarache*, p. 38.
20. Gilbert-Santamaría, *Writers on the Market*, p. 103: "Thus, *engaño*, or deception—in concert with its dialectical complement *desengaño* or disillusion—comes to embody more than just an important literary *topos* of the picaresque, as many have observed; it also provides the foundation for a new poetics that may be said to respond directly to the exhaustion of mimetic imitation as a poetic mode adequate to the *pícaro*'s peculiar experience of the world."
21. Cavillac, *Pícaros y mercaderes*, p. 16.
22. Alemán, *Guzmán de Alfarache*, vol. 2, p. 182.
23. Ibid. vol. 2, p. 192.
24. Ibid. vol. 2, pp. 198–9.
25. Bakhtin, "Discourse in the Novel," p. 333. Bakhtin's emphasis on the character in the novel as "an *ideologue*, and his words" as "*ideologemes*" highlights the inadequacy of his key concept of heteroglossia for an analysis of friendship in the picaresque, and arguably, Alemán's novel in general. Where Bakhtin's analysis focuses on the ideological foundation of novelistic discourse, the concept of private friendship that I propose here depends by definition on the individuality of particular personal narratives that may or may not have a larger social significance.
26. Alemán, *Guzmán de Alfarache*, vol. 2, p. 203.
27. Ibid. vol. 2, p. 203.
28. Ibid. vol. 2, p. 217.
29. Ibid. vol. 2, p. 217.
30. Johnson, "Defining the Picaresque," pp. 168–9.
31. Mariscal, *Contradictory Subjects*, p. 67, expresses this idea in the following terms: "Thus the idea of the family as an isolated group of nurturing individuals set in opposition to society, which seems to us both natural and historically constant, was in fact relatively alien to early modern culture."

32. Reiss, *Mirages of the Selfe*, p. 3. Reiss's concept here is drawn from his larger argument against modern notions of independent "subjectivity" and, by extension, against the conventional dichotomy between public and private life throughout this entire period. In light of this background, his passing reference, p. 468, to Montaigne's view of friendship in this context is particularly noteworthy: "for him [i.e. Montaigne], in an atypical anti-Ciceronian (and anti-Aristotelian) move, friendship was a strictly *private* affair." At the very least, that Reiss would make such a statement highlights an important distinction between private friendship and modern subjectivity. The first does not necessarily imply the second.
33. Alemán, *Guzmán de Alfarache*, vol. 2, p. 214.
34. Ibid. vol. 2, p. 215.
35. Ibid. vol. 2, pp. 242–3.
36. Ibid. vol. 2, p. 243.

Chapter 7

The Errantry of Friendship in *Don Quixote*

Based on the internal evidence of Cervantes's novel, there is reason to doubt whether the account of Don Quixote and Sancho Panza's travels even qualifies as a tale of friendship. From the very moment of Sancho's introduction into the novel, the relationship between the two is marked by a quasi-contractual arrangement through which Sancho agrees to serve as Don Quixote's squire for a price: "Decíale, entre otras cosas, don Quijote, que se dispusiese a ir con él de buena gana, porque tal vez le podía suceder aventura, que ganase, en quítame allá esas pajas, alguna ínsula, y le dejase a él por gobernador della [Don Quixote, among other things, told him he ought to be ready to go with him gladly, because any moment an adventure might occur that might win an island in the twinkling of an eye and leave him governor of it]."[1] Moreover, not only does Sancho's initial decision to serve his master rest almost entirely on his aspirations to this island governorship—"Con estas promesas y otras tales, Sancho Panza . . . dejó su mujer e hijos y asentó por escudero de su vecino [On these and the like promises Sancho Panza . . . left wife and children, and engaged himself as squire to his neighbor]"—this description of his first encounter with Don Quixote exposes Sancho's essential lack of fitness for the role of perfect friend. His inferior social status—he is described as merely a "labrador vecino"—his poverty, and his lack of intelligence mark a clear distinction with the idealized moral virtue of the Aristotelian model. Combined with Don Quixote's already established madness at this early point in the novel, the manner of Sancho's introduction into the narrative suggests that Cervantes's interest in writing about these two characters lies elsewhere.

Furthermore, from their first encounter throughout the rest of the novel, there is rarely any explicit attention paid to the evolving relationship between Don Quixote and Sancho Panza in terms that would suggest that anything has arisen between them beyond the original terms of their master-servant relationship.[2] Certainly, Don Quixote frequently refers to his companion as "amigo, Sancho," but the repetition of that formula belies a pervasive failure to engage seriously with the question of friendship as it might relate to the novel's two main characters. Where the narrative undertakes lengthy self-conscious debates on all manner of topics, from Don Quixote's long discourse on arms and letters to extended discussions with Sansón Carrasco and the canon of Toledo on matters of aesthetics, the question of friendship remains largely unremarked by either the characters or the narrator. Even the more specific question of Don Quixote and Sancho Panza's ongoing fellowship, without doubt a central focus of the narrative, is only rarely explored within the novel as an explicit topic of theoretical interest in its own right.

Mitigating against such a quick dismissal of a reading of the novel in terms of friendship, however, is the powerful fact of hundreds of pages devoted to describing the evolving terms of Don Quixote and Sancho's shared adventures. From Sancho's initial incredulity at his master's antics to his slow absorption into the world of Don Quixote's fantasies, the novel cannot be fairly assessed except through the continuing relationship between these two most unlikely of companions. That relationship, however, resists the kind of categorical definition that characterizes the narrative tradition of writing perfect friendship. Where nearly all the friendship narratives examined in this study operate within the clear framework of the Aristotelian ideal of the perfect friend, Cervantes's portrayal of his two protagonists exhibits a fluidity that thwarts attempts to characterize their relationship in a definitive way. Rather, Don Quixote and Sancho Panza's assumed roles of knight and squire, as will become clear later in this discussion, provide the conduit through which a far more idiosyncratic and particularized understanding of personal intimacy slowly takes shape. Where the perfect friend exists as an idealized type, the relationship between Don Quixote and Sancho Panza emerges through the very act of narration and, for this reason, may be said to represent nothing other than itself.

A full appreciation of this last assertion requires a more detailed elaboration of the poetic stakes of Cervantes's project, especially as they relate to two key concepts of Renaissance literary production: imitation and exemplarity. First, Don Quixote's commitment to resurrecting knight-errantry in the world already involves a radical reinterpretation of the Renaissance practice of *imitatio*. Writing in imitation of the great authors of the past here gives way in the figure of Don Quixote to the literal acting out of that which was formerly written. This defining gesture in Cervantes's novel not only anticipates a poetic practice that would derive its models from everyday life, it also presages the more ambitious declarations of the opening of Part II in which the world—at least as described by Sansón Carrasco—begins to imitate the narrative's fiction.[3] At the same time, however, the absurdity of Don Quixote's quest to resurrect knight-errantry hints at a second movement within Cervantes's poetic practice as the exemplary function so frequently associated with Renaissance literary production is revealed as pure folly. In its most literal application to the affairs of this world, knight-errantry provides a very poor model for human conduct, a conclusion that is reinforced repeatedly through Don Quixote's failed efforts to implant the values of chivalric fiction in his day-to-day existence. Not only do those failures highlight the incompatibility of fantastic fiction and everyday life, they serve to feed a more generalized suspicion of literary idealization that is arguably a major feature of the novel as a whole.[4]

At the same time, it is precisely this deflation of literary idealization that opens a space for a very different kind of representational project, one that will, in the end, offer new possibilities for the depiction of interpersonal intimacy. As *vecinos* in an unnamed village, Don Quixote and Sancho are subject to rules that impose rigid socially defined limits on their association. In the social context of their first encounter, the only relationship that may exist between the two is largely constrained by their very different standing in the social hierarchy. Furthermore, their new roles as knight-errant and squire would seem to perpetuate this underlying sense of social inequality, formalizing a hierarchical distinction that persists until the very end of the novel. And yet, unlike their former association as *labrador* and *hidalgo* in a small village, the framing of this new relationship is complicated in ways that, over the course of the narrative's evolution, slowly erode the explicit hierarchical distinction between the two. With constant reminders that the two protagonists are, in fact, playing roles founded in Don Quixote's madness, the narrative underscores the performative basis of their adopted identities as knight and squire.[5] In keeping with the Cervantine lemma that "cada uno es hijo de sus obras," the notion of identity as performance privileges the characters' actions over inherited claims to social status and, in the end, creates opportunities for self-determination that transcend the ostensible limits of their assigned roles.[6]

This emphasis on subjective autonomy within—or despite—the framework of Don Quixote's insistence on emulating roles derived from his reading of chivalric fiction infuses the narrative with a sense of unpredictability that is registered most clearly in the evolving relationship between the two main characters. Recalling the novel's more general ambivalence toward both literary *imitatio*—here understood primarily as intertextuality—and traditional notions of exemplarity, the narrative's episodic structure and fragmented plotting contribute to the sense of the relationship between these two unlikely companions as largely unscripted. The issue here, however, is not that of failed models for human comportment—as was the case for knight-errantry as a code of conduct—but rather the seemingly unsystematic proliferation of narrative details that fails to offer any models at all. Cervantes's more general aversion to overt didacticism—see, for example, the *Novelas ejemplares*—combines with a self-conscious privileging of the protagonists' autonomy in the depiction of a relationship whose defining attribute is its inimitability.

Critical to this analysis of Don Quixote and Sancho Panza's fellowship is the seemingly ceaseless flow of conversation between the two. As in real-life friendship, conversation functions as the primary means through which the protagonists experience their relationship and, over time, slowly develop a sense of mutual understanding.[7] In contrast to more contemporary novelistic discourse, Cervantes's narrator rarely, if ever, offers direct access to the characters' thoughts so that, in the end, insight into Don Quixote and Sancho Panza's interior life is almost exclusively derived from what they say to each other. Like the novel's itinerant structure, however, the dialogue between the knight and squire is presented consistently as a kind of self-generating reaction to the circumstances of their shared experiences. As Elias Rivers notes, "from the beginning to the end of their relationship, the two characters seem to be engaged in one long, complex dialogue, frequently interrupted by the intrusion of events or other people, but maintaining a continuity that is dependent, in part, upon reminiscent references to what may almost be called 'standing jokes,' that is, references to permanent topics of mutual interest."[8] To the extent that the characters may be said to get to know each other through their ongoing conversations, that process reinforces the impression of their relationship as developing from within the dynamic itself of their errant adventures.[9]

One indicator of the importance of conversation to Cervantes's project is Don Quixote's aborted attempt to impose a vow of silence on his loquacious companion. Fearful of the potential damage to his reputation after one especially embarrassing misadventure—the *batanes* episode to be considered below—Don Quixote invokes his role as master in order to control Sancho's speech:

> ... y está advertido de aquí adelante en una cosa, para que te abstengas y reportes en el hablar demasiado conmigo: que en cuantos libros de caballerías he leído, que son infinitos, jamás he hallado que ningún escudero hablase

tanto con su señor como tú con el tuyo. Y en verdad que lo tengo a gran falta, tuya y mía: tuya, en que me estimas en poco; mía, en que no me dejo estimar en más ... De todo lo que he dicho has de inferir, Sancho, que es menester hacer diferencia de amo a mozo, de señor a criado y de caballero a escudero. Así que, desde hoy en adelante, nos hemos de tratar con más respeto ...[10]

["... and one thing for the future bear in mind, that you curb and restrain your loquacity in my company; for in all the books of chivalry that I have read, and they are innumerable, I never met with a squire who talked so much to his lord as you do to yours; and in fact I feel it to be a great fault of yours and of mine: of yours, that you have so little respect for me; of mine, that I do not make myself more respected ... From all I have said you will gather, Sancho, that there must be a difference between master and man, between lord and lackey, between knight and squire: so that from this day forward in our intercourse we must observe more respect ..."]

Invoking their association as master and servant, the appeal to hierarchy in Don Quixote's drive to silence Sancho is tainted by the source of his claim to authority, namely, the "infinitos" fictional "libros de caballerías" that have addled his brain. At the very least, the passage ironizes Don Quixote's claim to social superiority, a conclusion that is largely confirmed a few chapters later when the vow of silence is finally lifted, never to be mentioned again.[11] Indeed, with Sancho's communicative impulse released anew, the narrative reasserts the centrality of dialogue to the fellowship between the knight and his squire. The result is not so much a rebuke of the social hierarchy as a recognition of its subordination to the more significant poetic force of dialogue within the trajectory of a growing bond of personal intimacy.

It is in this respect, too, that the representation of the relationship between Don Quixote and Sancho Panza intersects with Cervantes's more general interest in a poetic practice that privileges verisimilitude over literary *imitatio*. In the heterogeneous particularity of the conversations between his protagonists, Cervantes discovers a vehicle for expressing the idiosyncratic singularity of all human relationships, alluding to the possibility that the relationship between Don Quixote and Sancho Panza might ultimately stand for nothing other than itself. Such an interpretation of representational verisimilitude suggests a more general skepticism not just toward literary didacticism but, even more radically, toward the notion that such didacticism would accurately represent the nature of human experience. With a hint of nihilism, representational verisimilitude in Cervantes—as was seen earlier in "El curioso impertinente"—occasionally gestures toward the ultimate meaninglessness of human affairs.

Intrinsic to such an interpretation of the novel's central relationship is a recognition that Cervantes's primary interests lie in the realm of poetics.[12] In fact, Don Quixote's insistence that he and Sancho imitate the literary roles of knight-errant and squire so completely dominates the explicit terms of their formal association that even Sancho's self-interest is constituted in the language of chivalric fiction: Despite occasional references to his salary and other forms of remuneration, the single most important expression of that self-interest, repeated over and over throughout the novel, is the absurd promise of an island governorship. Moreover, even as Sancho becomes more adept—and aggressive—at manipulating Don Quixote, such manipulation always occurs within the established frame of his assigned role as squire to an illustrious knight, that is, a role that only truly exists in the fantastical world of the chivalric novel.[13]

For this same reason, the novel, to the extent that it offers a different approach to writing friendship, does so first and foremost as a literary matter. As E. C. Riley correctly cautioned over half a century ago, Cervantes's interest in representational verisimilitude must not be confused with realism, an idea that is later echoed by Martínez-Bonati: "Certainly the *Quixote* is a very profound image of life, and for that reason it is rightly known as *true*, but its image of life is not a *realistic* one."[14] In contrast, as B. W. Ife notes, verisimilitude and Aristotelian poetic ideas more generally in the Spanish Golden Age circulate around what he describes as "aesthetic belief," an idea that is complicated by "the widespread recognition that readers are convinced by the most unlikely things."[15] Writing more specifically about *Don Quixote*, Ife observes:

> The Canon of Toledo runs into precisely this problem. He says that the novels of chivalry are 'fuera del trato que pide la común naturaleza'—that is, they do not conform to verisimilitude—and then blames don Quixote for believing them. He thereby admits, or so it would seem, that belief is not a function of verisimilitude; one cannot reasonably call something incredible and at the same time complain that people believe in it. But by throwing the books across the room in disgust whenever he catches himself enjoying them in an unguarded moment the Canon makes an even more telling admission: they are infuriatingly attractive in spite of their lack of truth.[16]

Don Quixote's extreme beliefs about chivalric fiction reveal the inadequacy of representational verisimilitude as a measure of what Ife describes as the "probabilities of empirical reality."[17] Ife's analysis here exposes the underlying irony that inhabits Cervantes's engagement with Aristotelian poetic theory, especially his resistance to assimilating his work to the Aristotelian categories of poetry and history.[18] At the same time, the seductiveness of these fictions—even for an austere soul like the canon—suggests an entirely different way of thinking about the novel's poetic structure, as the "probabilities of empirical reality" give way to the more visceral experience of pleasure. Despite his rational objections to chivalric fiction on formal grounds, the canon finds himself entertained by these wildly fantastic narratives.

Such complications in Cervantes's approach to the problem of representational verisimilitude and, in particular, Aristotle's distinction between history and fiction present significant difficulties for a critical approach that would attempt to explain the relationship between Don Quixote and Sancho in terms of concrete historical phenomena, sociological or otherwise. Like the canon who flings books of chivalry against the wall when he realizes that "son todos mentira," the critic who would presume to find some historical truth in Cervantes's depiction of his protagonists must eventually come to terms with the fact that Don Quixote's self-reinvention derives from the same fantastically mendacious source.[19]

In assessing the representation of friendship in the primary relationship between Don Quixote and Sancho Panza, there remains the more specific question of the longer tradition of writing perfect friendship that has been the focus of this study so far. As the above discussion indicates, the relationship between Don Quixote and his squire lacks a formal basis in the Aristotelian model, a point that is supported by a more general insistence on the unprecedented nature of Cervantes's project in the prologue to the first part. Cervantes here represents himself as grappling with the lack of antecedents for his literary project, at which point a fictional friend interrupts his musings, dispelling his concerns through an acid critique of literary authority and, by extension, the Renaissance practice of literary *imitatio*.[20] To his friend, the fictionalized Cervantes expresses concerns about his book's lack of "acotaciones en las márgenes [quotations in the margin]" and "anotaciones en el fin del libro, como veo que están otros libros . . . tan llenos de sentencias de Aristóteles, de Platón y de toda la caterva de filósofos, que admiran a los leyentes y tienen a sus autores por hombres leídos, eruditos y elocuentes [annotations at the end, after the fashion of other books that I see . . . so full of maxims from Aristotle, and Plato, and the whole herd of philosophers, that they fill the readers with amazement and convince them that the authors are men of learning, erudition, and eloquence.]"[21] To such scruples the friend responds with a series of suggestions that trivialize beyond recognition the prestigious Renaissance tradition of literary *imitatio*. The complex problem of literary influence that lies at the heart of this Renaissance poetics is transformed into the stuff of parody. Dismissing any serious purpose in literary imitation, the friend encourages Cervantes to borrow at will from ancient sources in a shameless display of superficial erudition, an idea that he applies explicitly to the theme of friendship:

> Si de la amistad y amor que Dios manda que se tenga al enemigo, entraros luego al punto por la Escritura Divina, que lo podéis con tantico de curiosidad y decir las palabras, por lo menos, del mismo Dios: «*Ego autem dico vobis: diligite inimicos vestros.*» ... Si de la inestabilidad de los amigos, ahí está Catón, que os dará su dístico: «*Donec eris felix, multos numerabis amicos. / Tempora si fuerint nubila, solus eris.*» Y con estos latinicos y otros tales os tendrán siquiera por gramático; que serlo no es de poca honra y provecho el día de hoy.[22]

["If it be friendship and the love God bids us bear to our enemy, go at once to the Holy Scriptures, which you can do with a very small amount of research, and quote no less than the words of God himself: "Ego autem dico vobis: diligite inimicos vestros" ... If of the fickleness of friends, there is Cato, who will give you his distich: "Donec eris felix multos numerabis amicos / Tempora si fuerint nubila, solus eris." With these and such like bits of Latin they will take you for a grammarian at all events, and that nowadays is no small honor and profit"]

The mixture of audacity and derision here is impressive. Citing the authority of Cato and even God, Cervantes's fictional friend transforms the authoritative voices of the Bible and classical antiquity into purveyors of "latinicos" that may be invoked in the service of an empty self-presentation of erudition. One of the novel's few instances of direct engagement with friendship as a topic of discussion in its own right, this passage underscores Cervantes's disregard for inherited traditions, an attitude that clearly extends to the representation of friendship. At the same time, the cynicism on display in this passage is amplified by its staging within a conversation between Cervantes and his fictional friend. Here, before the action of the novel has even begun, friendship is already associated with morally dubious practical advice. In advocating a break with established literary practice, the unnamed friend's irreverent exploitation of classical and biblical sources in order to lend a false sense of authority to Cervantes's novel anticipates the ethical ambiguity that will inform nearly every aspect of Don Quixote's relationship with his squire.

In the end, then, what clues the prologue offers as to the representation of the central relationship between Don Quixote and Sancho Panza are largely negative. The rejection of literary idealization in the prologue prefaces a statement on the novelty of Cervantes's project that is, in fact, constituted in highly ambiguous terms. In the wake of his cynical assessment of classical *auctoritas*, the friend concludes with a vague appeal to imitation: "Sólo tiene que aprovecharse de la imitación en lo que fuere escribiendo; que, cuanto ella fuere más perfecta, tanto mejor será lo que se escribiere [In what you are writing you have only to make use of imitation, and the more perfect the imitation the better your writing will be]."[23] Given the friend's earlier insistence on the novelty of Cervantes's project, the term imitation here must be recalibrated to the circumstances of what is, according to the discourse of the prologue, an unprecedented literary experiment. Exactly what form that recalibration should take and how it might influence the representation of the novel's two main characters is, based on the information provided in the prologue, highly uncertain.

This last observation leads to the other major premise of this chapter, namely, that the representation of friendship in the relationship between Don Quixote and Sancho Panza emerges as a second-order consequence of Cervantes's poetic practice.[24] Where formal structure in the tale of two friends tradition invariably functions in response to the requirements of the Aristotelian model for perfect friendship and therefore frequently appears scripted and pre-determined, Cervantes's depiction of the relationship between Don Quixote and Sancho develops from within the process itself of narration, a largely unanticipated outcome of Cervantes's poetic practice that is also one of the most significant manifestations of that practice.[25] In contrast to the Aristotelian categorical ideal, friendship in *Don Quixote*, like the novel's poetics more generally, is subject to constant renegotiation in a dynamic process, the defining feature of which is, as indicated above, its idiosyncratic singularity.[26]

Key to this interpretation of the relationship between the two main characters is the underlying indeterminacy of the novel's treatment of matters of form. The ambiguous reference to imitation in the prologue, just like the repeated appeals to abstract notions of truth and representational verisimilitude throughout the novel as a whole, are symptomatic of a compositional style that eschews prescriptive poetic principles. There are in *Don Quixote* moments of direct engagement with early modern poetic ideas, but such encounters rarely lead to unambiguous prescriptive statements that might account for what Cervantes does in his novel. Moreover, what is true for the novel overall is even more valid for the relationship between the two main characters. For where the novel at least engages occasionally in explicit speculation on matters of literary composition, it largely ignores any direct encounter with the problem of friendship as a topic worthy of independent analysis—with the one notable exception of the tale of "El curioso impertinente," a story, it will be recalled, that ends with a wholesale repudiation of the tradition of writing perfect friendship.

In the absence of any systematic account of the nature of the relationship between Don Quixote and Sancho, one is left to contemplate the diffuse evidence of the text's representation of their shared adventures. Against the deliberate statements of Cervantes's hero in support of his project to resurrect chivalry in the world, those adventures underscore the knight-errant's itinerant nature, his wandering from scene to scene providing the circumstances within which his relationship with his squire slowly unfolds. Whether deliberate or not, each new adventure opens up the relationship between Don Quixote and Sancho in ways that feel spontaneous, as if the narrative were generating the substance of that relationship in the process of its composition. It is here, as well, that one begins to appreciate the uniqueness of the relationship between these two characters not only as a manifestation of the novel's unusual subject matter, but more fundamentally, as a direct consequence of the evolving dynamic through which that relationship is given shape. In place of the static vision of perfect Aristotelian friendship, one encounters in the communion between Don Quixote and Sancho Panza a relationship in the process of becoming, in which definitive statements of meaning give way to narrative as testimonial, as an ongoing act of witnessing that resists summary statements of meaning.

Moreover, to the extent that Cervantes acknowledges some ultimate plan in his literary project, those affirmations take on the character of *ex post facto* revelations. On the matter of friendship, the most important example of this occurs midway through the novel's second part, at the residence of the Duke and Duchess, where the conditions for Dulcinea's disenchantment are laid out for the knight and his squire. A theme that is referenced repeatedly in the final chapters of the novel, the disenchantment of Dulcinea re-enacts—albeit in an altered form—the essential elements of the more traditional narrative of perfect friendship: Don Quixote's love interest is here, in her last major appearance in the novel, transformed into the objectified point of contention between Cervantes's two main characters. Setting out the conditions for Dulcinea's disenchantment, namely, that Sancho, of his own will, must inflict "tres mil azotes y trecientos / en ambas sus valientes posaderas . . . [three thousand three hundred lashes / on both of his brave buttocks]," the narrative provides Sancho with an opportunity to demonstrate his devotion to Don Quixote through an act of conscious self-sacrifice.[27] Echoing the conventional test of friendship, the problem of Dulcinea's disenchantment—whether intentional or not—provides the most concrete focus for comparison between Cervantes's novel and the tale of two friends tradition.

The inclusion of this episode—of which a fuller account will be provided later—illuminates the broader implications of the relationship between Don Quixote and Sancho Panza for the long tradition of writing perfect friendship. As with the tale of "El curioso impertinente," the force of this reprise of the tale of two friends tradition is largely negative, the staging of this opportunity to test Sancho's devotion to his traveling companion ultimately failing to provide the desired confirmation of selfless devotion within the bonds of perfect friendship. Instead, Sancho's venality not only betrays the principles of Aristotelian perfect friendship, but indeed, the longer trajectory of this important subplot leads to the final unraveling of both characters' role-playing within the pretended resurrection of chivalric values.

Compared with the highly deliberate encounter with the tradition of writing Aristotelian perfect friendship in "El curioso impertinente," the subplot that grows up around the absurd prescription for Dulcinea's disenchantment seems almost incidental in its engagement with that tradition. For one thing, the timing of the episode reflects the evolving nature of the relationship between Don Quixote and Sancho Panza and, more specifically, the fact that only here, midway in the novel's second part, has the sense of shared intimacy between the two grown to the point where a full comparison with the discourse of perfect friendship is finally possible. Unlike the more paradigmatic case of narrative perfect friendship, where perfect harmony between friends is the assumed starting point for a predictable tale of conflict and the final reaffirmation of the Aristotelian ideal, in this instance the starting point is, in fact, the beginning of the end. The timing of the test of friendship—so central to the earlier narrative tradition—suggests that it is, in some fundamental sense, superfluous to the underlying substance of Don Quixote and Sancho's fellowship. Ultimately, the notion of singular, defining acts of self-sacrifice cannot compete with the far more tangible evidence of hundreds of pages documenting the myriad details of their shared experience.

Part I

Don Quixote cannot get far without a companion.[28] In his first sally without Sancho, the representation of Don Quixote's aspirations is limited by his lack of an appropriate interlocutor. Marked by frequently aggressive declarations of his knightly vocation, Don Quixote's early verbal exchanges are riddled with failures to communicate that almost invariably lead to violence. In these early episodes, Don Quixote's chivalric quest is reduced to the surface of pure performance, his verbal claims to knight-errantry recalling the theatrical hyperbole that characterizes so much of the Spanish *comedia*. In contrast, with Sancho's arrival, the possibility of a deeper understanding of Don Quixote's peculiar condition becomes possible. With his willingness to engage Don Quixote on his own terms, Sancho generates new poetic possibilities as rhetorical posturing yields to dialogue that revels in the complexity of both characters' inner lives.[29] This is arguably what Auerbach has in mind when he suggests that "the experience of Don Quijote's personality is not received by anyone as completely as it is by Sancho; it is not assimilated pure and whole by anyone as it is by him."[30]

Yet the emergence of such psychic complexity is not instantaneous, and, in fact, a close reading of Don Quixote's first adventure with his new squire reveals the distance that will still have to be traveled before the two can claim anything like the status of friendship. In the iconic windmill episode, the dialogue between the knight and his squire still elicits a sense of Sancho's almost complete alienation from his master and his strange madness:

En esto, descubrieron treinta o cuarenta molinos de viento que hay en aquel campo, y así como don Quijote los vio, dijo a su escudero:
— La ventura va guiando nuestras cosas mejor de lo que acertáramos a desear; porque ves allí, amigo Sancho Panza, donde se descubren treinta, o pocos más, desaforados gigantes, con quien pienso hacer batalla y quitarles a todos las vidas, con cuyos despojos comenzaremos a enriquecer; que ésta es buena guerra, y es gran servicio de Dios quitar tan mala simiente de sobre la faz de la tierra.
— ¿Qué gigantes?—dijo Sancho Panza.
— Aquellos que allí ves—respondió su amo—de los brazos largos, que los suelen tener algunos de casi dos leguas.
— Mire vuestra merced—respondió Sancho—que aquellos que allí se parecen no son gigantes, sino molinos de viento, y lo que en ellos parecen brazos son las aspas, que, volteadas del viento, hacen andar la piedra del molino.[31]

[At this point they came in sight of thirty or forty windmills that there are on that plain, and as soon as Don Quixote saw them he said to his squire, "Fortune is arranging matters for us better than we could have shaped our desires ourselves, for look there, friend Sancho Panza, where thirty or more monstrous giants present themselves, all of whom I mean to engage in battle and slay, and with whose spoils we shall begin to make our fortunes; for this is righteous warfare, and it is God's good service to sweep so evil a breed from off the face of the earth."

"What giants?" said Sancho Panza.

"Those you see there," answered his master, "with the long arms, and some have them nearly two leagues long."

"Look, your worship," said Sancho; "what we see there are not giants but windmills, and what seem to be their arms are the sails that turned by the wind make the millstone go."

In aligning Sancho with the narrator who affirms a material world of windmills and not giants, Cervantes reveals the fundamental divide that separates these two characters at the outset of their adventures. Having all but excluded any substantive interest in the social distinction between the two, Cervantes uses dialogue here to record the simple fact of Sancho's incredulity in the face of Don Quixote's strange visions as the privileged perspective in this scene. Like nearly everyone else Don Quixote meets, Sancho remains at this point in the novel a mere spectator for whom Don Quixote's madness registers as pure phenomenon.[32]

Furthermore, to the extent that there is a power dynamic at work in this scene, it largely serves as an equalizing force in the relationship between the two characters. Emulating the omniscient narrator, Sancho's words are endowed with an authority that reaches its fullest expression in the wake of Don Quixote's failed attempt to vanquish his imagined foe: "¿No le dije yo a vuestra merced que mirase bien lo que hacía, que no eran sino molinos de viento, y no lo podía ignorar sino quien llevase otros tales en la cabeza? [Did I not tell your worship to mind what you were about, for they were only windmills and no one could have made any mistake about it but one who had something of the same kind in his head?]"[33] Flaunting his superior understanding of the material world, Sancho's invocation of his master's madness here erodes the hierarchical inequalities of their original association as squire and knight-errant. At the same time, the fact itself of their dialogue anticipates the formal mechanism through which, over time, the relationship between the two will slowly evolve. While Sancho's intervention here is hardly effective—Don Quixote at this point is unable to hear Sancho in any meaningful way—it nevertheless generates the conditions for a possible response and with that, the potential for a more consequential dialogue in the future.

The first sign of this new potential comes into view only a few chapters later, in Don Quixote and Sancho's visit with the anonymous goatherds in the scene that culminates with the famous speech on the Golden Age.[34] Invited to share a meal with these seemingly rustic characters, Don Quixote implores Sancho to sit at his side as a sign of the "bien que en sí encierra la andante caballería, y cuán a pique están los que en cualquiera ministerio della se ejercitan de venir brevemente a ser honrados y estimados del mundo . . . [the good that knight-errantry contains in itself, and how those who fill any office in it are on the high road to be speedily honored and esteemed by the world . . .]"[35] Don Quixote's point, as he goes on to explain, is to show how knight-errantry, like love, is an equalizing force in the world. In a previous study, I emphasized the implicit violence in Don Quixote's insistence that his squire sit with him as an equal: After Sancho politely refuses his master's request, Don Quixote nevertheless forces the matter, "asiéndole por el brazo." In light of the speech extolling the communal values of the Golden Age that Don Quixote delivers a bit later in the episode, his actions toward his squire come off as ironic, if not hypocritical.[36] Read from the perspective of friendship, however, Don Quixote's insistence that Sancho sit with him and be "una mesma cosa" nevertheless possesses a certain efficacy: The physical circumstances of Sancho's move to his master's side constitutes an important localized geographical fact that is made possible by the more expansive geographical circumstances of their itinerancy.

Beyond the equalizing impulse that Don Quixote associates with knight-errantry, the deepening connection between the knight and his squire finds support of a different kind in the goatherds who are the only witnesses to this peculiar exchange between the two protagonists. From the outset these rustic men are presented as completely alien to Don Quixote's world, so much so that they are unable to detect in the knight's strange discourse the underlying pathology that, for Sancho, is the key to understanding his master: "No entendían los cabreros aquella jerigonza de escuderos y de caballeros andantes, y no hacían otra cosa que comer y callar, y mirar a sus huéspedes . . . [The goatherds did not understand this jargon about squires and knights-errant, and all they did was to eat in silence and stare at their guests . . .]."[37] Here, the curious language of knight-errantry—"aquella jerigonza"—creates a bond between Don Quixote and his squire that is defined, at least in part, by way of contrast with the goatherds' mystified silence.[38] Understood through the lens of classical paradigms for perfect friendship, Cervantes's protagonists may be said to share a secret discourse that renders them unknowable to those whom they encounter in their travels. In this instance, however, this sense of unknowability arises not from an Aristotelian claim to superior virtue but out of Don Quixote's madness, that is, from an impulse to self-idealization that is contested by almost every other character in the novel.

In creating the circumstances for what will later emerge as a peculiarly Cervantine vision of private friendship, the formal conventions of novelistic discourse play an especially important role. Like Sancho, the reader has access to privileged information about Don Quixote's mental state. Having already experienced the knight-errant's madness in a variety of contexts, the reader easily assimilates these new delusions and is thus brought into the circle of intimacy between the two protagonists. This assimilation within the fold of an evolving private relationship between Don Quixote and Sancho Panza works particularly well in the fictional space of the novel, with its conventions of individual private reading.[39] Even madness, with its tendency toward hyperbolic displays—like Don Quixote's extravagant speech on the Golden Age—is made accessible to the intimate space of personal communion in the fictionalized world of the novel where, in the end, all action is reduced to movements of the reader's imagination.

If the scene with the goatherds helps to establish the boundaries of Don Quixote and Sancho's private fellowship against an uninitiated public, the full integration of Sancho into his master's fantasy life depends on a secondary movement *within* their relationship. In the windmill episode, Sancho remains, despite his official status as Don Quixote's squire, aloof from the active pursuit of chivalric valor. This soon changes, however, as Sancho's evolving communion with his master leads him to take on a far more active role in many subsequent adventures as his integration into Don Quixote's living fantasy increases.

The first clear and arguably most straightforward example of this may be observed in the knight and squire's encounter with the *yangüeses*, an episode that begins not with Don Quixote's fantastical imaginings but with the romantic dalliances of his decrepit mount, Rocinante, whose unrequited attentions to a group of mares soon arouses the ire of their owners who, in turn, beat Don Quixote's horse mercilessly—"tantos palos le dieron, que le derribaron malparado en el suelo [and laid into him so hard that he was soon on the ground in a very sorry state]."[40] Don Quixote's response to Rocinante's beating opens the door to a new level of participation for Sancho within the action of the novel. Asserting that Rocinante's assailants are not "caballeros, sino gente soez y de baja ralea [not knights but base folk of low birth]," Don Quixote rationalizes in the logic of chivalric fiction a request for Sancho's aid in his plan for vengeance: "Dígolo porque bien me puedes ayudar a tomar la debida venganza del agravio que delante de nuestros ojos se le ha hecho a Rocinante [I mention it because you can lawfully aid me in taking due vengeance for the insult offered to Rocinante before our eyes]."[41] Here, then, for the first time, the rules of chivalry create a space for Sancho to emulate his master so that, despite his awareness of the precariousness of their situation—"¿Qué diablos de venganza hemos de tomar . . . si estos son más de veinte . . . [What the devil vengeance can we take . . . if they are more than twenty . . .]"—he nonetheless accedes to Don Quixote's request, "incitado y movido del ejemplo de su amo [incited and impelled by the example of his master]," and is thereby transformed from witness into active collaborator in this act of mad valor.[42]

The notion of active imitation in this episode constitutes a significant evolution beyond the earlier scene with the perplexed goatherds. Linguistic fellowship in that scene creates a nascent intimacy between knight-errant and squire defined against the background of the world's indifference to their strange discourse. In contrast, Sancho's charge into battle with the *arrieros* provokes an active hostility between our two adventurers and the world around them: Don Quixote and Sancho attack the *yangüeses*, who, with their greater numbers, return in kind, "dejando a los dos aventureros de mala traza y de peor talante [leaving the two adventurers a sorry sight and in sorrier mood]."[43] This direct experience of violence informs a renewed dialogue in the wake of their beating that illuminates the important role of shared participation in the events depicted in this scene:

> ... respondió Sancho—... apenas puse mano a mi tizona, cuando me santiguaron los hombros con sus pinos, de manera, que me quitaron la vista de los ojos y la fuerza de los pies, dando conmigo adonde ahora yago, y adonde no me da pena alguna el pensar si fue afrenta, o no, lo de los estacazos, como me la da el dolor de los golpes, que me han de quedar tan impresos en la memoria como en las espaldas.
>
> —Con todo eso, te hago saber, hermano Panza—replicó don Quijote—, que no hay memoria a quien el tiempo no acabe, ni dolor que muerte no le consuma.
>
> —Pues ¿qué mayor desdicha puede ser—replicó Panza—de aquella que aguarda al tiempo que la consuma y a la muerte que la acabe? Si esta nuestra desgracia fuera de aquellas que con un par de bizmas se curan, aun no tan malo; pero voy viendo que no han de bastar todos los emplastos de un hospital para ponerlas en buen término siquiera.
>
> —Déjate deso y saca fuerzas de flaqueza, Sancho—respondió don Quijote—, que así haré yo, y veamos cómo está Rocinante; que, a lo que me parece, no le ha cabido al pobre la menor parte desta desgracia.[44]

> [... answered Sancho, "... for hardly had I laid hand on my *tizona* when they signed the cross on my shoulders with their sticks in such style that they took the sight out of my eyes and the strength out of my feet, stretching me where I now lie, and where thinking of whether all those stake-strokes were an indignity or not gives me no uneasiness, which the pain of the blows does, for they will remain as deeply impressed on my memory as on my shoulders."
>
> "For all that let me tell you, brother Panza," said Don Quixote, "that there is no recollection which time does not put an end to, and no pain which death does not remove."

"And what greater misfortune can there be," replied Panza, "than the one that waits for time to put an end to it and death to remove it? If our mishap were one of those that are cured with a couple of plasters, it would not be so bad; but I am beginning to think that all the plasters in a hospital almost won't be enough to put us right."

"No more of that: pluck strength out of weakness, Sancho, as I mean to do," returned Don Quixote, "and let us see how Rocinante is, for it seems to me that not the least share of this mishap has fallen to the lot of the poor beast."]

Sancho's description of his injuries articulates a new point of commonality between the two characters, the fact of physical violence providing the opportunity for a shared experience of pain that transcends social difference. Don Quixote underscores this reading in two ways, first through his appeal to a popular *refrán*—"no hay memoria a quien el tiempo no acabe, ni dolor que muerte no le consuma"—that infuses their recent misfortune with a universal character and later, at the end of the passage above, in his attempt to console his squire: "Déjate deso y saca fuerzas de flaqueza, Sancho, que así hare yo . . ." In a manner that is arguably much more effective because of its subtlety, these final words mark a move beyond the exemplarity with which the episode commences. The imitative function implicit in Sancho's decision to follow his master into battle is here replaced by Don Quixote's sympathetic plea that they overcome their shared suffering, that is, by words that already assume Sancho's active integration into the fantasy world of chivalric adventure.

The evolving relationship between Don Quixote and Sancho Panza in this episode furnishes a heterodox response to the canonical paradigm of narrative perfect friendship and the Aristotelian foundation upon which it is built. Certainly, the shift from Don Quixote's exemplary function at the outset of the episode with the *yangüeses* to his open expression of commiseration with Sancho's pain at the end of that scene reveals an equalizing tendency that mitigates not only the hierarchy of their newly professed identities as knight and squire but also, more significantly, the stratification of their former relations as neighbors from different classes within an ossified social hierarchy. This process of equalization gestures toward a key Aristotelian condition for ideal friendship and, in doing so, highlights the peculiar mix of representational verisimilitude and fantasy that characterizes Cervantine poetics. Cervantes's vision of friendship, even as it rejects the more extreme prerequisites of the Aristotelian ideal, nonetheless recognizes the impossibility of friendship between two such dissimilar characters in their normal social roles. An admixture of fantasy based in madness thus provides the necessary first step in the evolving friendship between these two unlikely companions. Thus, while Cervantes's novel respects the formal requirements of a poetics based in representational verisimilitude—there are no "real" giants in Cervantes's narrative—it nonetheless requires Don Quixote's fantasy world in order to escape the oppressive social constraints that would otherwise render a deeper communion between his characters difficult, if not impossible.[45] This is just one of the many ways in which the discourse of friendship and Cervantine poetics are inextricably intertwined.

Beyond the leveling effect of Sancho's initiation into Don Quixote's fantasy life, however, Cervantes's peculiar brand of representational verisimilitude continues in its rejection of other attributes of the Aristotelian model in keeping with a more general dismissal of all forms of poetic idealism that might claim ontological priority. Simply put, Don Quixote's idealizing fantasies, because they always play out in juxtaposition to a much less sparkling material background, never escape an ironic frame that evaporates their claim to truth, but not their appeal as fantasies. The friendship between Don Quixote and Sancho is not immune to these poetic pressures, the cumulative effect of which is to cast the ideal back onto the material world time and time again. Thus, while the relationship between Don Quixote and Sancho arguably crystallizes within the ethereal space of an idealized chivalric existence, the real work of friendship only becomes visible against the background of the material circumstances of their adventures. The same fantasy life that allows both characters to escape the stultifying air of village life is not in itself adequate to the requirements of the friendship that emerges as a result of that escape, but rather depends on a concomitant and somewhat paradoxical return to the practical concerns of everyday life. From this perspective, the relationship between Don Quixote and Sancho is revealed as wholly incompatible with the most extreme feature of the Aristotelian model, namely the apotheosis of the ideal friend against the background of the *vulgo*. Indeed, through his merciless irony, Cervantes not only rejects this transcendent vision of friendship, he renders it absolutely meaningless to his own poetic project.

Rather than a return to the Aristotelian ideal, the leveling effect of Cervantes's peculiar juxtaposition of fantasy and representational verisimilitude pushes the relationship between Don Quixote and Sancho in directions that are without precedent in the narrative tradition of writing perfect friendship. Only five chapters after their encounter with the *yangüeses*, the knight-errant and squire are discovered in the midst of an adventure whose anticlimactic ending opens up entirely uncharted territory in the discourse of early modern friendship. The adventure of the *batanes* leaves Sancho cowering in the dark in fear of a mysterious hammering sound while Don Quixote makes his plan to engage this latest opportunity to demonstrate his knightly valor. Such is Sancho's fear that, in one of his first acts of subterfuge against his master, he immobilizes Rocinante, tying his legs together. When, in the next paragraph, Don Quixote attempts to set out to meet whatever challenge is awaiting him in the night, he discovers Rocinante's paralysis, for which Sancho offers a hasty explanation: "—Ea, señor, que el cielo, conmovido de mis lágrimas y plegarias, ha ordenado que no se pueda mover Rocinante; y si vos queréis porfiar, y espolear, y dalle, será enojar a la fortuna y dar coces, como dicen, contra el aguijón [See there, *señor!* Heaven, moved by my tears and prayers, has so ordered it that Rocinante cannot stir; and if you will be obstinate, and spur and strike him, you will only provoke fortune, and kick, as they say, against the pricks]."[46]

Sancho's clever manipulation of Don Quixote's knightly ambitions demonstrates, once again, how Cervantes frames the chivalric ideal against the nagging backdrop of a poetics that draws its inspiration from the material world.[47] Even more significant in the present context, Sancho's trick points to the evolving trajectory of his relationship with Don Quixote. Through his deception, Sancho is able to take the upper hand, subverting the hierarchy that would reduce him to the role of Don Quixote's servant; Don Quixote may be the master, but in this instance, his squire has all the power. Yet Cervantes here is not interested in the question of power for its own sake, nor even in a critique of early modern social hierarchies—whatever that might mean in this case. Instead, as was evident in the previous example, the deeper implications of this new twist in their shared experience emerges in the apparent paradox of a growing interpersonal bond: Sancho's ultimate motivation for duping Don Quixote is a fear that registers as a kind of separation anxiety. As the episode progresses, both Sancho's manipulation of Don Quixote and his unwillingness to be parted from his companion reveal entirely new if not always unambiguously positive depths in their relationship.

Signs of this change are already evident in the conversation leading up to Sancho's *engaño*. In pleading with Don Quixote not to abandon him in pursuit of this new adventure, Sancho first appeals to Don Quixote's reason—"así que no es bien tentar a Dios acometiendo tan desaforado hecho [so it is not right to tempt God by trying so tremendous a feat]"—and then, as his long speech on the matter develops, to a sense of pity for his timid squire: "Y cuando todo esto no mueva ni ablande ese duro corazón, muévale el pensar y creer que apenas se habrá vuestra merced apartado de aquí, cuando yo, de miedo, dé mi ánima a quien quisiere llevarla [and if all this does not move or soften that hard heart, let this thought and reflection move it, that you will have hardly quitted this spot when from pure fear I shall yield my soul up to anyone that will take it]."[48] With these last words, Sancho speaks to precisely the same sense of commiseration that informed Don Quixote's earlier response to Sancho's suffering in the scene with the *yangüeses*. While the language of friendship is never used, Sancho's reasoning in this passage necessarily implies an expectation that Don Quixote may be swayed by his sense of obligation to his weak-kneed companion. As a measure of friendship, pity for fear is completely alien to the classical idea. And yet, as a symptom of a mode of interpersonal relations based in mutual sympathy, Sancho's apparent belief that such considerations might carry some weight implies that something of this nature has emerged.

Such pleading on the basis of mutual sympathy might seem to be at odds with Sancho's final resolution to trick his master into believing that he has been enchanted. Certainly, neither impulse rises anything close to the demands of Aristotelian perfect friendship and, to the contrary, both highlight Sancho's complete inadequacy to any kind of heroic action. Nevertheless, as a measure of intimacy, Sancho's weakness arguably provides the opening for a different kind of response in an audience willing—and historically prepared—to engage with Cervantes's fictional universe less on the basis of its fulfillment of conventional literary expectations and more through its appeal, by way of representational verisimilitude, to the reader's emotional sympathies.

The *batanes* episode also highlights a second key element in the evolving friendship between knight and squire: Like the pathos of shared suffering, humor in the novel consistently deflates Don Quixote's idealized aspirations through a return to the material world of everyday life. Repeatedly exposing the unbridgeable gulf between knightly fantasies and the mundane affairs that frame them, Cervantes rarely wastes an opportunity to exploit the comic potential of Don Quixote's absurd madness. In the *batanes* episode, this particular mode of humor—like the violence witnessed earlier—contributes to the leveling effect between master and servant, transforming the idealized discourse of Don Quixote's heroic pretensions into a very human weakness—be it mental affliction, narcissism, or just plain arrogance—that renders his behavior intelligible within the discourse of the novel's peculiar poetics.

At daybreak, Sancho releases Rocinante from his contrived enchantment and the two adventurers set out to find the source of the mysterious sounds that Don Quixote had taken as cause for knightly intervention. What they discover is a fulling mill, a water-driven mechanism for pounding textiles "que con sus alternativos golpes aquel estruendo formaban." Here, in the clearest terms, a more mundane seventeenth-century reality imposes itself, dispelling the fantasies that had reigned in the darkness of night. But unlike previous adventures—the windmills, the *yangüeses*—the result is not violence, but comic ridicule. Sancho Panza's other principal role in the novel comes to the fore at this point, his response to this new turn of events exposing the scene's comic potential:

> Cuando don Quijote vio lo que era, enmudeció y pasmóse de arriba abajo. Miróle Sancho y vio que tenía la cabeza inclinada sobre el pecho, con muestras de estar corrido. Miró también don Quijote a Sancho, y viole que tenía los carrillos hinchados, y la boca llena de risa, con evidentes señales de querer reventar con ella, y no pudo su melanconía tanto con él, que a la vista de Sancho pudiese dejar de reírse; y como vio Sancho que su amo había comenzado, soltó la presa de manera, que tuvo necesidad de apretarse las ijadas con los puños, por no reventar riendo. Cuatro veces sosegó, y otras tantas volvió a su risa, con el mismo ímpetu que primero; de lo cual ya se daba al diablo don Quijote, y más cuando le oyó decir, como por modo de fisga:—«Has de saber, ¡oh Sancho amigo!, que yo nací por querer del cielo en esta nuestra edad de hierro para resucitar en ella la dorada, o de oro. Yo soy aquel para quien están guardados los peligros, las hazañas grandes, los valerosos fechos . . .»[49]

> [When Don Quixote perceived what it was, he was struck dumb and rigid from head to foot. Sancho glanced at him and saw him with his head bent down upon his breast in manifest mortification; and Don Quixote glanced at Sancho and saw him with his cheeks puffed out and his mouth full of laughter, and evidently ready to explode with it, and in spite of his vexation he could not help laughing at the sight of him; and when Sancho saw his master begin he let go so heartily that he had to hold his sides with both hands to keep himself from bursting with laughter. Four times he stopped, and as many times did his laughter break out afresh with the same violence as at first, at which Don Quixote grew furious, above all when he heard him say mockingly, "You must know, friend Sancho, that of Heaven's will I was born in this our iron age to revive in it the golden or age of gold; I am he for whom are reserved perils, mighty achievements, valiant deeds."]

The exemplarity that was cited in Sancho's decision to follow his master into battle against the *yangüeses* is transformed in the final lines above into self-conscious mocking. With his words uttered in the style of Don Quixote, Sancho demonstrates mastery of the language through which the mad hero constructs his knightly identity and, perhaps more significantly, a willingness to completely undermine the hierarchy of their formal association. In ridiculing Don Quixote's knightly vocation, Sancho upends the high-minded Renaissance of *imitatio*—implicated from the outset of Don Quixote's quasi-literary project to resurrect the values of chivalric fiction—recasting it as a light parody that has the serious effect of reminding the reader of the novel's foundation in representational verisimilitude.

For a study of friendship, however, the more pertinent impact of Sancho's mirth is paradoxically realized in a solidification of their personal bond as Don Quixote, despite his *melanconía*, is nevertheless swept up in the contagion of Sancho's hilarity—"y no pudo su melanconía tanto con él, que a la vista de Sancho pudiese dejar de reírse." These words both humanize Don Quixote and underscore the depth of his connection with the jolly Sancho. Not only is he able—in spite of himself—to laugh at his own folly, his sympathy with Sancho is such that he cannot help but be drawn into Sancho's comic assessment of the previous night's events. Here, then, one discovers a new way of thinking about the commiseration between Cervantes's adventurers, a new basis for their shared intimacy.[50]

This final point also helps to explain the chapter's denouement. After a spontaneous outburst of anger at Sancho's mocking imitation of his way of speaking, Don Quixote finally acknowledges the grain of truth in his squire's humor: "—No niego yo—respondió don Quijote—que lo que nos ha sucedido no sea cosa digna de risa; pero no es digna de contarse; que no son todas las personas tan discretas, que sepan poner en su punto las cosas ['I do not deny,' said Don Quixote, 'that what happened to us may be worth laughing at, but it is not worth making a story about, for it is not everyone that is shrewd enough to hit the right point of a thing']."[51] Significantly, this acknowledgment of the humor in their predicament is accompanied by an appeal to secrecy. Don Quixote is obsessed with controlling his narrative, and the impulse to silence those aspects of the story that are less favorable to his image must be understood in this light. In this particular instance, however, the exhortation to secrecy necessarily accentuates the complicity of both characters in this presumed cover-up which, in turn, only serves to intensify the sense of their personal connection in opposition to everyone else from whom Don Quixote would rather keep secret the less flattering episodes in his story. In this way, friendship as a private matter reveals, once again, its dependence on an external world defined through a *lack* of knowledge of the intimate circumstances of idiosyncratic personal fellowship.

The contrast with the tale of two friends tradition could not be more stark. Where the representation of ideal friendship invariably acknowledges the public character of such relationships—as the narrator in "El curioso impertinente" puts it, "los dos amigos eran llamados"—the emerging bond between Don Quixote and Sancho in this episode comes to depend on an inherent antagonism to public recognition.[52] Thus, even as Don Quixote actively strives for fame as a knight-errant, his relationship with Sancho Panza is defined within a fictionalized space of private life whose integrity depends on an implicit resistance to public recognition. Eschewing the exemplary function of perfect friendship—with all its attendant flaws—Cervantes presents his reader with a new vision of friendship founded on the verisimilitudinous representation of private life.[53]

At this point, it is useful to emphasize, once again, Don Quixote and Sancho's relationship as a second-order consequence of the novel's poetic commitments. While the importance of the friendship between Don Quixote and Sancho is, perhaps, obvious in retrospect, the specific contours of its evolution and even its centrality to the narrative's formal structure are not prescribed by some external ideological imperative. There is almost always room in Cervantes for the unexpected. Perhaps this explains Don Quixote's appeal to the influence of fortune in his life, a concept that is re-energized by Cervantes's interest in representational verisimilitude both as a measure of the unpredictability of human affairs—in matters both pedestrian and transcendent—and as a clever device for holding the reader's attention in the uncertain expectation of what will happen next. Narratives depicting the classical ideal frequently struggle with the transcendent determinism of Aristotelian perfect friendship, with the fact that the underlying formal structure of this highest form of friendship is largely fixed in categorical terms and is, therefore, resistant to narrativization. Not so for the relationship between Don Quixote and Sancho Panza, which, like the meandering path of the novel's episodic form, is both dynamic and unpredictable. Like the adventures that fill Cervantes's narrative, knight and squire are constantly renegotiating the terms of their fellowship, revealing new insights into a phenomenon that they themselves have conjured into existence.

The subtlety of such insights may be glimpsed in a brief exchange between Don Quixote and his squire late in the first part of the novel. Having witnessed the collusion between the priest and the barber in a scheme to imprison Don Quixote under the guise of enchantment and bring him back to his village, ostensibly in order to restore his mental health, Sancho engages Don Quixote in a conversation that lends new depth to their mutual understanding. Pointing out that Don Quixote, unlike the truly enchanted, is able to eat, drink, sleep, and converse, Sancho encourages him to break free from his imprisonment:

>   —Pues con todo eso—replicó Sancho—digo que para mayor abundancia y satisfación sería bien que vuestra merced probase a salir desta cárcel, que yo me obligo con todo mi poder a facilitarlo, y aun a sacarle della, y probase de nuevo a subir sobre su buen Rocinante, que también parece que va encantado, según va de malencólico y triste; y, hecho esto, probásemos otra vez la suerte de buscar más aventuras."[54]

["Still for all that," replied Sancho, "I say that, for your greater and fuller satisfaction, it would be well if your worship were to try to get out of this prison (and I promise to do all in my power to help, and even to take you out of it), and see if you could once more mount your good Rocinante, who seems to be enchanted too, he is so melancholy and dejected; and then we might try our chance in looking for adventures again."]

The subtext here is subtle, but unmistakable: Only Sancho Panza recognizes the suffering of his master, channeled here through a comparison with Rocinante who, like his master, "va de malencólico y triste." In offering to help Don Quixote in his attempt at freedom, Sancho locates the real remedy for his master's ills, as he will express again at Don Quixote's deathbed, in a return to adventuring, to that liberating escape from the mundane reality of village life.

Even more significant, however, Sancho ends his exhortation with a pledge to join his master in his imprisoned state in the event that his plan for escape fails: "y si no nos sucediese bien, tiempo nos queda para volvernos a la jaula, en la cual prometo a ley de buen y leal escudero de encerrarme juntamente con vuestra merced [and if we have no luck there will be time enough to go back to the cage; in which, on the faith of a good and loyal squire, I promise to shut myself up along with your worship]."[55] More a gesture of commiseration than self-sacrifice—of the kind typically witnessed in the more traditional tale of two friends—the promise to accompany Don Quixote in his suffering is steeped in a pathos that negates the optimistic narrative of perfect friendship. In the end, that promise constitutes a recognition of failure and not, as in the older tradition, a means to greater glory. Sancho's willingness to suffer with his master with no hope of recompense, while noble in its own right, nonetheless serves to frame the conclusion to the novel's first part with a reality that is anything but heroic.[56]

The pathos and melancholy of Sancho's words provide an excellent measure of the dynamic nature of Cervantes's new, more modern vision of friendship. Far from the highly stylized, hyperbolic impulse to self-sacrifice that characterizes the tradition, Don Quixote's spiritual and bodily suffering functions, if only temporarily, as the new *status quo* for their relationship: What both Sancho and Don Quixote imagine is a future for their friendship within the imprisonment—itself a metaphor for a return to the claustrophobic anonymity of life in a small unnamed Manchegan village. With his promise to join his master in his cage, Sancho expresses a willingness to remain faithful not just despite suffering, but rather with an acceptance of suffering as the prevailing condition of their fellowship. In contrast to the more familiar rhetorical posturing in the name of an Aristotelian ideal, Sancho's pledge embodies the aspirations of a friendship that embraces the profound limitations of human existence in the imperfect reality that serves as the novel's ultimate foundation.

Part II

As suggested earlier in this analysis, the evolving relationship between Don Quixote and Sancho Panza is largely constituted through the dialogue between the two adventurers. In each of the episodes discussed so far, the most important evidence of the status of the fellowship between the two main characters derives from what they say about their shared experiences. From the earliest failure of communication in the wake of Don Quixote's unfortunate encounter with the windmills to Sancho's promise to join his master in his imprisonment at the end of the first part, changes in the quality of their relationship are nowhere more fully registered than in the novel's dialogue. In the novel's second part, the central role of dialogue is reaffirmed and even heightened, arguably a reflection of the increased complexity of the dynamic between the two main characters, the simple master-servant binary giving way to a language of contestation that impedes facile characterizations of the nature of their relationship.

In fact, the novel's second part opens with one of the few instances in which the knight and squire discuss the status of their relationship in explicit terms. Echoing his insistence on the equalizing power of knight-errantry in his comments on the Golden Age in the earlier scene with the goatherds from Part I, Don Quixote sustains hierarchical distinctions even as he insists on his shared experience with his squire as a leveling force:

> —... juntos salimos, juntos fuimos y juntos peregrinamos; una misma fortuna y una misma suerte ha corrido por los dos: si a ti te mantearon una vez, a mí me han molido ciento, y esto es lo que te llevo de ventaja.
> —Eso estaba puesto en razón—respondió Sancho—, porque, según vuestra merced dice, más anejas son a los caballeros andantes las desgracias que a sus escuderos.
> —Engáñaste, Sancho—dijo don Quijote—, según aquello, *quando caput dolet* . . ., etcétera.
> —No entiendo otra lengua que la mía—respondió Sancho.
> —Quiero decir—dijo don Quijote—que, cuando la cabeza duele, todos los miembros duelen; y así, siendo yo tu amo y señor, soy tu cabeza, y tú mi parte, pues eres mi criado; y por esta razón el mal que a mí me toca, o tocare, a ti te ha de doler, y a mí el tuyo.

—Así había de ser—dijo Sancho—; pero cuando a mí me manteaban como a miembro, se estaba mi cabeza detrás de las bardas, mirándome volar por los aires, sin sentir dolor alguno; y pues los miembros están obligados a dolerse del mal de la cabeza, había de estar obligada ella a dolerse dellos.[57]

["... We sallied forth together, we took the road together, we wandered abroad together; we have had the same fortune and the same luck; if they blanketed you once, they belaboured me a hundred times, and that is the only advantage I have of you."

"That was only reasonable," replied Sancho, "for, by what your worship says, misfortunes belong more properly to knights-errant than to their squires."

"You are mistaken, Sancho," said Don Quixote, "according to the maxim *quando caput dolet*, etc."

"I don't understand any language but my own," said Sancho.

"I mean to say," said Don Quixote, "that when the head suffers all the members suffer; and so, being your lord and master, I am your head, and you a part of me as you are my servant; and therefore any evil that affects or shall affect me should give you pain, and what affects you give pain to me."

"It should be so," said Sancho; "but when I was blanketed as a member, my head was on the other side of the wall, looking on while I was flying through the air, and did not feel any pain whatever; and if the members are obliged to feel the suffering of the head, it should be obliged to feel their sufferings."]

Unlike the earlier scene from Part I, in which Don Quixote's grandiose attempts to link knight-errantry with the myth of the Golden Age remain largely uncontested by his newly appointed squire, Sancho's rejoinder in this exchange displays a cutting sarcasm that disables Don Quixote's attempt to formulate a serious theory of the master-servant relationship. Intentionally misappropriating Don Quixote's words in their literal sense, Sancho's absurd account of his "cabeza" looking on with indifference as his "miembros" fly through the air deflates not only Don Quixote's theorizing but, perhaps more significantly, the claim to authority that would presumably lend that theorizing legitimacy. Undermining Don Quixote's attempt at clarifying the hierarchical basis of their relationship, Sancho's witty response illustrates the extent to which their dialogue has become the more accurate indicator of the underlying state of their relationship.

The significance of this scene, however, goes beyond the mere fact of Sancho's contestation of Don Quixote's defense of the hierarchical basis of their relationship. Rather, the rhetorical dexterity that he displays in neutralizing Don Quixote's theorizing here underscores his clear understanding of both his traveling companion and the complexities of the interpersonal dynamic that has emerged over their long-shared experience.

Indeed, in ridiculing Don Quixote's attempt at theorizing their association in the facile language of masters and servants, Sancho not only subverts the hierarchical basis of the knight-errant's original claim, he calls into question the reductive tendency of all such categorical labels when applied to the idiosyncratic particularity of their relationship. Read in this way, the substance of Don Quixote's theorizing is finally revealed as little more than a foil to the narrative's reassertion in the opening chapters of the second part of its continued interest in dialogue as the space in which Cervantes's protagonists experience their relationship in an ongoing process of self-articulation.

A further measure of both the centrality of dialogue and the novel's commitment to continuity arises a few chapters later in the chapter documenting Sancho's homecoming to his wife, Teresa. Written almost entirely as a conversation between the squire and his *oíslo*, the chapter devoted to this family reunion explores Sancho's metamorphosis from *labrador* to *escudero* as reflected in a complete breakdown in his attempts to communicate with his wife. As Teresa puts it near the beginning of the chapter, "después que os hicistes miembro de caballero andante habláis de tan rodeada manera, que no hay quien os entienda [ever since you joined on to a knight-errant you talk in such a roundabout way that there is no understanding you]."[58] Teresa's reaction recalls the earlier scene of Don Quixote and Sancho's shared meal with the goatherds from the first part: Like the goatherds who listen on in mystified silence to the knight-errant's *jerigonza*, Teresa's inability to make sense of Sancho's speech constitutes a mark of exclusion. Here, however, the consequences are far more radical, the breakdown in communication from within the bounds of marriage signaling a rupture within the deepest recesses of private life. The intimacy of Sancho's family life, it would seem, has been replaced by the newfound intimacy of his relationship with Don Quixote. And once again, dialogue—or, in this case, the failure of dialogue—provides the most accurate measure of this profound shift in Sancho's personal commitments.

Understood from the traditional perspective of writing perfect friendship, Sancho's homecoming intensifies the conventional exaltation of friendship over all other relationships, as was evident, for example, in Tito's long harangue to Sofronia's family in the *Decameron*. Yet unlike his predecessors, for whom the prioritization of perfect friendship depends almost exclusively on an abstract idealization of the friend's intrinsic virtue, Sancho's alienation from his wife signals a change *within* the squire's psychic life. In place of virtue as a prerequisite for friendship, Sancho's relationship with Don Quixote is predicated on the possibility of individual transformation that is less about abstract values and more about the power of personal influence as a motive force in character development.

This last point becomes abundantly clear as the chapter advances. Beyond the initial fact of Teresa's difficulty in understanding her husband's way of speaking, she displays a fierce resistance to the values of knight-errantry. When Sancho suggests that she might some day become the wife of a governor with all the attendant privileges, Teresa withdraws into a strong defense of her peasant identity: "Teresa me pusieron en el bautismo, nombre mondo y escueto, sin añadiduras ni cortapisas, ni arrequives de *dones* ni *donas* . . . y con este nombre me contento, sin que me le pongan un *don* encima . . . [They called me Teresa at my baptism, a plain, simple name, without any additions or tags or fringes of *Dons* or *Doñas* . . . and I am content with this name without having the '*Don*' put on top of it . . .]"[59] With her insistence on her identity as fixed and immutable, Teresa posits an essentialist understanding of the self that contests not only Sancho's squirely ambitions but, indeed, the very idea of personal transformation that makes those ambitions possible. The contrast between the two could not be more starkly drawn: Teresa's dogged adherence to the rigid—one is tempted to say medieval—social and political hierarchy of village life embodies precisely those structural constraints that Sancho's embrace of his squirely vocation attempts to transcend. Read against Teresa's stultifying sense of social conformity, Sancho's will to remake himself as expressed in this chapter underscores the strength of his alliance with Don Quixote as well as the radical potential inherent in their now shared project to resurrect knight-errantry.[60]

From the practical point of view of a reader who may be taking up the novel's second part for the first time—potentially after a hiatus of several years—the explicit privileging of Sancho's relationship with Don Quixote helps recall the shared history between the two main characters that will serve as the foundation for their new adventures.[61] This emphasis on the connection between the two parts of the novel creates a sense of continuity that, by this point in the narrative, is essential to understanding the peculiar nature of Sancho's bond with his would-be knight-errant companion. Above all, Sancho's homecoming with his wife serves as a reminder that the novel's second part begins *in medias res*, the claims for a pre-existing relationship between the two protagonists a direct outgrowth of the long narrative account of that same relationship published ten years previously.

This sense of continuity is also key to understanding an important development midway through the novel's second part. With the unique dynamic of Don Quixote and Sancho's relationship well established over the course of hundreds of pages, the appearance of the Duke and Duchess at a point deep within the second part finally leads to a set of circumstances that may be read productively—if not definitively—as an attempt to relate Cervantes's unique literary vision to the long narrative tradition of writing Aristotelian friendship. Despite their gentility, the Duke and Duchess are arguably the most unsympathetic characters in the entire novel. Subjecting the unwitting Don Quixote and Sancho to a series of elaborate pranks, the aristocratic couple transforms the knight-errant's fantastic beliefs into a source of mocking humor. Some of these pranks are innocuous enough, but others involve great cruelty, and none more so than the ruse by which the thematics of a more traditional narrative of perfect friendship finally bursts into the novel's main storyline.

The scenario authored by the Duke and Duchess for Dulcinea's disenchantment parallels the conflicts observed in almost every antecedent friendship narrative examined in this study. Dulcinea comes to inhabit the familiar role of the objectified lover, here distorted by Sancho's casting not as Don Quixote's rival but rather as the bizarrely chosen instrument for her salvation: In an elaborately staged performance, the magician Merlin declares that in order to disenchant Dulcinea—whom Don Quixote believes has been transformed into a rustic peasant woman—and restore her former beauty, Sancho must of his own will apply three thousand three hundred lashes to his "valientes posaderas."[62] Despite the novelty of Merlin's demand, an essential congruity links this scene to the long tradition of narrative friendship. By empowering Sancho as the sole agent for Dulcinea's restoration, the Duke and Duchess strip the love triangle down to what is truly essential for it to operate as a test of friendship: In this modified rendering of traditional plotting, the requirement for self-sacrifice is necessarily painful and self-willed.

The importance of this last observation soon becomes apparent in an exchange between Sancho and Don Quixote that follows Merlin's account of the conditions for Dulcinea's disenchantment:

—¡Voto a tal!—dijo a esta sazón Sancho—. No digo yo tres mil azotes; pero así me daré yo tres como tres puñaladas. ¡Válate el diablo por modo de desencantar! ¡Yo no sé qué tienen que ver mis posas con los encantos! ¡Par Dios que si el señor Merlín no ha hallado otra manera como desencantar a la señora Dulcinea del Toboso, encantada se podrá ir a la sepultura!

—Tomaros he yo—dijo don Quijote—, don villano, harto de ajos, y amarraros he a un árbol, desnudo como vuestra madre os parió, y no digo yo tres mil y trecientos, sino seis mil y seiscientos azotes os daré, tan bien pegados, que no se os caigan a tres mil y trecientos tirones. Y no me repliquéis palabra, que os arrancaré el alma.[63]

["By all that's good," exclaimed Sancho at this, "I'll just as soon give myself three stabs with a dagger as three, not to say three thousand, lashes. The devil take such a way of disenchanting! I don't see what my backside has got to do with enchantments. By God, if *Señor* Merlin has not found out some other way of disenchanting the lady Dulcinea del Toboso, she may go to her grave enchanted."

"But I'll take you, Don Clown stuffed with garlic," said Don Quixote, "and tie you to a tree as naked as when your mother brought you forth, and give you, not to say three thousand three hundred, but six thousand six hundred lashes, and so well laid on that they won't be got rid of if you try three thousand three hundred times; don't answer me a word or I'll tear your soul out."]

In place of the exaggerated displays of courtesy and a will to self-sacrifice that characterize earlier narratives of perfect friendship, Sancho's outright refusal to undertake the required self-flagellation is met with threats of violence, even murder. More than hyperbolic grandstanding—of the kind that was observed earlier in various theatrical works, for example—these threats are suggestive of visceral anger that is less about histrionics and more a reflection of a serious and very personal conflict between Cervantes's two protagonists.

With Sancho's absolute refusal to comply with the terms of Merlin's demands and Don Quixote's threats of violence, the text sabotages the expected confirmation of perfect friendship. The test of friendship here leads not to an exaltation of the Aristotelian ideal but to an affirmation of the profound imperfection of Cervantes's unlikely heroes. Sancho, in particular, is poorly suited to sustained gestures of self-sacrifice—despite his claims to the contrary in the scene at the end of the novel's first part discussed above—so that the matter of Dulcinea's disenchantment soon becomes a recurring feature in the narrative as Sancho's aversion to pain continually runs up against Don Quixote's dogged determination to restore his *doncella* to her pristine state.

Moreover, when this ongoing dispute finally reaches what would appear to be a resolution, the means employed involve a radical distortion of the more familiar narrative of hyperbolic self-sacrifice. In one of the last episodes of the novel, the knight-errant and his squire finally come to an agreement based in economic remuneration: Don Quixote will pay Sancho "un cuartillo" for each lash.[64] In a previous analysis of this episode, I suggested that Don Quixote's offer of payment to secure Dulcinea's disenchantment marks the definitive end of his chivalric quest. By conceding to a market-based deal to achieve what he has been unable to accomplish through an appeal to virtue, Don Quixote debases his knightly vocation, undermining the nobility of purpose that had long served to mitigate some of the morally problematic aspects of his mad fantasies.[65]

Similarly, from the perspective of Aristotelian perfect friendship, the proposed solution to the conflict over Dulcinea's disenchantment makes a mockery of the central principle of self-sacrifice. In place of the test of friendship that allows the good friend to show selfless devotion, Don Quixote's agreement to pay Sancho points to the huge gulf between the idealized discourse of Aristotelian perfect friendship and the practical necessities of Cervantes's commitment to representational verisimilitude. Sancho, in particular, reveals his inadequacy to the demands of his appointed role in this rewriting of the friendship tradition as the requirements of Cervantes's poetics supplant the structural demands of a more conventional rendering of the tale of two friends. Indeed, in the literary universe of those poetics, the very notion of self-sacrifice comes under pressure, as the idea of unmotivated magnanimity runs up against the practical reality of everyday life in which actions are invariably motivated by self-interest of one kind or another.

Yet even as it debunks the impractical expectations of the Aristotelian ideal, the narrative posits the possibility of a more sympathetic take on the relationship between Don Quixote and his squire. In place of rigid categorical definitions for friendship that stagnate in predicable narratives, the awkward economic solution to Dulcinea's imagined disenchantment slowly gives way to a recognition—particularly on Don Quixote's part—of the more substantive bond of intimacy that has grown up between these two characters. The movement here is slow, and Cervantes takes pains to further intensify Don Quixote's selfishness before finally creating an opportunity for reconciliation. Nevertheless, the end result is an unambiguous embrace of a radically different aspirational vision of friendship based in a distinctly modern notion of intimacy that acknowledges the mutability of the human condition.

The intensification of Don Quixote's selfishness comes with Sancho's first attempt at self-flagellation in the wake of his new contract with his master. After Sancho withdraws behind a thicket of trees to commence his beating, Don Quixote expresses his concern that his squire might expire before administering the required number of lashes—". . . no quieras apresurarte tanto en la carrera, que en la mitad della te falte el aliento; quiero decir que no te des tan recio, que te falte la vida antes de llegar al número deseado [. . . do not be in so great a hurry as to run yourself out of breath midway; I mean, do not lay on so strenuously as to make your life fail you before you have reached the desired number]."[66] Don Quixote's false compassion for Sancho's well-being exudes a bitter skepticism at the prospect of true friendship. In demoting his relationship with Sancho to one of pure instrumentalism after so many chapters of shared intimacy, Don Quixote's words here would appear to deny even the possibility of friendship between these two unlikely companions, the result of a hard landing in a material world that frustrates humanity's nobler aspirations. For even if Dulcinea is nothing more than a fantasy, the material fact of more than 3,000 lashes is most certainly something quite real.

The apparent degeneration in the relationship between the knight-errant and his squire deepens with Sancho's response to his master's continued cajoling. Having commenced with a small number of lashes, Sancho quickly tires of his appointed task and, as frequently occurs in difficult situations involving his master, employs deception in order to ease his self-inflicted suffering: "Pero el socarrón dejó de dárselos en las espaldas, y daba en los árboles, con unos suspiros de cuando en cuando, que parecía que con cada uno de ellos se le arrancaba el alma [But the rogue no longer laid them on his shoulders, but laid on to the trees, with such groans every now and then, that one would have thought at each of them his soul was being plucked up by the roots]."[67] Viewed from the perspective of the highest values of perfect friendship, Sancho's decision to trick his master arguably constitutes a fundamental betrayal of whatever trust might be said to exist between the two characters. Unlike the earlier instances of deception—as was witnessed in the *batanes* episode, for example—Sancho's feigned lashes involve a cynical subversion of the central conceit of Don Quixote's knightly identity: his absolute and unconditional devotion to Dulcinea.

With his scheme to escape the bind of his promised self-flagellation, Sancho's relationship with Don Quixote reaches a nadir that reveals with exquisite clarity the fragility of Cervantine friendship. Rather than fortify the indissoluble bond with one's second self, the pressure of Merlin's formula for Dulcinea's disenchantment leads each of Cervantes's protagonists to withdraw into the narrowly drawn space of his separate and incompatible self-interest. Yet this moment of essential selfishness—for both Sancho and Don Quixote—also marks the starting point for a kind of redemption as the breakdown in their shared commitments clears the way for a new kind of intimacy that might transcend this recognition of their essential otherness. In an echo of the empathy exhibited by the squire in his offer to join his imprisoned master at the end of Part I, Don Quixote's earlier concern that Sancho might expire before achieving Dulcinea's disenchantment is abruptly displaced by a powerful rejection of the entire enterprise: "—No permita la suerte, Sancho amigo, que por el gusto mío pierdas tú la vida, que ha de servir para sustentar a tu mujer y a tus hijos: espere Dulcinea mejor coyuntura; que yo me contendré con los límites de la esperanza propincua, y esperaré que cobres fuerzas nuevas, para que se concluya este negocio a gusto de todos [Heaven forbid, Sancho my friend, that to please me you should lose your life, which is needed for the support of your wife and children; let Dulcinea wait for a better opportunity, and I will content myself with a hope soon to be realized, and have patience until you have gained fresh strength so as to finish off this business to the satisfaction of everybody]."[68] The knight-errant's willingness here to subordinate Dulcinea to Sancho through an explicit recognition of Sancho's financial obligations to his family, signals a renewal of their friendship through Don Quixote's privileging of his real-world companion's material needs over the requirements of his knight-errant fantasies.[69]

At the same time, Don Quixote's expression of empathy may be said to constitute an understated, but arguably sincere return to a modified discourse of self-sacrifice that flourishes in spite of his essential selfishness. Indeed, given his hyperbolic passion for his beloved Dulcinea, Don Quixote's change of heart at this moment would be incredible were it not for the fact of his relationship with Sancho. Where Dulcinea—not unlike Aristotelian perfect friendship—exists in the realm of abstract ideals, Sancho occupies the material world of Don Quixote's here and now, that is, a fictionalized version of the world beyond the text in which real-life friendships form. As Carroll Johnson observes, when finally forced to choose between an imagined lover and his imperfect worldly squire, Don Quixote opts for his friend Sancho.[70]

The relative lack of self-consciousness with which the topic of friendship permeates this episode necessarily undermines its rhetorical force. As a function of Cervantes's poetics, friendship loses its exemplary status, its capacity to represent an ideal that, however problematically, is held up as a model for imitation. The relationship between Don Quixote and Sancho is, in a very real sense, inimitable even as it depends on a new kind of imitative poetics for its very existence. A deep well of lived experience informs a poetics based in representational verisimilitude that is, to borrow from Aristotle in a very different sense, a function of the probable, now understood as a species of the idiosyncratic. Clearing away the fantasies that comprise Don Quixote's peculiar madness, one is left with the dynamic process of rapprochement between knight and squire that possesses credibility precisely to the extent that it rejects claims to exemplary authority. This is not to say that one may not learn something from the relationship between Don Quixote and Sancho, but rather that what is learned cannot be generalized into a principle or rule for conduct that might, even in a theoretical way, provide a guide for friendship.

The intimacy that is the ultimate measure of modern friendship thus exists in *Don Quixote* beyond or beneath the narrative's ostensible interest in repudiating chivalric literature. It emerges slowly, over hundreds of pages, through the gradual accumulation of experience that defines the relationship between Don Quixote and his squire. Its relative invisibility against the backdrop of the novel's open engagement with all manner of themes only underscores its importance, the fact of its assumed nature as part of the poetic structure of the narrative, the consequence not of an explicit theoretical project but rather of an accretion of a way of writing that makes modern friendship possible, that, indeed, transforms the voluntary intimacy between Don Quixote and Sancho Panza into the symptom of an alternative way of rendering fictional lives.

Perhaps the best, final sign of this alternative vision of friendship may be witnessed in a rare instance in which the two companions find themselves separated. In a private audience with the Duchess in the middle of the second part, Sancho attempts an explanation of his continued devotion to Don Quixote despite their never-ending misadventures:

—Par Dios, señora—dijo Sancho—que ese escrúpulo viene con parto derecho; pero dígale vuesa merced que hable claro, o como quisiere; que yo conozco que dice verdad: que si yo fuera discreto, días ha que había de haber dejado a mi amo. Pero esta fue mi suerte, y esta mi malandanza; no puedo más, seguirle tengo: somos de un mismo lugar; he comido su pan; quiérole bien; es agradecido; diome su pollinos, y, sobre todo, yo soy fiel; y, así, es imposible que nos pueda apartar otro suceso que el de la pala y azadón.[71]

["By God, *señora*," said Sancho, "but that doubt comes timely; but your grace may say it out, and speak plainly, or as you like; for I know what you say is true, and if I were wise I should have left my master long ago; but this was my fate, this was my bad luck; I can't help it, I must follow him; we're from the same village, I've eaten his bread, I'm fond of him, I'm grateful, he gave me his ass-colts, and above all I'm faithful; so it's quite impossible for anything to separate us, except the pickaxe and shovel."]

In explaining why he stays with Don Quixote despite his master's obvious madness, Sancho speaks in terms that evoke a kind of negative reconstitution of the traditional association of perfect friendship with the forces of destiny, frequently understood in terms of divine providence. Such negativity, however, is steeped in irony, as Sancho goes on to describe his relationship with his master in the language of shared experiences and an affective bond that while hardly able to boast of the heroics that attend ideal friendship in the longer narrative tradition, nevertheless carries the promise of fidelity until death.[72] Despite the inherent imperfections of this alternative understanding of friendship, there nonetheless persists a sense of the life-altering power of the bonds of intimacy that link such unlikely companions as Don Quixote and Sancho Panza.

This last observation hints at the Cervantine optimism that discovers within the limits of human experience the possibility of a kind of transcendence based in the quotidian, an idea that is captured most succinctly in the metonymic image of a shared meal. After their common origins in the same small village, this is what finally defines their relationship for Sancho, followed in the logical sequence of the passage above by the affective declaration, "quiérole bien." While complicated by obvious self-interest, like the gift of *pollinos* that arguably stands in for all of Sancho's material expectations from his employment with Don Quixote, this simple fellowship based in a shared day-to-day existence is never undermined by these other considerations. Unlike the hyperbolic idealism on display in more traditional narratives of perfect friendship, Sancho's relationship with Don Quixote does not demand purity and, as suggested by this passage, can coexist with the more venal aspects of the squire's personality. Cervantes thus offers his reader a more complex, practical vision of the often conflicting impulses through which modern human friendships are brought into being.

In the end, however, what stands out most in this meditation on the nature of the relationship between Don Quixote and Sancho is its final inadequacy to the experience itself of that relationship. Where the traditional friendship narrative attempts to give representational form to an ideal that is defined *a priori* in clear conceptual terms, the relationship between Don Quixote and Sancho is constituted in the very act of storytelling. A pale approximation of the thing in itself, Sancho's attempt to explain his decision to remain with his master underscores the impossibility of describing their friendship in categorical terms. While everything that he says to the Duchess is arguably true, Sancho's words are no substitute for the practice of friendship. Like the knight and squire's wandering through the Iberian countryside, that friendship is itself a kind of errantry, conjured by the reader's movement through the pages of a book, each of which describes a unique but passing moment within the long trajectory of their shared adventures.

Notes

1. Cervantes, *Don Quixote*, I.7. Spanish is adapted from the Rodríguez Marín edition. Except where noted, English translations are adapted from the Ormsby edition, which I have selectively modernized and modified for readability and accuracy, especially with respect to pronouns.

2. As a response to what he sees as the pervasive "sentimentalization" of the relationship between Don Quixote and Sancho (p. 838), Williamson, "The Power-Struggle Between Don Quixote and Sancho," p. 839, provides one of the more emphatic critiques of the power dynamic operating between Cervantes's protagonists: "Nevertheless, I will argue that the relationship between the protagonists is best characterized as a power-struggle, and that once it is perceived as such it becomes possible to identify certain crises which advance the narrative at strategic junctures."
3. Cervantes, *Don Quixote*, II.3: "—Eso no—respondió Sansón—; porque es tan clara, que no hay cosa que dificultar en ella: los niños la manosean, los mozos la leen, los hombres la entienden y los viejos la celebran; y, finalmente, es tan trillada y tan leída y tan sabida de todo género de gentes, que apenas han visto algún rocín flaco, cuando dicen: 'Allí va Rocinante.'"
4. Alter, *Partial Magic*, p. 4, for example, highlights the contrast between those "many generations of readers" who "have rhapsodized over Don Quixote as a timeless image of humanity," and the novel's explicit self-consciousness: "Cervantes takes pains, on the other hand, to make us aware also that the knight is merely a lifelike model of papier-maché, a design in words, images, invented gestures and actions, which exists between the covers of a book by Miguel de Cervantes."
5. Alter, *Partial Magic*, p. 5, notes: "This novel, like so many others after it, presents us a world of role-playing, where the dividing lines between role and identity are often blurred, and almost everyone picks up the cues for his role from the literature he has read." In a somewhat different vein, Spitzer, "Linguistic Perspectivism in the *Don Quijote*," pp. 70–1, writes: "In the second part of the novel, when the Duke and Duchess ask to see the by now historical figures of Quijote and Panza, the latter says to the Duchess: 'I am Don Quijote's squire who is to be found also *in the story* and who is called Sancho Panza—unless they have changed me in the cradle—I mean to say, at the printer's.' In such passages, Cervantes willingly destroys the artistic illusion: he, the puppeteer, lets us see the strings of his puppet show: 'see, reader, this is not life, but a stage, a book: art; recognize the life-giving power of the artist as a thing distinct from life!'"
6. Durán, *La ambigüedad en el Quijote*, p. 241, highlights the connection between action and identity in *Don Quixote:* "Mientras que el Licenciado Vidriera funciona en papel de oráculo, el caballero manchego, en lugar de permanecer pasivo, tratando de ponerse en contacto con alguna fuente de sabiduría ultraterrena, se esfuerza en *convertirse en sí mismo*, en llegar a ser 'hijo de sus obras'; y esta actividad a la que se lanza con toda energía se convierte a la vez en expresión de su yo interno y en forma de moldearlo con mayor precisión desde un ámbito exclusivamente terrestre."
7. Murillo, "Diálogo y dialéctica en el siglo XVI español," pp. 35–6, identifies the originality of the characters that populate *Don Quixote* with Cervantes's innovative use of dialogue: "En toda su historia, desde Platón, no había variado el arte del diálogo; en cada caso el dialogar representaba el discurso racional elaborado dentro de una idea, ya fuera Cicerón, San Augustín o

Petrarca y sus distintos interlocutores, o los personajes de Tasso o de Giordano Bruno. Sólo con el *Quijote* de Cervantes adquiere nueva dimensión; aquí el discurso es la concentrada y conservada esencia del personaje desde su intimidad; es la vida misma estabilizada para siempre por el arte." Murillo's association of Cervantine dialogue with "intimacy" is especially relevant to my analysis here.

8. Rivers, *Quixote Scriptures*, p. 118. The trivializing force of his reference to "standing jokes" and "topics of mutual interest" notwithstanding, Rivers correctly identifies the central role of private dialogue in forging a personal bond of friendship between Don Quixote and Sancho despite social difference.

9. Mancing, *The Chivalric World of* Don Quijote, pp. 49–50, alludes to this idea in an analysis of Don Quixote's speech: "On his first sally, Don Quijote traveled all day until he and Rocinante were exhausted, his only conversation being with himself as he imagined how his history would be written by a benevolent wizard and as he invoked (with appropriate chivalric archaism) the support of Dulcinea. In contrast, his second sally begins with a conversation with Sancho Panza that deals partly with the *ínsula* that the squire is to receive and partly with the nature of the latter's wife. This discussion contains no archaism. Luis Rosales has shown how beginning with this conversation an essential change in Don Quijote's character takes place. Previously he has employed a 'borrowed' language, using only his chivalric style and never really communicating with anyone. Now, with the simultaneous introduction of Sancho Panza and practical social dialogue, Don Quijote becomes more humanized. One of the the main reasons why Don Quijote's frequency of archaic speech declines is that it is simply not practical to sustain such an artificial style in his conversations with Sancho."

10. Cervantes, *Don Quixote*, I.20.

11. See Ibid. I.25: "—Señor don Quijote, vuestra merced me eche su bendición y me dé licencia; que desde aquí me quiero volver a mi casa y a mi mujer y a mis hijos, con los cuales por lo menos, hablaré y departiré todo lo que quisiere; porque querer vuestra merced que vaya con él por estas soledades de día y de noche, y que no le hable cuando me diere gusto, es enterrarme en vida . . ." Faced with Sancho's possible abandonment of his squirely vocation, Don Quixote relents and, despite a statement to the contrary, the command of silence is never really enforced after this point in the novel.

12. This emphasis on poetics arguably distinguishes this study from other recent scholarship on friendship in *Don Quixote*. Gil-Osle, for example, who has written extensively about friendship in the Spanish early modern period, relates the relationship between Don Quixote and Sancho to the more purely historical phenomena of "mecenazgo," "clientelismo" and "fuedalismo." See especially, *Amistades imperfectas: Del Humanismo a la Ilustración con Cervantes*, pp. 34–5.

13. Urbina's analysis of *Don Quixote* as parody hinges on a reading of Sancho in connection with the literary figure of the *escudero* from chivalric fiction. See Urbina, *El sin par Sancho Panza*, pp. 13–14: "Lejos de ser un factor

marginal bajo el cual han de buscarse significados ocultos trascendentes de muy diverso signo, la parodia es factor dominante y determinante de toda la ficción, de su estilo, de su estructura y de su sentido. La parodia así entendida—la parodia de la figura del escudero—ha de dar lugar a la válida interpretación de Sancho Panza como personaje literario y, en definitiva, a la del *Quijote* como obra paródico-seria, a la vez crítica y creativa." Urbina's study begins with an overview of previous writings on Sancho Panza, all of which focus on the character's status as a purely literary creation.

14. Martínez-Bonati, Don Quixote *and the Poetics of the Novel*, p. 5. Riley, *Cervantes's Theory of the Novel* addresses this confusion on at least two separate occasions in his classic study of Cervantine poetics. In the first instance, he highlights the complexities of Cervantes's approach to the relationship between "art" and "nature," noting, p. 57, that the simple formula that "art imitates nature" is complicated, among other things, by the "complementary notion that art perfected nature," all of which, he suggests, "serves also as a reminder that imitation did not imply what we now understand by 'realism.'" Later in a discussion of decorum in *Don Quixote* and idealization in the *Persiles*, p. 140, he points to the tendency in Cervantes toward associations—like the notion, and here he cites the *Persiles* directly, that "'bodily beauty is often a sign of beauty of soul'"—that would appear "to make nonsense of the repeated insistence of Cervantes on verisimilitude." He continues: "But we must not make the mistake of confusing verisimilitude with realism. These unlikely characters are, for Cervantes, poetically true. The ideal is a poeticization of reality without being, as fantasy is, essentially untrue. Yet literary idealization caused him uneasiness on account of the eulogistic, hyperbolical procedures involved. What it meant indeed was the subjection of one sort of verisimilitude (what 'could be') to another (what 'ought to be')." This last point is of particular relevance to *Don Quixote*, where the distrust of literary idealizations is most powerfully on display. Martínez-Bonati, pp. 4–5, also observes: "What critical commonplace has been repeated more often than the assertion of the *Quixote's* 'stupendous realism'? It is true that many Cervantes studies question such a characterization. Distinctions have been drawn between the Golden Age's 'verisimilitude' and the 'realism' of the nineteenth and twentieth centuries. But the analysis of these concepts, which will prove useful for understanding the nature of the novelistic world of the *Quixote*, has been precarious. As a consequence, this novel is considered in relation to aesthetic ideals (such as the realism of the image of life) that are not its own . . ."

15. Ife, *Reading and Fiction in Golden-Age Spain*, p. 52. Ife's notion of "aesthetic belief" echoes Forcione's earlier analysis of verisimilitude in *Cervantes, Aristotle, and the* Persiles, pp. 96–7: "The canon makes the same assumption, for, after claiming that works must be composed so that 'they astonish, hold, excite, and entertain,' he adds that 'none of this can be achieved by anyone departing from verisimilitude or from that imitation of nature in which lies the perfection of all that is written.' Since verisimilitude depends ultimately

on the capacity or willingness of the reader to believe, the poet's task is to choose and to construct his inventions or 'lies' carefully, giving them enough semblance of truth so that the reader's willingness to believe is strained but not destroyed . . ."
16. Ibid. p. 52. Ife's analysis focuses in particular on the Platonic critique of neo-Aristotelian poetic theory.
17. Ibid. p. 52.
18. One is reminded in this respect of the various framing devices that Cervantes uses to construct his fictional narrative as a kind of history, all of which serve to undermine the stability of the text's relationship to either category.
19. Martínez-Bonati, Don Quixote *and the Poetics of the Novel*, pp. 11–12, provides a forceful defense of this idea: "And regarding the repeated assertion that construes the *Quixote* as a complete picture of the Spanish society of its times, I think, as Erich Auerbach does, that it suffices to examine a historiographical vision of the sixteenth and seventeenth centuries in Spain to understand that the severe, somber, multiple face of that peninsular society is not *shown* in the *Quixote* . . . What leads to the (deceptive) impression of a complete social panorama is the pictorial variety of social types: high nobility, hidalgos, merchants, ecclesiastics, peasants, soldiers, students, vagabonds, criminals, and so on. But the characters who assume these conditions and offices are not there primarily to expound the framework of the social organization and its vital relationships by exemplifying its roles . . . Fundamentally, the *Quixote*'s characters incarnate figures from the tradition of comedy: imposters, *milites gloriosi*, plain dealers, clowns, rustics, gallants, maidens, and so forth. The complete universe that the work offers us is not that of historical society. It is the archetypal universe of literature, whose relationship with real life is more indirect and abstract than that of a sociographic representation, or than that of realistic literature."
20. In describing the friend as fictional, I am following the lead of Presberg, *Adventures in Paradox*, p. 87, who identifies the introduction of this new character in the prologue as a sign of the prologue's status as pure fiction: "Further, the timely arrival of the 'witty and learned friend,' whose comments perfectly suit the narrator's purposes, strikes me as transparently implausible . . . Moreover, the language of the 'dialogue' between the narrator and the friend is bookish in the extreme, a form of written discourse rather than oral speech, and seems less than credible as a verbal exchange between friends. In paradoxical terms, their 'conversation' is made to 'sound' like pure print—a paradox involving the *written* version of what purports to be *oral* speech, which is more plausibly an *imitation* of *written* discourse."
21. Cervantes, *Don Quixote*, I.Prologue.
22. Ibid. I.Prologue.
23. Ibid. I.Prologue. The translation here is from Cohen, who captures the literal sense of Cervantes's original better than Ormsby.
24. Maravall, *Utopía y contrautopía en el «Quijote»*, pp. 14–15, captures this idea most succinctly: "No es infrecuente el caso de un escritor que comienza

concibiendo su libro con un sentido determinado, y a medida que avanza su tarea va adquiriendo aquél una significación propia que acaba imponiéndose a la que su autor anticipó proyectivamente al empezar. Cuando mayor es la relevancia que adquiere en la historia una obra literaria, más acusadamente se da en ella el fenónemo que hemos señalado."

25. As both an "unanticipated outcome" and "one of the most significant manifestations of" Cervantes's poetic practice, friendship also resembles what might be described as an emergent property of the novel's internal structure. It is inseparable from the novel's formal conceits but also irreducible to those conceits. Rather, it represents something new, a phenomenon whereby the sum of the whole is greater than the parts. It is for this reason, perhaps, that it is difficult to speak of friendship between Don Quixote and Sancho as a concrete concept in the novel that might exist independent of the process of narration that gives it life.

26. While focusing more on the role of madness in shaping the relationship between Don Quixote and Sancho Panza, Shuger's analysis nevertheless shares with my own a recognition of the dynamic nature of the association between Cervantes's protagonists. See especially *Don Quixote in the Archives*, pp. 133–47.

27. Cervantes, *Don Quixote*, II.35. The translation here is mine.

28. Mancing, *The Chivalric World of* Don Quixote, p. 49, writes, "The most important single event in Cervantes's novel, after the original exposition, is the introduction of Sancho Panza."

29. There is a significant tradition of reading the *Quixote* through psychoanalytical theories of one kind or another. See, for example, *Quixotic Desire: Psychoanalytic Perspectives on Cervantes*, eds. El Saffar and Wilson; Johnson, *Madness and Lust: A Psychoanalytical Approach to Don Quixote*; Sullivan, *Grotesque Purgatory: A Study of Cervantes's* Don Quixote, *Part II*. In contrast, I am more interested in the representation of the characters' inner lives as a function of Cervantes's innovative use of language, especially dialogue. Rather than probe the recesses of Don Quixote and Sancho's psyche, I will be concerned with the rhetorical techniques that make the appearance of their psychic lives even possible. For this reason, my reading of Don Quixote's madness is more in line with that of Williamson and Auerbach. Williamson, *The Half-Way House of Fiction*, p. 92, writes: "All we are told about Don Quixote's madness is that it was induced by excessive reading of romances of chivalry, which led him to believe that everything written in them was literally true. Cervantes fastens on this simple cause and provides no further explanation. Medical or psychological theories of insanity—whether modern or contemporary—would offer very little that could be relevant to an understanding of the nature of the *hidalgo*'s madness."

30. Auerbach, "The Enchanted Dulcinea," p. 353, continues: "The others all wonder about him, are amused or angered by him, or try to cure him. Sancho lives himself into Don Quijote, whose madness and wisdom become productive in him. Although he has far too little critical reasoning power to

form and express a synthetic judgment upon him, it still is he, in all his reactions, through whom we best understand Don Quijote." Auerbach's final point here underscores the extent to which the discovery of Don Quixote's "personality" registers its ultimate meaning in the reader.
31. Cervantes, *Don Quixote*, I.8.
32. This characterization of Sancho's early interactions with Don Quixote overlaps somewhat with Mancing's analysis of the windmill scene in *The Chivalric World of Don Quixote*, p. 49: "First, and most important, is the squire's role as 'Reality Instructor.' Sancho's nagging voice asking '¿Qué gigantes?' ('What giants?') and adding more specifically, 'Mire vuestra merced ... que aquellos que allí se parecen no son gigantes, sino molinos de viento' ('Look, your worship ... What we see there are not giants but windmills'), can never be effectively silenced by Don Quijote's mere will ... The knight's chivalric fantasy must from now on attempt to withstand repeated assaults of reality from his squire."
33. Cervantes, *Don Quixote*, I.8.
34. Ibid. I.11.
35. Ibid. I.11. The goatherds are *seemingly* rustic at this point. Later, several of them will reveal a high level of cultural attainment, reminiscent more of the pastoral than a verisimilitudinous representation of rural life in early seventeenth-century Spain. Nevertheless, the fact that Cervantes waits to reveal this information is arguably important to the creation of the effect described in the analysis offered here.
36. Gilbert-Santamaría, *Writers on the Market: Consuming Literature in Early Seventeenth-Century Spain*, pp. 170–1.
37. Cervantes, *Don Quixote*, I.11.
38. On the etymology of the word *jerigonza*, see Moralejo Laso, "Para la etimología de la palabra *jerigonza*," p. 330: "Para Corominas *jerigonza* es sinónimo de *jerga* y por primera vez se lee en el *Lazarillo* (1554), pero a mediados del siglo XIII se halla *girgonz*. La voz *jerga* le parece un derivado retrógrado del occitano antiguo *gergon*, salido a su vez del francés antiguo *jargon* o *gergon* (dialectal *gargon*, primitivamente «gorjeo de los pájaros», de donde «habla incomprensible»), de la onomatopeya GARG- «hablar confusamente, tragar», etc., en relación con la garganta."
39. In fact, Cervantes's writings contain examples of both public and private reading. The priest's reading to the collected guests at the inn of the "El curioso impertinente" is perhaps the most famous depiction of public reading in early modern Spain. A contrasting representation of private reading occurs at the end of "El casamiento engañoso," in the *Novelas ejemplares*. As Ife notes in *Reading and Fiction in Golden-Age Spain*, p. 9, "When Campuzano gives Peralta the *Coloquio de los perros* to read, he reads it silently although he is not alone, and there is no suggestion that he should or could have done otherwise. It is impossible to say when the balance began to tilt, but it seems reasonable to associate the consolidation of silent reading with the age of the printed book."

40. Cervantes, *Don Quixote*, I.15. The translation here is taken from Cohen's edition. The term *yangüeses* is used only in the title to chapter 15; throughout the text of chapter 15, these characters are referred to as *gallegos*.
41. Ibid. I.15.
42. Ibid. I.15.
43. Ibid. I.15.
44. Ibid. I.15.
45. This idea echoes Close's assertion in *Cervantes and the Comic Mind of his Age*, p. 158, that Cervantes in his "heroic fiction" (i.e. the *Quixote*) "conscientiously strives to contain the extraordinary within the bounds of what he understands by 'common nature' (*Don Quijote* I.49; i.578)." Referencing the notion of *admiratio* from romance and epic, Williamson, *The Half-Way House of Fiction*, pp. 90–1, reaches a similar conclusion by way of Don Quixote's madness: "Where his predecessors sought to retain *admiratio* by effecting some sort of compromise between the marvellous and verisimilitude, Cervantes effectively redefines the nature of the marvellous by seeking it, not in the supernatural, but in the madness of his protagonist: although the madness is consistently mocked, it is used all the same to turn the tables on the reader, whose common sense is never actually confounded but neither is it ever decisively triumphant over the knight's inspired lunacy." This idea has been echoed more recently by Shuger, *Don Quixote in the Archives*, p. 133, who references both Williamson and Menéndez Pidal: "Edwin Williamson, building on Ramón Menéndez Pidal's theory of the evolution of *Don Quixote*, characterises the decision to present a mad protagonist, and then to give him a sidekick, as 'fortuitous', because it provided 'a creative space beyond verisimilitude' in which Cervantes could 'assert the freedom of his imagination.'"
46. Cervantes, *Don Quixote*, I.20.
47. If there were any doubt about the privileged role of the material world, it is quickly remedied in this episode by Sancho's soiling himself out of fear. That fear, and that soiling, possesses a force—one might call it a reality—that is wholly independent of Don Quixote's own projected fantasies.
48. Cervantes, *Don Quixote*, I.20.
49. Ibid. I.20.
50. Hutchinson, "Affective Dimensions in *Don Quijote*," p. 82, expands on this idea in a recent study of emotion in *Don Quixote*: "This Olympian laughter, generated out of bodies, looks, perceptions, and awareness, banishes all the fear and melancholy of the night before. One thing that happens in this chapter is that the characters' emotion, highly dialogic in nature, orients their actions and conversations to such an extent that emotion itself becomes a central theme of reflection and debate for the characters, and actually redefines their relationship." The emphasis on how dialogue functions in this episode is particularly relevant to my analysis.
51. Cervantes, *Don Quixote*, I.20. In his analysis of this episode through the lens of the "power-struggle" between Cervantes's protagonists, Williamson,

"The Power-Struggle between Don Quixote and Sancho," p. 841, focuses on Don Quixote's anger and Sancho's subsequent acquiescence to his master's authority. In contrast, my reading here emphasizes the points of commiseration between the two in this important scene, the way in which the two characters are drawn closer together despite their different social positions.
52. Ibid. I.33.
53. There is, of course, a paradox in such claims to privacy, as revealed in the chapter's curiously ironic subtitle: "*De la jamás vista ni oída aventura que con más poco peligro fue acabada de famoso caballero en el mundo, como la que acabó el valeroso don Quijote de la Mancha.*" Beyond the more obvious fact that this embarrassing spectacle hardly fits the definition of an adventure, these words capture the underlying tension between public and private discourse that is a key component of novelistic fiction in general. On the one hand, in its formal capacity as a label attached to the "novel" *Don Quixote*, the reference to this "jamás vista ni oída aventura" exposes the inherent conflict between the representation of personal intimacy and the formal requirements of a genre that is, in the end, destined for public consumption. While the fictional space of Don Quixote and Sancho's private relationship opens up to include the reader as witness to hidden events known only to the initiated, the novel by definition circulates within a commercial space that necessarily exposes such embarrassing mishaps to public scrutiny. Put another way, the reader's role as witness to an evolving personal intimacy between Cervantes's characters depends on a concurrent suppression of the formal circumstances of that role, a "suspension of disbelief" that paradoxically links the poetics of representational verisimilitude to the reader's willful refusal to acknowledge the formal requirements of those same poetics. The representation of a new kind of friendship thus depends on the reader's occupation of the awkward and even paradoxical position of complicit witness to a fictional intimacy that is itself constructed through a medium that is the object of public consumption. Ife, *Reading and Fiction in Golden-Age Spain*, pp. 58–9, links Coleridge's expression with Cervantes through the Spanish verb *suspender*. Noting that "this verb . . . does duty for many aspects of the reading process, conveying both the rapture which fiction inspires in its audience, and the willing or unwilling suspension of the rational and critical faculties which is what ultimately brings that rapture about," he goes on to suggest, "English usage echoes the Spanish by speaking of the 'suspension of disbelief.'"
54. Cervantes, *Don Quixote*, I.49.
55. Ibid. I.49.
56. This observation finds further support in Don Quixote's initial resistance to Sancho's plea for escape: That resistance is based in Don Quixote's unwillingness to acknowledge the sordid reality of his imprisonment, that is, the fact that it is not a manifestation of magical forces in the world, but merely a form of material degradation.

57. Cervantes, *Don Quixote*, II.2.
58. Ibid. II.5.
59. Ibid. II.5.
60. It is for this reason that the historical significance of this moment in Cervantes's text is best understood more abstractly, in terms of Sancho's advocacy for a more robust understanding of his own agency over and against Teresa's more conservative embrace of social identity as fixed and unchanging. In this episode in particular, Sancho's presumed subordination to his master is far less significant than the transformative power of Don Quixote's larger project in boosting Sancho's belief in his ability to radically alter his social circumstances, even as that belief is tinged with a significant measure of Cervantine irony.
61. It should be noted that the framing of this chapter as apocryphal introduces an element of irony in Sancho's assertion of self-willed social mobility. In arguing in II.5 that "en él habla Sancho Panza con otro estilo del que se podía prometer su corto ingenio," the narrator calls into question the veracity of Sancho's new claim to subjective autonomy. As with so much else in Cervantes's novel, this ironizing counter-current creates an inescapable ambiguity around the problem of identity that necessarily impedes attempts at definitive readings of the chapter's significance. Yet despite the narrator's misgivings as to the chapter's status, there nevertheless persists the inescapable impact of the dialogue's representation of Sancho's alienation from his wife. No amount of ironic posturing can fully undo the fact of that dialogue.
62. Cervantes, *Don Quixote*, II.35.
63. Ibid. II.35.
64. Ibid. II.71.
65. Gilbert-Santamaría, *Writers on the Market*, p. 186: "The contract [to accomplish Dulcinea's disenchantment] between knight-errant and squire arguably represents don Quijote's most important capitulation to the claims of the new social and economic order. In this respect, the episode is more significant than don Quijote's defeat by the *caballero de la blanca luna*. That defeat, while it obligates don Quijote to give up his self-proclaimed profession of knight-errantry, still functions within the logic of chivalric romance. While it leads to the end of don Quijote's career, it is an end conceived from within the paradigm of don Quijote's fantastic quest. In contrast, the episode of Dulcinea's disenchantment involves an essential corruption of the chivalric model. The contract between don Quijote and his *escudero* contaminates the very essence of their relationship with the encroaching values of the economic market." For a somewhat different take on this same episode, see Johnson, *Cervantes and the Material World*, pp. 32–6.
66. Cervantes, *Don Quixote*, II.71.
67. Ibid. II.71.
68. Ibid. II.71.

69. Johnson, *Cervantes and the Material World*, p. 35 emphasizes the fact that this reconciliation between Cervantes's protagonists "takes place in an environment defined by economics." Following up on Johnson's observation, I note in *Writers on the Market*, p. 188, "that rather than a withdrawal from the new economic logic that has infected his relationship with Sancho, don Quijote's gesture of friendship may be understood as an attempt to find some way to save their personal communion *despite* that economic logic." What the present analysis adds to that earlier interpretation is a recognition that in choosing Sancho over Dulcinea, Don Quixote is also embracing his friendship with his squire over the chivalric fantasy that has been the driving force behind nearly everything he does in the novel.
70. Johnson, *Cervantes and the Material World*, p. 35. Shuger's reading of this scene in *Don Quixote in the Archives*, pp. 144–5, underscores its pivotal role in the evolution of the relationship between Cervantes's protagonists: "This time the inversion of roles—the master asking the servant to stop the discipline that he himself had ordered, and then covering up the servant with his own cloak—is initiated by Don Quixote. Both characters, by this point, have come to place the physical and mental well-being of the other above their own desires and above society's dictates. They have become friends."
71. Cervantes, *Don Quixote*, II.33.
72. This sense of fidelity is echoed in Don Quixote's assessment of his *escudero* in his final deathbed speech in II.74: ". . . y si como estando yo loco fui parte para darle el gobierno de la ínsula, pudiera agora, estando cuerdo, darle el de un reino, se le diera, porque la sencillez de su condición y fidelidad de su trato lo merece."

Works Cited

Alemán, Mateo. *Guzmán de Alfarache*. Ed. Julio Cejador y Frauca. Madrid: Renacimiento, 1913.
Alfonso, Pedro. *Die Disciplina clericalis des Petrus Alfonsi*. Ed. Werner Söderhjelm and Alfons Hika. Heidelberg: C. Winter, 1911.
Alfonso, Pedro. *The* Disciplina Clericalis *of Petrus Alfonsi*. Ed. Eberhard Hermes. Trans. P. R. Quarrie. Berkeley: University of California Press, 1977.
Alfonso, Pedro. *The Scholar's Guide: A Translation of the Twelfth-Century* Disciplina Clericalis *of Pedro Alfonso*. Trans. Joseph Ramon Jones and John Esten Keller. Toronto: The Pontifical Institute of Mediaeval Studies, 1969.
Alter, Robert. *Partial Magic: The Novel as a Self-Conscious Genre*. Berkeley: University of California Press, 1975.
Arellano, Ignacio. "Del relato al teatro: la reescritura de *El curioso impertinente* cervantino por Guillén de Castro." *Criticón* 72 (1998): 73–92.
Aristotle. *Nicomachean Ethics*. Trans. Terence Irwin. Indianapolis: Hackett Publishing Company, 1985.
Aubrun, Charles-Vincent. *La comedia española (1600–1680)*. 2nd edn. Madrid: Taurus Ediciones, S. A., 1968.
Auerbach, Erich. "The Enchanted Dulcinea." In *Mimesis: The Representation of Reality in Western Literature*. Trans. Willard R. Trask. Princeton: Princeton University Press, 1953, pp. 334–58.
Avalle-Arce, Juan Bautista. "El cuento de los dos amigos." In *Deslindes cervantinos*. Madrid: Edhigar S. L., 1961, pp. 163–235.
Avalle-Arce, Juan Bautista. "*La Galatea*: The Novelistic Crucible." In *A Celebration of Cervantes on the Fourth Centenary of* La Galatea, *1585–1985*, special issue of *Cervantes: Bulletin of the Cervantes Society of America* 8 (1988): 7–15.
Avalle-Arce, Juan Bautista. *La novela pastoril*. 2nd. edn. Ediciones Istmo, 1974.
Avalle-Arce, Juan Bautista. "Una tradición literaria: El cuento de los dos amigos." *Nueva Revista de Filología Hispánica* 11.1 (1957): 1–35.
Bakhtin, M. M. "Discourse in the Novel." In Michael Holquist, ed., *The Dialogic Imagination*. Trans. Caryl Emerson and Michael Holquist. Austin: University of Texas Press, 1981, pp. 259–422.

Barbagallo, Antonio. "Los dos amigos, *El curioso impertinente* y la literatura italiana." *Anales Cervantinos* 32 (1994): 207–19.
Bayliss, Robert. *The Discourse of Courtly Love in Seventeenth-Century Spanish Theater.* Lewisburg: Bucknell University Press, 2008.
Bayliss, Robert. "Feminism and María de Zayas's Exemplary Comedy, *La traición en la amistad.*" *Hispanic Review* 76.1 (2008): 1–17.
Blackbourn, Barbara L. "The Eighth Story of the Tenth Day of Boccaccio's *Decameron.*" *Italian Quarterly* 27.106 (1986): 5–13.
Boccaccio, Giovanni. *The Decameron.* 2nd edn. Trans. G. H. McWilliam. London: Penguin Books, 2003.
Boccaccio, Giovanni. *The Decameron.* Trans. J. M. Rigg. 2 vols. London: H. F. Bumpus, 1906.
Boccaccio, Giovanni. *Decameron.* Ed. Vittore Branca. 2 vols. Florence: Felice Le Monnier, 1960.
Boyle, Margaret E. *Unruly Women: Performance, Penitence, and Punishment in Early Modern Spain.* Toronto: University of Toronto Press, 2014.
Brancaforte, Benito. *Guzmán de Alfarache: ¿Conversión o proceso de degradación?* Madison: Hispanic Seminary of Medieval Studies, 1980.
Brown, Katherine A. *Boccaccio's Fabliaux: Medieval Short Stories and the Function of Reversal.* Gainesville: University Press of Florida, 2014.
Cavillac, Michel. *Pícaros y mercaderes en el* Guzmán de Alfarache. Trans. Juan M. Azpitarte Almagro. Granada: Universidad de Granada, 1994.
Castro, Américo. *El pensamiento de Cervantes.* Nueva edición ampliada y con notas del autor y de Julio Rodríguez-Puértolas. Barcelona: Editorial Noguer, S. A., 1972.
Castro, Guillén de. *El curioso impertinente.* Ed. Christiane Faliu-Lacourt and María Luisa Lobato. Kassel: Edition Reichenberger, 1991.
Castro, Guillén de. *El curioso impertinente.* Ed. Francisco Martínez y Martínez. Valencia: Manuel Pau, 1908.
Cervantes Saavedra, Miguel de. *The Adventures of Don Quixote.* Trans. J. M. Cohen. New York: Penguin Books, 1950.
Cervantes Saavedra, Miguel de. *Don Quijote de La Mancha.* Ed. Francisco Rico. Barcelona: Instituto Cervantes, 1998.
Cervantes Saavedra, Miguel de. *Don Quijote de La Mancha.* Ed. Francisco Rodríguez Marín. 6 vols. Madrid: Revista de Archivos, Bibliotecas y Museos, 1916–17.
Cervantes Saavedra, Miguel de. *Don Quixote of La Mancha.* Trans. Walter Starkie. New York: Signet Classic, 1970.
Cervantes Saavedra, Miguel de. *La Galatea.* Ed. Juan Bautista Avalle-Arce. Madrid: Espasa-Calpe, S. A., 1987.
Cervantes Saavedra, Miguel de. *La Galatea.* Ed. Rodolfo Schevill and Adolfo Bonilla. 2 vols. Madrid: Imprenta de Bernardo Rodríguez, 1914.
Cervantes Saavedra, Miguel de. *The Ingenious Gentleman Don Quixote of La Mancha.* 4 vols. Ed. and trans. John Ormsby. New York: Dodd, Mead and Company, 1887.

Cicero. *De amicitia*. In *Cicero: De senectute, De amicitia, De divinatione*. Ed. Jeffrey Henderson. Trans. William Armistead Falconer. Cambridge, MA: Harvard University Press, 1923.
Cicero. *Cicero:* On Old Age *and* On Friendship. Trans. Frank O. Copley. Ann Arbor: The University of Michigan Press, 1967.
Close, Anthony. *Cervantes and the Comic Mind of his Age*. Oxford: Oxford University Press, 2000.
Cros, Edmond. *Protée et la gueux: Recherches sur les origines et la nature du récit picaresque dans Guzmán de Alfarache*. Paris: Didier, 1967.
Damiani, Bruno M. "The Rhetoric of Death in *La Galatea*." In Juan Bautista Avalle-Arce, ed., La Galatea *de Cervantes cuatrocientos años después*. Newark: Juan de la Cuesta, 1985, pp. 53–70.
Dunn, Peter N. *Spanish Picaresque Fiction*. Ithaca: Cornell University Press, 1993.
Durán, Manuel. *La ambigüedad en el Quijote*. Xalapa: Universidad Veracruzana, 1960.
Eden, Kathy. *The Renaissance Rediscovery of Intimacy*. Chicago: The University of Chicago Press, 2012.
Egginton, William. *How the World Became a Stage: Presence, Theatricality, and the Question of Modernity*. Albany: State University of New York Press, 2003.
Egido, Aurora. *Cervantes y las puertas del sueño: Estudios sobre* La Galatea, *El* Quijote, y *El* Persiles. Barcelona: Promociones y Publicaciones Universitarias, S. A., 1994.
El Saffar, Ruth. *Distance and Control in* Don Quixote: *A Study in Narrative Technique*. Chapel Hill: North Carolina Studies in the Romance Languages and Literature, 1975.
El Saffar, Ruth Anthony and Diana de Armas Wilson, eds. *Quixotic Desire: Psychoanalytic Perspectives on Cervantes*. Ithaca: Cornell University Press, 1993.
Faliu-Lacourt, Christiane. "Formas variantes de un tema recurrente: 'El curioso impertinente' (Cervantes y Guillén de Castro)." *Criticón* 30 (1985): 169–81.
Flores, R. M. "'El curioso impertinente' y 'El captián cautivo,' novelas ni sueltas ni pegadizas." *Cervantes: Bulletin of the Cervantes Society of America* 20.1 (2000): 79–98.
Flores, R. M. "Formación del personaje femenino en *El curioso impertinente*." *Revista de Estudios Hispánicos* 34.2 (May 2000): 331–49.
Forcione, Alban K. *Cervantes, Aristotle, and the* Persiles. Princeton: Princeton University Press, 1970.
Frenk, Margit, "'Lectores y oidores': La difusión oral de la literatura en el Siglo de Oro." *Actas del Séptimo Congreso de la Asociación Internacional de Hispanistas* (Venice, 1980). Vol. 1. Ed. Guiseppe Bellini. Rome: Bulzoni Editore, 1982.
Friedman, Edward H. "Insincere Flattery: Imitation and the Growth of the Novel." *Cervantes: Bulletin of the Cervantes Society of America* 20.1 (2000): 99–114.

García Martín, Manuel. *Cervantes y la comedia española en el Siglo XVII.* Salamanca: Ediciones Universidad de Salamanca, 1980.
Garcilaso de la Vega. *Égloga I.* In Elías L. Rivers, ed., *Poesía lírica del Siglo de Oro.* 18th. edn. Madrid: Cátedra, 1999, pp. 83–98.
Gerli, E. Michael. "Truth, Lies, and Representation: The Crux of 'El curioso impertinente.'" In Francisco LaRubia-Prado, ed., *Cervantes for the 21st Century = Cervantes para el siglo XXI: Studies in Honor of Edward Dudley.* Newark: Juan de la Cuesta, 2000, pp. 107–22.
Gilbert-Santamaría, Donald. "Love and Friendship in Montemayor's *La Diana.*" *Bulletin of Hispanic Studies* 84.6 (2007): 745–60.
Gilbert-Santamaría, Donald. *Writers on the Market: Consuming Literature in Early Seventeenth-Century Spain.* Lewisburg: Bucknell University Press, 2005.
Gil-Osle, Juan Pablo. *Amistades imperfectas: Del Humanismo a la Ilustración con Cervantes.* Madrid: Iberoamericana, 2013.
Gil-Osle, Juan Pablo. "La Edad de Hierro en *La traición en la amistad* de María de Zayas." *Neophilologus* 98.2 (2014): 275–86.
Girard, René. *Deceit, Desire and the Novel.* Trans. Yvonne Freccero. Baltimore: Johns Hopkins University Press, 1965.
Gónzalez Echevarría, Roberto. *Love and the Law in Cervantes.* New Haven: Yale University Press, 2005.
Gorfkle, Laura. "Female Communities, Female Friendships and Social Control in María de Zayas's *La traición en la amistad*: A Historical Perspective." *Romance Languages Annual* X (1999): 615–20.
Greenblatt, Stephen. *Renaissance Self-Fashioning: From More to Shakespeare.* Chicago: The University of Chicago Press, 1980.
Greene, Thomas M. *The Light in Troy: Imitation and Discovery in Renaissance Poetry.* New Haven: Yale University Press, 1982.
Hahn, Juergen. "*El curioso impertinente* and Don Quijote's Symbolic Struggle against *Curiositas.*" *Bulletin of Hispanic Studies* 49.2 (1972): 128–40.
Hollander, Robert. *Boccaccio's Dante and the Shaping Force of Satire.* Ann Arbor: The University of Michigan Press, 1997.
Hutchinson, Steven. "Affective Dimensions in *Don Quijote.*" *Cervantes: Bulletin of the Cervantes Society of America* 24.2 (2004): 71–91.
Hutson, Lorna. *The Usurer's Daughter: Male Friendship and Fictions of Women in Sixteenth-Century England.* London: Routledge, 1994.
Hyatte, Reginald. *The Arts of Friendship: The Idealization of Friendship in Medieval and Early Renaissance Literature.* Leiden: E. J. Brill, 1994.
Ife, B. W. "Cervantes, Herodotus and the Eternal Triangle: Another Look at the Sources of *El curioso impertinente.*" *Bulletin of Hispanic Studies* 82.5 (2005): 671–81.
Ife, B. W. *Reading and Fiction in Golden-Age Spain: A Platonist Critique and Some Picaresque Replies.* Cambridge: Cambridge University Press, 1985.
Jehenson, Yvonne. "*Masochisma* versus *Machismo* or: Camila's Re-writing of Gender Assignations in Cervantes's *Tale of Foolish Curiosity.*" *Cervantes: Bulletin of the Cervantes Society of America* 18.2 (1998): 26–52.

Johnson, Carroll B. *Cervantes and the Material World*. Urbana: University of Illinois Press, 2000.
Johnson, Carroll B. "Defining the Picaresque: Authority and the Subject in *Guzmán de Alfarache*." In Giancarlo Maiorino, ed., *The Picaresque: Tradition and Displacement*. Minneapolis: University of Minnesota Press, 1996, pp. 159–82.
Johnson, Carroll B. *Inside Guzmán de Alfarache*. Berkeley: University of California Press, 1978.
Johnson, Carroll B. *Madness and Lust: A Psychoanalytical Approach to Don Quixote*. Berkeley: University of California Press, 1983.
Johnson, Carroll B. "Montemayor's *Diana*: A Novel Pastoral." *Bulletin of Hispanic Studies* 48.1 (1971): 20–35.
Jurado Santos, Agapita. *Obras teatrales derivadas de las novelas cervantinas (Siglo XVII)*. Kassel: Edition Reichenberger, 2005.
Kartchner, Eric J. "Playing Doubles: Another Look at Alemán's Vengeance on Martí." *Cincinnati Romance Review* 16 (1997): 16–23.
Kirkham, Victoria. *The Sign of Reason in Boccaccio's Fiction*. Florence: L. S. Olschki Editore, 1993.
Langer, Ullrich. *Perfect Friendship: Studies in Literature and Moral Philosophy from Boccaccio to Corneille*. Geneva: Librairie Droz S. A., 1994.
Lapesa, Rafael. *La trayectoria poética de Garcilaso: Edición corregida y aumentada*. Madrid: Ediciones Istmo, 1985.
Larson, Catherine. "Gender, Reading, and Intertextuality: Don Juan's Legacy in María de Zayas's *La traición en la amistad*." *INTI: Revista de Literatura Hispánica* 40–1 (1994–5): 129–38.
Lauer, A. Robert. "*Honor/Honra* Revisited." In Hilaire Kallendorf, ed., *A Companion to Early Modern Hispanic Theater*. Leiden: Brill, 2014, pp. 77–90.
Lee, A. C. *The Decameron: Its Sources and Analogues*. London: David Nutt, 1909.
López Estrada, Francisco. *La "Galatea" de Cervantes: Estudio crítico*. La Laguna de Tenerife, 1948.
Luján de Sayavedra, Mateo [Juan Martí]. "Vida del pícaro Guzmán de Alfarache." In *Novelistas anteriores a Cervantes*. 3rd edn. Madrid: M. Rivadeneyra, 1850, pp. 363–430.
Mancing, Howard. *The Chivalric World of Don Quijote: Style, Structure, and Narrative Technique*. Columbia: University of Missouri Press, 1982.
Maravall, José Antonio. *La cultura del barroco: Análisis de una estructura histórica*. Barcelona: Editorial Ariel, 1975.
Maravall, José Antonio. *La literatura picaresca desde la historia social (Siglos XVI y XVII)*. Madrid: Taurus Ediciones, S. A., 1986.
Maravall, José Antonio. *Utopía y contrautopía en el «Quijote»*. Santiago de Compostela: Editorial Pico Sacro, 1976.
Marcus, Millicent Joy. *An Allegory of Form: Literary Self-Consciousness in the Decameron*. Saratoga: Anma Libri & Co., 1979.

Mariscal, George. *Contradictory Subjects: Quevedo, Cervantes, and Seventeenth-Century Spanish Culture*. Ithaca: Cornell University Press, 1991.
Maroto Camino, Mercedes. "María de Zayas and Ana Caro: The Space of Women's Solidarity in the Spanish Golden Age." *Hispanic Review* 67.1 (1999): 1–16.
Martínez-Bonati, Félix. *Don Quixote and the Poetics of the Novel*. Trans. Dian Fox. Ithaca: Cornell University Press, 1992.
Mazzotta, Guiseppe. *The World at Play in Boccaccio's Decameron*. Princeton: Princeton University Press, 1986.
McGrady, Donald. *Mateo Alemán*. New York: Twayne Publishers, 1968.
Montemayor, Jorge de. *Los siete libros de La Diana*. Ed. Asunción Rallo. Madrid: Cátedra, 1999.
Moralejo Laso, Abelardo. "Para la etimología de la palabra *jerigonza*." *Revista de Filología Española* 60.1/4 (1980): 327–31.
Mujica, Barbara. "Antiutopian Elements in the Spanish Pastoral Novel." *Kentucky Romance Quarterly* 26.3 (1979): 263–82.
Muñoz Sánchez, Juan Ramón. "Un ejemplo de interpolación Cervantina: El espiodio de Timbrio y Silerio de *La Galatea*." *Anuario de Estudios Filológicos* 26 (2003): 279–97.
Murillo, Luis Andrés. "Diálogo y dialéctica en el siglo XVI español." In *Estudios sobre el diálogo renacentista español: Antología de la crítica*. Malaga: Universidad de Málaga, 2006, pp. 25–36.
Orozco Díaz, Emilio. *¿Qué es el «Arte nuevo» de Lope de Vega?* Salamanca: Ediciones Universidad de Salamanca, 1978.
Pangle, Lorraine Smith. *Aristotle and the Philosophy of Friendship*. Cambridge: Cambridge University Press, 2003.
Parker, A. A. "Tema e imagen de la *Égloga I* de Garcilaso." In Elias L. Rivers, ed., *La poesía de Garcilaso: Ensayos críticos*. Barcelona: Editorial Ariel, 1974, pp. 197–208.
Pérez, Ashley Hope. "Into the Dark Triangle of Desire: Rivalry, Resistance, and Repression in 'El curioso impertinente.'" *Cervantes: Bulletin of the Cervantes Society of America* 31.1 (2011): 83–107.
Pérez, Luis C. and Federico Sánchez Escribano. *Afirmaciones de Lope de Vega sobre preceptiva dramática a base de cien comedias*. Madrid: Consejo Superior de Investigaciones Científicas, 1961.
Plato. *The Collected Dialogues of Plato*. Ed. Edith Hamilton and Huntington Cairns. Princeton: Princeton University Press, 1961.
Presberg, Charles D. *Adventures in Paradox: Don Quixote and the Western Tradition*. University Park: The Pennsylvania State University Press, 2001.
Price, A. W. *Love and Friendship in Aristotle and Plato*. Oxford: Clarendon Press, 1989.
Regueiro, José M. "Textual Discontinuities and the Problems of Closure in the Spanish Drama of the Golden Age." In Marina S. Brownlee and Hans Ulrich Gumbrecht, eds., *Cultural Authority in Golden Age Spain*. Baltimore: The Johns Hopkins University Press, 1995, pp. 28–50.

Reiss, Timothy J. *Mirages of the Selfe: Patterns of Personhood in Ancient and Early Modern Europe*. Stanford: Stanford University Press, 2003.
Rhodes, Elizabeth. "Sixteenth-century Pastoral Books, Narrative Structure, and *La Galatea* of Cervantes." *Bulletin of Hispanic Studies* 66.4 (1989): 351–60.
Riley, E. C. *Cervantes's Theory of the Novel*. Oxford: Clarendon Press, 1962.
Rivers, Elias L. *Quixote Scriptures: Essays on the Textuality of Hispanic Literature*. Bloomington: Indiana University Press, 1983.
Shannon, Laurie. *Sovereign Amity: Figures of Friendship in Shakespearean Contexts*. Chicago: The University of Chicago Press, 2002.
Shuger, Dale. *Don Quixote in the Archives: Madness and Literature in Early Modern Spain*. Edinburgh: Edinburgh University Press, 2012.
Sieber, Harry. "On Juan Huarte de San Juan and Anselmo's *Locura* in 'El curioso impertinente.'" *Revista Hispánica Moderna* 36.1/2 (1970–1): 1–8.
Sorieri, Louis. *Boccaccio's Story of* Tito e Gisippo *in European Literature*. New York: Institute of French Studies, 1937.
Soufas, Teresa Scott. *Dramas of Distinction: A Study of Plays by Golden Age Women*. Lexington: The University Press of Kentucky, 1997.
Spitzer, Leo. "Linguistic Perspectivism in the *Don Quijote*." In *Linguistics and Literary History: Essays in Stylistics*. Princeton: Princeton University Press, 1948, pp. 41–85.
Stroud, Matthew D. "Love, Friendship, and Deceit in *La traición en la amistad*, by María de Zayas." *Neophilologus* 69.4 (1985): 539–47.
Struever, Nancy S. *Theory as Practice: Ethical Inquiry in the Renaissance*. Chicago: The University of Chicago Press, 1992.
Sullivan, Henry W. Henry. *Grotesque Purgatory: A study of Cervantes's* Don Quixote, *Part II*. University Park: The Pennsylvania State University Press, 1996.
Thacker, Jonathan. *Role-Play and the World as Stage in the* comedia. Liverpool: Liverpool University Press, 2002.
Tolan, John. *Petrus Alfonsi and His Medieval Readers*. Gainesville: University Press of Florida, 1993.
Unamuno, Miguel de. *Vida de Don Quijote y Sancho*. Madrid: Alianza Editorial, 1987.
Urbina, Eduardo. *El sin par Sancho Panza: Parodia y creación*. Barcelona: Editorial Anthropos, 1991.
Venier, Martha Elena. Review of *Cervantes y la melancholia: Ensayos sobre el tono y la actitud cervantinos*, by Javier García Gibert. In *Nueva Revista de Filología Hispánica* 48.1 (2000): 146–8.
Vollendorf, Lisa. "Desire Unbound: Women's Theater of Spain's Golden Age." In Joan F. Cammarata, ed., *Women in the Discourse of Early Modern Spain*. Gainesville: University of Florida Press, 2003, pp. 272–91.
Wardropper, Bruce W. "The Pertinence of *El curioso impertinente*." *PMLA* 72.4 (1957): 587–600.
Weiger, John G. "Sobre la originalidad e independencia de Guillén de Castro." *Hispanófila* 31 (1967): 1–15.

Wilcox, Amanda. *The Gift of Correspondence in Classical Rome*. Madison: The University of Wisconsin Press, 2012.

Williams, Craig A. *Reading Roman Friendship*. Cambridge: Cambridge University Press, 2012.

Williamson, Edwin. *The Half-Way House of Fiction: Don Quixote and Arthurian Romance*. Oxford: Clarendon Press, 1984.

Williamson, Edwin. "The Power-Struggle between Don Quixote and Sancho: Four Crises in the Development of the Narrative." *Bulletin of Spanish Studies* 84.7 (2007): 837–58.

Williamson, Edwin. "Romance and Realism in the Interpolated Stories of the *Quixote*." *Cervantes: Bulletin of the Cervantes Society of America* 2.1 (1982): 43–67.

Wilson, Diana de Armas. "'Passing the Love of Women': The Intertextuality of *El curioso impertinente*." *Cervantes: Bulletin of the Cervantes Society of America* 7.2 (1987): 9–28.

Zayas y Sotomayor, María de. *La traición en la amistad*. Ed. Valerie Hegstrom. Trans. Catherine Larson. Lewisburg: Bucknell University Press, 1999.

Zayas y Sotomayor, María de. *La traición en la amistad*. 2nd edn. Ed. Michael J. McGrath. Newark: European Masterpieces, 2007.

Index

Page numbers followed by n refer to notes

Abel, Lionel, 132–3n
Aelred of Rievaulx, 24n
"aesthetic belief," 181
Alemán, Mateo, *Guzmán de Alfarache*, 158–75
Alfarache, Guzmán de (character), 158–75
Alfonso, Pedro
  Disciplina clericalis, 27–30, 37, 40–1, 45, 46–7n, 47n
  Exemplum de integro amico, 27–31, 43, 45–6, 59, 89
Alter, Robert, *Partial Magic*, 211n
alter ego
  Anselmo and Lotario, 89, 96, 111–12
  comedia, 132n
  friend as, 4–5, 14
  Laura and Marcia, 150, 156n
  Silerio and Timbrio, 60, 66
  Tito and Gisippo, 35
alter idem (second self), 14–15
Anselmo and Lotario (characters), 9–10, 84–101, 104–8n, 111–31, 133–6n, 137, 154n
Aquinas, Thomas, 12, 105n
Arellano, Ignacio, "Del relato al teatro," 134–5n

Ariosto, 88
  Orlando furioso, 104–5n, 108n
Aristotelian ideal of perfect friendship
  allegory, 145–6
  Anselmo and Lotario, 112–15
  Camila (character), 117, 128–9
  Don Quixote and Sancho Panza, 177, 184, 186, 192–3, 206
  good will, 58–9
  and love, 56
  Marcia and Laura (characters), 150
  and marriage, 86
  moral virtue, 152–3
  Silerio and Timbrio, 65–7
  Sofronia (character), 63
  Tito and Gisippo, 37–44, 46, 48n, 51n, 74–5n
  unknowable friend, 124
  virtue, 105n
Aristotle
  categories of friendship, 19–20
  friends as second self, 160
  good will, 55–6, 59, 61
  hierarchy of three levels of friendship, 10–11
  history and fiction, 181–2
  inherent good, 92–3, 98–9, 121

Aristotle (*Cont.*)
  Nicomachean Ethics, 2–5, 10–12, 14–17, 50n, 173n
  poetic theory, 181–2
  Poetics, 132n
  and scholasticism, 25n, 33–4
  selflessness, 29
  virtue, 81, 90
arrieros, 191
Atticus, 17–18
Aubrun, Charles-Vincent, *La comedia española*, 132n, 133–4n
auctoritas, 3, 184
audience, 109–10
Auerbach, Erich, 23n, 187, 214n, 215n
  "The Enchanted Dulcinea," 215–16n
Augustine, 12
Avalle-Arce, Juan Bautista
  Alfonso, Pedro, 27–8, 30–2
  Cervantes, Miguel de, 8–10
  "fiction," 38
  "La Galatea: La Novelistic Crucible," 73n
  La novela pastoril española, 72n, 74n
  public opinion, 58
  "tale of two friends" tradition, 1–2, 6–7, 13, 98

"bad" friend, 138–42, 147–9, 151
Bakhtin, M. M., 167
  "Discourse in the Novel," 174n
batanes, 193–4, 195, 207
Battaglia, Salvatore, 23n
Bayliss, Robert, 139
  The Discourse of Courtly Love, 132n
  "Feminism and María de Zayas's Exemplary Comedy," 154–6n

Blackbourn, Barbara L., "The Eighth Story of the Tenth Day of Boccaccio's *Decameron*," 48n
Boccaccio, Giovanni
  and Cervantes, 74n, 76n, 89
  Decameron, 7, 23n, 27–51, 47–51n, 84–7, 202
  divine will, 61–5
  free will, 55–6
  parody, 74–5n
  poetic innovation, 6
  separation of perfect friend and other relations, 58–9
  subjective self-control, 92
Boyle, Margaret E., 141
  Unruly Women, 154n, 155n
Brancaforte, Benito, 158
  Guzmán de Alfarache: ¿Conversión o proceso de degradación?, 173n
Brown, Katherine A., *Boccaccio's Fabliaux*, 47n
Burckhardt, Jacob, 6–7, 21

Camila (character), 85, 89–100, 106–8n, 110–11, 115–1, 132–5n
  gender roles, 137
  subjective self-control, 142
  "wife testing," 154n
Camino, Mercedes Maroto, 146
Candaules and Gyges (characters), 105n
Carino (character), 54
Carrasco, Sansón (character), 77–80, 101n, 177, 178
Castro, Américo, *El pensamiento de Cervantes*, 101–2n, 107n
Castro, Guillén de, 109–136, 138
  El curioso impertinente, 137, 142
Cavillac, Michel, 165
Cervantes (as character), 182–3
Cervantes, Miguel de
  Avalle-Arce, Juan Bautista, 9–10

Index

Don Quixote, 176–220
  aspirational model of friendship, 121
  Avalle-Arce, Juan Bautista, 9–10
  and Castro, 134n
  exemplarity, 7
  new poetics of friendship, 124
  "tale of two friends" tradition, 152
  unknowable friend, 14, 19–21, 25–6n
  "El curioso impertinente," 77–108
  Avalle-Arce, Juan Bautista, 9–10, 31
  Camila (character), 128
  and Castro, 120–3, 135n
  classical *auctoritas*, 183–4
  confessional storytelling, 145
  exemplarity, 7
  as interpolated story, 23n, 154n
  public opinion, 58, 197–8
  public reading, 216n
  "tale of two friends" tradition, 149, 155n, 186
  honor, 113
  La Galatea, 5–6, 7, 9, 52–76, 84
  Novelas ejemplares, 179, 216n
  Persiles, 213n
chivalric fiction, 181–2, 196–7, 212–13n
Cicero
  audience, 114, 115
  De amicitia, 2–5, 7–8, 14–17, 29–30, 85, 89, 173n
  Epistulae ad familiares, 25n
  free will, 55–6, 92
  friendship as aspirational, 40
  letters, 17–19, 124
  'natural fraternity', 48n
  oratory, 51n
  Orestes and Pylades, 9, 22–3n, 37, 84, 90

Close, Anthony, *Cervantes and the Comic Mind of his Age*, 217n
comedia
  audience, 109
  closure, 135–6n, 156n
  gender roles, 137
  hyperbole, 128–9, 132n, 187
  hyperbolic moralism, 147
  moral self-righteousness, 157n
  representational verisimilitude, 153
  sonnets, 133–4n
  vulgo, 115
  see also Castro, Guillén de: *El curioso impertinente*; Zayas, María de: *La traición en la amistad*
commiseration, 198–9
"communal mode," 155n
confessional storytelling, 142–4, 146–7, 154n
continuity, 203–4
conversation, 179–80, 200–20
Cros, Edmond, *Protée et le Gueux*, 174n

Damiani, Bruno, "The Rhetoric of Death in *La Galatea*," 73n
Dante, 107n
deception, 34–5
  Anselmo and Lotario, 93, 112, 120–2, 125–6
  Camila (character), 97
  Don Quixote and Sancho Panza, 194, 207
  Fenisa (character), 140, 144, 154n
  gender roles, 156n
  Guzmán and Sayavedra, 162–3, 166–8, 170–2
  Liseo (character), 151
  picaresque, 174n
  Sofronia (character), 65
desengaño, 101, 174n

dialogue, 211–12n, 212n, 214n, 215n
division between private and public life, 117, 165–75, 174–5n, 218n
"domestic interior space," 146–7
Don Quixote (character), 6, 20, 21, 70, 78–80, 176–220
"dulce lamentar," 52–4
Dulcinea (character), 185–6, 204–8, 212n, 219n
Durán, Manuel, *La ambigüedad en el Quijote*, 211n

Eden, Kathy, 17–19, 22, 25n, 40
The Renaissance Rediscovery of Intimacy, 25n
Egginton, William, *How the World Became a Stage*, 132n
Egido, Aurora, 62
Cervantes y las puertas del sueño, 73–4n, 75n
egoism, 141–2
Elicio and Erastro (characters), 54, 73–4n
engaño, 97–8, 150–1, 172, 174n, 194–5
entertainment, 27–8, 102–3n
Erastro and Elicio (characters), 54, 73–4n
exemplarity, 1–3
  Alfonso, Pedro, 27–8
  audience, 114, 120
  "bad" friend, 147
  Cicero, 7–8
  Don Quixote and Sancho Panza, 179
  Filomena (character), 38
  hyperbole, 110–11
  La traición en la amistad, 152
  marriage and friendship, 86
  negative, 154–5n
  public opinion, 84–5
  self-sacrifice for a friend, 30
  Sofronia (character), 35

Faliu-Lacourt, Christiane, 132n
  El curioso impertinente, 134n
  "Formas vicariantes de un tema recurrente," 134n
farce, 118, 122
Favelo (character), 166, 170–1
female friends, 137–57
Fenisa (character), 138–57, 153–6n
  as Don Juan, 153–5n
"fiction," 43, 48n
  "lie of fiction," 141
  "pleasant fictions," 30, 47n
Flores, R. M., "Formación del personaje femenino en e*l curioso impertinente*," 108n
Forcione, Alban K., *Cervantes, Aristotle and the* Persiles, 213–14n
Francesca and Paolo (characters), 107n
free will, 55–6, 146, 154n
Frenk, Margit, «Lectores y oidores», 102n
Friedman, Edward H., 158

Gadamer, Hans-Georg, *Truth and Method*, 18
García Martín, Manuel, *Cervantes y la comedia española*, 135n
Garcilaso de la Vega, *Égloga I*, 52–3, 71n
gender roles, 137–57
Gerardo (character), 147–9, 155–6n
Gerli, E. Michael, "Truth, Lies, and Representation," 107n
"gift exchange," 16
Gilbert-Santamaría, Donald, *Writers on the Market*, 174n, 219n, 220n
Gil-Osle, Juan Pablo, 212n
Gisippo and Tito (characters), 31–46, 47–51n

Aristotelian ideal of perfect friendship, 74–5n
deception, 151
divine will, 152
exemplarity, 160
free will, 55–6
Sofronia (character), 63–5
superiority of perfect friendship, 81, 84–7, 202
"tale of two friends" tradition, 26n, 74n, 130
goatherds (characters), 188–90, 216n
"good" friend, 137–57
Gorfkle, Laura, "Female Communities, Female Friendships and Social Control," 155n
Greenblatt, Stephen, 26n
Gyges and Candaules (characters), 105n

Hahn, Juergen, "*El curioso impertinente* and Don Quijote's Symbolic Struggle against Curiositas," 104n, 108n
Hegstrom, Valerie, 153n, 155n
La traición en la amistad, 156n
Herodotus, 105n
History, 108n
Hollander, Robert, 31–2, 38–9, 42–5, 50n, 56
Boccaccio's Dante and the Shaping Force of Satire, 47–51n
honor, 104n, 105n, 113–14, 134–5n, 153, 155–6n
Hutchinson, Steven, "Affective Dimensions in *Don Quijote*," 217n
Hutson, Lorna, *The Usurer's Daughter*, 49n
Hyatte, Reginald, *The Arts of Friendship*, 24n, 49n, 50–1n

hyperbole
Anselmo and Lotario, 126, 128–31
"antonomasia," 84
comedia, 132n, 157n
Don Quixote and Sancho Panza, 205
El curioso impertinente, 109–22
female friends, 137–8
happy ending, 67
madness, 190
moralism, 147
Pacuvius, 8
pastoral lovers, 53–4
self-sacrifice for a friend, 11, 13–14
violence and death, 73n

identity as performance, 178–9, 211n
"*ideologemes*," 174n
Ife, B. W., 181–2
"Cervantes, Herodotus and the Eternal Triangle," 104–5n
Reading and Fiction in Golden-Age Spain, 213–14n, 216n, 218n
imitatio, 2–3, 20, 30, 55, 177–83, 196–7
intertextuality
Anselmo and Lotario, 86, 100
Don Quixote, 21
imitatio, 3, 22n, 30, 55, 179
intimacy
Castro, Guillén de, 109–36
personal, 137–57, 155n, 160, 172
private, 137–57
Renaissance, 17–19, 25n

Jehenson, Yvonne, "*Masochisma* versus *Machismo*," 106n, 108n
jerigonza, 189, 202, 216n

Johnson, Carroll B., 169
   Cervantes and the Material World, 220n
   "Montemayor's *Diana*: A Novel Pastoral," 71n
Jones, Joseph Ramon, 30
   The Scholar's Guide, 46–7n

Keller, John Esten, 30
   The Scholar's Guide, 46–7n
Kermode, Frank, 31, 48n
Kirkham, Victoria, 45
   The Sign of Reason, 48n
knight-errantry, 80–1, 177–9, 184, 186–220, 219n

Landau, Marcus, 47n
Langer, Ullrich
   Aristotelian ideal of perfect friendship, 46
   epistolary tradition, 18, 24n
   Perfect Friendship, 24n, 26n
   scholasticism, 11–14, 25n, 105n
   second self, 34
   unknowable friend, 16, 19–20, 28, 39–40, 58
Larson, Catherine, 151
   "Gender, Reading and Intertextuality," 155n, 157n
Lauer, A. Robert, "*Honor/Honra* Revisited," 105n
Laura and Marcia (characters), 138–7, 155–7n
Lee, A. C., *The Decameron: Its Sources and Analogues*, 47n
Lisandro (character), 55, 56, 73n
Liseo (character), 139–47, 149–51, 155n, 156n
Lobato, María Luisa, 132n
   El curioso impertinente, 134n
Lombard, Peter, 12
Lope de Vega, 132n, 133–4n

El arte nuevo de hacer comedias en este tiempo, 109, 115, 131n
López Estrada, Francisco, 62, 74n
   La "Galatea" de Cervantes, 75n, 76n
Lotario and Anselmo (characters), 9–10, 84–101, 104–8n, 111–31, 133–6n, 137, 154n
Luján de Sayavedra, Mateo, 158

madness, 92–3, 171–2, 187–90, 192–3, 195, 209–10, 215–17n
Mancing, Howard, *The Chivalric World of Don Quijote*, 212n, 215n, 216n
Maravall, José Antonio, 80, 159
   La literatura picaresca desde la historia social, 173n
   Utopía y contrautopía en el «Quijote», 214–15n
Marcia and Laura (characters), 138–57, 155–7n
Marcus, Millicent Joy, *An Allegory of Form*, 23n
Mariscal, George, 169
   Contradictory Subjects, 174n
Maritornes (character), 81–2, 85
Martí, Juan, 158
Martínez-Bonati, Félix, 181
   Don Quixote and the Poetics of the Novel, 213n, 214n
master-servant relationship, 176–220
Mazzotta, Giuseppe, 39
   The World at Play, 49n, 50n
Melloni, Alessandra, 153n
Menéndez Pidal, Ramón, 217n
metatheatre, 132–3n, 133n
Montaigne, Michel de, 175n
Montemayor, Jorge de, *Los siete libros de la Diana*, 52–3, 71n, 72n
moralism, 28, 138, 146, 147, 151–2
morality tale, 108n

Mujica, Barbara, "Antiutopian Elements in the Spanish Pastoral Novel," 72n, 76n
Muñoz Sánchez, Juan Ramón, "Un ejemplo de interpolación cervantina," 74n
Murillo, Luis Andrés, "Diálogo y dialéctica en el siglo XVI español," 211–12n
mutual purification, 165
mutual recognition, 160, 163–4
mutual understanding, 179
"mythmaking," 32, 38–9, 43, 44–5, 48n, 56

"negative exemplarity," 154–5n
Neoplatonism, 55, 72n, 73–4n
Nísida (character), 62–70, 75–6n

Orestes and Pylades (characters)
  audience, 42, 114
  Cicero, 22–3n
  exemplarity, 9, 28, 37, 84–5, 90
  Laelius, 3–5
  mythic status, 29–30
  self-identification, 8
  unknowable friend, 81
Orozco Díaz, Emilio, 109
  ¿Qué es el «Arte nuevo» de Lope de Vega?, 131n
"Otro yo," 158–75

Pacuvius
  audience, 42, 114
  Cicero, 22–3n
  exemplarity, 9, 28, 115
  Laelius, 4–5, 7
  mythic status, 29–30
  self-identification, 8
Panza, Sancho (character), 6, 19–20, 21, 78–9, 176–220
Paolo and Francesca (characters), 107n
parody, 44–5, 55, 74–5n, 182–3, 212–13n
pastoral lovers, 52–76
"pastoral novel," 55–76, 71n
Paun de García, Susan, 153n
Pérez, Ashley Hope, "Into the Dark Triangle of Desire," 106–7n
Pérez de Montalbán, Juan, 153n
Pérez, Luis C., Afirmaciones de Lope de Vega, 132n
perfect friendship, 2–22, 24n, 55–6, 110–11
personal intimacy, 137–57, 155n, 160, 172
Petrarch, 17–19, 20, 22, 124
picaresque, 158–75, 174n
picaro as protean figure, 164, 174n
plagiarism, 158, 174n
poetic idealism, 193
poetics, 181, 206, 208, 212n, 215n
power-struggle, 211n, 217–18n
Presberg, Charles D., Adventures in Paradox, 214n
Price, A. W., 11–12, 50n
private friendship, 159–75
private intimacy, 137–57
private relationship, 190, 218n
"probabilities of empirical reality," 181–2
public opinion, 58, 79–80, 84, 98–9, 105n, 114
public reputation, 142

radical alienation, 141–2
realism, 181, 213n
Regueiro, José M., "Textual Discontinuities and the Problems of Closure in the Spanish Drama of the Golden Age," 135–6n
Reiss, Timothy J., 169
  Mirages of the Selfe, 174–5n
Renaissance courtly love, 149

Renaissance self-fashioning, 21, 26n
representational verisimilitude *see* verisimilitude
Rhodes, Elizabeth, 54
  "Sixteenth-century Pastoral Books, Narrative Structure, and *La Galatea* of Cervantes," 71n, 72–3n
Riley, E. C., 181
  Cervantes's Theory of the Novel, 102–3n, 103n, 213n
Rivers, Elias L., 179
  Quixote Scriptures, 212n
Rocinante (character), 190–1, 194, 195, 199, 212n
role-play, 116, 132–3n, 133n, 186, 211n
Rosales, Luis, 212n

Sánchez Escribano, Federico, *Afirmaciones de Lope de Vega*, 132n
Sancho Panza (character) *see* Panza, Sancho (character)
Sannazaro, Jacopo, *Arcadia*, 52, 72n
Sayavedra (character), 158–75
scholasticism, 12–16, 25n, 32–4, 38, 41, 105n
second self, 162–3, 172, 173n
  Guzmán and Sayavedra, 158
self-identification, 160, 163–4
selfishness, 140, 206–8
self-sacrifice for a friend
  Anselmo and Lotario, 129–30
  Boccaccio, Giovanni, 11–12
  Don Quixote, 20
  Don Quixote and Sancho Panza, 205–6
  Exemplum de integro amico, 29–30
  Laelius, 4–5
  Laura and Marcia, 140, 149
  Orestes and Pylades, 14
  Tito and Gisippo, 35, 37, 44
separation anxiety, 194–5
service to God, 2, 12, 89
shared adventures, 21, 177, 179, 185–6, 200–20
shared experience of pain, 191–2
shared humor, 195, 197, 217n
shared identity, 112, 156n
shared interest, 58
Sherberg, Michael, *The Governance of Friendship*, 48n
Shuger, Dale, 215n
  Don Quixote in the Archives, 217n, 220n
Sieber, Harry, 92
  "On Juan Huarte de San Juan and Anselmo's *Locura* in 'El curioso impertinente'," 105n
Silerio and Timbrio (characters), 9, 57–70, 74–6n, 84, 130
sincerity, 142–4
Smith, Barbara Herrnstein, 135–6n
social alienation, 161, 164
social stereotype, 167–9
Sofronia (character), 33–6, 39–43, 49n
  deception, 151
  divine will, 63
  superiority of perfect friendship, 81, 87, 202
"soledad," 159
solidarity in crime, 165–9
Sorieri, Louis, *Boccaccio's Story of Tito e Gisippo*, 47n
Soufas, Teresa Scott, *Dramas of Distinction: A Study of Plays by Golden Age Women*, 156n

spiritual friendship, 2, 24n
Spitzer, Leo, "Linguistic Perspectivism in the *Don Quijote*," 211n
'standing jokes,' 179, 212n
Struever, Nancy, 18–19, 20, 22
Theory as Practice, 25n
subjective self-control, 142–5
"subjectivity"
  Camila (character), 111, 115–17, 138
  Don Quixote, 20–1
  Fenisa (character), 141, 142
  pastoral lovers, 53
  Reiss, Timothy, 174–5n
  Sofronia (character), 49n
  Tito and Gisippo, 63

"tale of two friends" tradition
  alienation, 14
  Avalle-Arce, Juan Bautista, 6–7
  Don Quixote and Sancho Panza, 184, 197–8
  history, 2
  idealism, 111
  Silerio and Timbrio, 74n
  unknowable friend, 16, 19
Teresa (character), 202–3, 219n
Thacker, Jonathan, 116
  Role-Play and the World as Stage in the comedia, 132–3n, 133n
Timbrio and Silerio (characters), 9, 57–70, 74–6n, 84, 130
Tito and Gisippo (characters), 31–46, 47–51n
  Aristotelian ideal of perfect friendship, 74–5n
  deception, 151
  divine will, 152
  exemplarity, 160
  free will, 55–6

Sofronia (character), 63–5
superiority of perfect friendship, 81, 84–7, 202
"tale of two friends" tradition, 26n, 74n, 130
Tolan, John, *Petrus Alfonsi and His Medieval Readers*, 47n
Torcato (character), 111, 132n
tragedy, 108n
"tragicomedia," 132n

unknowable friend, 16, 19, 28, 58, 142
Urbina, Eduardo, *El sin par Sancho Panza*, 212–13n
utilitarianism, 28–9, 159, 161, 162, 173n

verisimilitude, 2–3, 5–6, 132n
  "aesthetic belief," 213–14n
  Anselmo and Lotario, 100, 130
  Boccaccio, Giovanni, 32, 42
  Camila (character), 115–16, 117, 125, 128–9, 137
  Castro, Guillén de, 109–10
  Cervantes, Miguel de, 55–7, 59, 62, 64, 67, 192–3, 208, 213n
  Don Quixote and Sancho Panza, 180–4, 192–3, 195
  Guzmán and Sayavedra, 164–5
  imitatio displaced by, 20–1, 196–8
  Laura and Marcia, 141, 146, 150–1
  pastoral lovers, 64
  picaresque, 169
  self-identification, 8–9
  Silerio and Timbrio, 70
  "tale of two friends" tradition, 22
Zayas, María de, 153

virtue
  Anselmo and Lotario, 88–91, 93, 113–16
  Aristotle, 11–12
  Boccaccio, Giovanni, 51n
  Camila (character), 97–8, 111, 118, 120, 128
  Cervantes, Miguel de, 81
  Cicero, 15
  Don Quixote and Sancho Panza, 176, 202–3, 205–6
  La traición en la amistad, 152
  perfect friendship, 5
  public opinion, 58, 105n
  Sofronia (character), 49n
  Tito and Gisippo, 38, 43, 45, 48n
"voluntad," 145
vulgo, 81, 83, 85, 103n, 115, 193

Wardropper, Bruce W., 23n, 71n
  "The Pertinence of *El curioso impertinente*," 77–8, 101–2n, 101n, 107n

Weiger, John G., "Sobre la originalidad e independencia de Guillén de Castro," 135n
"wife testing," 88, 90–1, 99, 104–5n, 107n, 108n, 154n
Wilcox, Amanda, 16–17
Williams, Craig A., 4, 14, 16
  Reading Roman Friendship, 22–23n, 25n
Williamson, Edwin
  The Half-Way House of Fiction, 215n, 217n
  "The Power-Struggle Between Don Quixote and Sancho," 211n, 217–18n
Wilson, Diana de Armas, "'Passing the Love of Women'," 104–5n, 106n

yangüeses, 191–3, 195, 196

Zayas, María de, *La traición en la amistad*, 137–57

EU representative:
Easy Access System Europe
Mustamäe tee 50, 10621 Tallinn, Estonia
Gpsr.requests@easproject.com